OUTPOST

Also by Dan Richards

Holloway (with Robert Macfarlane and Stanley Donwood)
The Beechwood Airship Interviews
Climbing Days

OUTPOST

a journey to the
wild ends of the earth

Dan Richards

CANONGATE

For David

This paperback edition published in Great Britain in 2020 by Canongate Books

First published in Great Britain, the USA and Canada in 2019
by Canongate Books Ltd,
14 High Street, Edinburgh EH1 1TE

Distributed in the USA by Publishers Group West
and in Canada by Publishers Group Canada

canongate.co.uk

3

British Library Cataloguing-in-Publication Data
A catalogue record for this book is available on
request from the British Library

ISBN 978 1 78689 157 0

Typeset in Garamond by Biblichor Ltd, Edinburgh

Printed and bound in Great Britain by Clays Ltd, Elcograf S.p.A.

CONTENTS

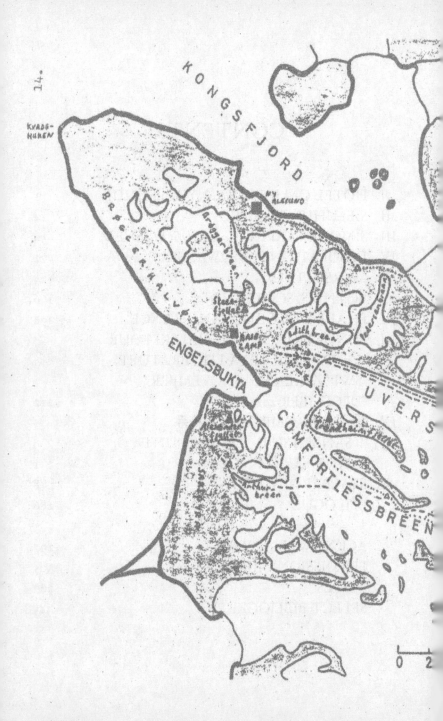

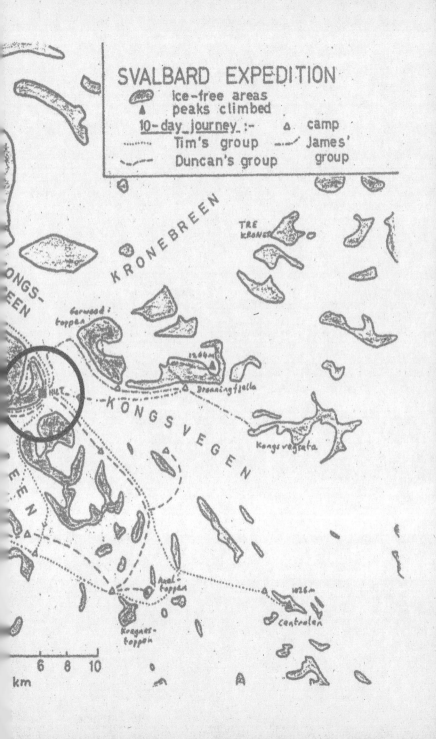

SVALBARD EXPEDITION

- ice-free areas
- ▲ peaks climbed

10-day journey :-
.... Tim's group   △ camp
— · — James' group
— — — Duncan's group

KRONEBREEN

TRE KRONER

KONGS-
BREEN

Garwood-
toppen

1366m

hut

Dronningfjella

KONGSVEGEN

Kongsvegstta

BREEN

Axel-
toppen

1025m

Kragnes-
toppen

centrelen

6 8 10

km

The Peace of Wild Things

When despair for the world grows in me
and I wake in the night at the least sound
in fear of what my life and my children's lives may be,
I go and lie down where the wood drake
rests in his beauty on the water, and the great heron feeds.
I come into the peace of wild things
who do not tax their lives with forethought
of grief. I come into the presence of still water.
And I feel above me the day-blind stars
waiting with their light. For a time
I rest in the grace of the world, and am free.

– Wendell Berry[1]

I

HOTEL CALIFORNIA,
NY-ÅLESUND

Hotel California, Ny-Ålesund, Svalbard, 1982. Photograph: Tim Richards

Dear Dan Richards,

   your travels will not be easy, but I think you have a
fascinating project in the making . . . I wish you all the
best, in particular in the Svalbard archipelago.

   Best,

   Werner Herzog[1]

I grew up fascinated by the polar bear pelvis in my father's study.

My mother, Annie, tells me that when my father, Tim, returned from his final Arctic expedition, a month before my birth, it was night and raining hard. From Svalbard he'd flown down to Tromsø, then Luton, caught several trains to reach Swansea and finally a bus to Penclawdd – a village on the Gower in Wales where my parents lived. Annie had sat by the window all evening, waiting, and now she could see him walking up the shining road, pack on his back. She was listening to Gladys Knight & the Pips, a cassette. Once home he was amazed to see how pregnant she was, how round her belly. He was also very taken with the carpet, she recalls – it felt so good on his tired feet.

Tim had been away for several months on Svalbard – a Norwegian archipelago in the Arctic Ocean, situated north of mainland Europe, about halfway between continental Norway and the North Pole – exploring the Brøgger peninsula and the glaciers, fjords and mountains east of Ny-Ålesund, the northernmost civilian functional settlement at 78° 55′ N.

Next morning he unpacked his bag. Everything smelled of smoke. The smell permeated the whole house – Trangia smoke and unwashed man – and from deep in the stuffed mix of wool and down he drew out the pelvis, abstract, sculptural, bleached, and placed it on the table. Strange object from another world.

Years later, he told me that he'd found the bony frame on the ice and glaciers of Kongsfjorden although, as time passed, the story changed and he'd swapped it for cake and kit with the expedition doctor. The pelvis lived in the study of our

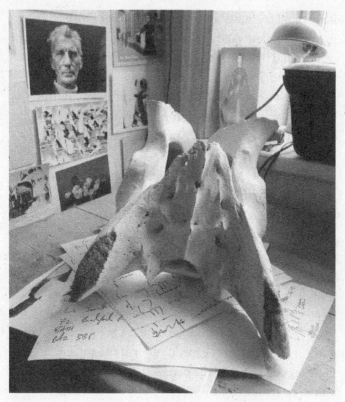

Polar bear pelvis, Bath, 2016. Photograph: Dan Richards

various houses throughout my childhood; less trophy, more alien artefact. It looked so pure, supernaturally white. When held it was heavier than one might expect. It enthralled me; an almost feathered line of peaks ran over the sacrum and coccyx, the broken ends of the flaring hips revealed a coral interior. The hollow eyes of the femur cups, the sinuous lines of the iliac crest, its conch shell-like fissures, cracks and apertures – all these tactile features thrilled and intrigued. The idea of my father having discovered it on a glacier – an impossibly far-flung landscape of mythical beasts – caught my imagination. And the names! Ny-Ålesund: I rolled the word round like a marble in my mouth; Svalbard: it sounded so cold; and Spitsbergen: somehow colder still.[*]

The pelvis was full of story. To hold it was to think of Tim as a young man in that great white silence, imagine polar bears, the life of that particular bear, and feel my horizons expand.

There's a photograph of Tim on his expedition. In it, he stands with four others outside the front door of a small wooden shed. A sixth, unseen behind the camera, takes the shot. Everyone smiles. Behind and around them stretch moonland cliffs and dunes. On the back of the photograph is written *Hotel California, Ny-Ålesund*. Tim, dressed in a wool hat and striped jumper, dark trousers and big boots, stands holding two pans. At his elbow, leant against the shed, is a long black rifle, for bears. Or rather, *in case of bears* ... He was the expedition marksman and took a shooting course before the party left England but never fired a shot, he reassured me.

They never met a bear.

Which is lucky, because Hotel California doesn't look like it would stand up to a bear.[†] An unremarkable garden shed, the only thing that makes it a shed of note is the fact it's there, stood on Svalbard. Once you notice the shed, the sheer blunt ordinary shed-ness of the shed, it's hard to see anything else. It has the sheepish air of a shed out of place,

---

[*] Prior to 1925 Svalbard was known by its Dutch name, Spitsbergen – still the name of its largest island.

[†] It is sobering to remember of polar bears that, as Peter Cook once observed, *strictly speaking, they're not vegetarians.*

a lost shed stumbled into a shot. The idea of six people sleeping inside it seems implausible and rather eccentric. Yet they gave it a name and called it home and there they are, Tim's party, stood beaming outside their shed, an incongruous cabin at the top of the world.

What has become of that shed? As time went on it became inseparable from the pelvis in my imagination, part of an Arctic triptych – my father, the pelvis, the shed. It stood clear of the mêlée of his recollections. The anecdotes about his team being buzzed by Ranulph Fiennes's spotter plane,* climbing mountains, an incident with a boat full of advocaat, sleeping out in the midnight sun, keeping watch for bears, receiving a care package from Annie – fruitcake and tea wrapped in newspapers posted up to the world's northernmost post office – all these recollections subtly shifted and changed as the years went on but the fact(s) Tim went to Svalbard, stayed in a shed and brought home a polar bear pelvis remained solid.

I'd read that in recent years, due to melting permafrost, wooden buildings in the far north have begun to thaw and rot for the first time. Has the shed gone the way of that bear on the ice – fallen down, picked apart, disappeared? At some point I decided to go and discover for myself.

———

* Between 1979 and 1982 Ranulph Fiennes, Charles R. Burton and Oliver Shepard attempted to journey around the world on its polar axis using only surface transport – land, sea, ice – in a quest named the Transglobe Expedition. Part of the trip involved negotiating the Northwest Passage in an open boat, to which end they employed a spotter plane to look for clear water. In the periods between surveying the ice the plane crew seem to have taken great pleasure in making low-level passes over Tim's expedition, *North by Northwest*-style.

During the course of climbing and researching my last book, *Climbing Days*, I stayed in a number of high mountain huts. Some were new and state of the art, some, like the Bertol Hut above Arolla in Switzerland, had been rebuilt on the site of earlier sheds, and some stood apparently unchanged since my great-great-aunt and uncle, Dorothea and Ivor, were mountaineering in the 1920s and 30s.

I found such cabins, often perched on the edge of sharp landscapes, to be a set of secret worlds. These were slightly arcane altitudinous hostels full of enthusiasts and eccentrics – the deeply-tanned leathery fellow in his seventies who took me through his idiosyncratic lethal-looking gear one breakfast, explaining each gizmo and tool in turn with obvious pride and glee; the Swiss guardians who sat in crow's-nest judgement – their duties of care and hospitality tempered by the immediate assessment of the shape and possible liability of everybody who crossed their threshold.

This was a very different setup from the unmanned refuges I'd encountered in Snowdonia and the Lake District – bothy *Marie Celeste*s which I always found empty of people but full of their traces – chairs pushed back in the act of leaving, scuff marks on the floor, faint cooking smells . . . The interior lives of these austere short-stay cells put me in mind of Philip Larkin's poem 'Home is so sad':

> It stays as it was left,
> Shaped to the comfort of the last to go
> As if to win them back.[2]

When Dorothea and Ivor stayed in the Bertol Hut it was little more than a wooden Wendy house set up on a crest of rock overlooking the Mont Miné Glacier. Dorothea captioned a photograph of it in her memoir as *'The Bertol Hut (11,155 ft.) perched like a medieval castle'*.[3]

I'm not sure it ever looked like a medieval castle. Examining the picture again it looks another case of a bewildered shed dragooned into service. *'Adjoining potting sheds on a silver rock mohawk'* might have been a better caption, although 'perched' is exactly right.

Today, the sheds are gone, replaced with a multi-storey insulated concrete bunk-fort. *Now* Bertol looks like a castle or, rather, the sort of monstrous research station inhabited by scientists at the poles. Run as a business, it is staffed half the year, sleeping eighty on four levels in five dormitories of sixteen beds equipped with 'duvets Nordic' and has a panoramic dining room. Things have changed.

Back in the early twentieth century Bertol had no guardian. Like Tim's Svalbard hut, it stood empty and unmanned, without running water; an off-grid refuge containing emergency food supplies. Every September, once the staff have departed, locking their quarters and kitchen behind them, Bertol reverts back to its essential spartan state known in German as *Biwakschachtel* or *Bivouac*.

Bivouac means different things in different countries. To the English it carries an elemental improvised quality: '*n*. the resting at night of soldiers (or others) in the open air, instead of under cover in camp. – *v.i.* to pass a night in the open air.' In Switzerland, Germany and many Nordic countries, however, bivouac refers to a more substantial built refuge. So, whilst my father and I might optimistically refer to the night we spent on the side of Dent Blanche as *bivouacking*, the Swiss would say that we just sat down. Indeed I discovered first hand that they have no special name or term for this beyond 'stopped due to fatigue and incompetence'.*

It would be wrong, however, to see these structures as escape pods alone; panic rooms for the injured or unprepared. Very few buildings in wilderness are designed as places to stop, recover, then phone a helicopter out – although they can fulfil this role in an emergency. Rather, they are often places of respite enabling one to keep going under one's own steam, part of a bigger picture instead of ends in themselves. I think the likes of Hotel California on Svalbard and the Bertol Hut in Switzerland are best understood as staging posts. Perhaps the gift such buildings really endow, their highest and ultimate function, is to allow mankind a foothold in otherwise inhospitable terrain.

'No man should go through life without once experiencing healthy, even bored solitude in the wilderness,' wrote Jack Kerouac of his time as a wildfire-spotter on Desolation Peak, 'finding himself depending solely on himself and thereby learning his true and hidden strength.'[4]

Human shelters in the wilderness are – perhaps ironically – necessary for this kind of immersion. Here is Antoine de Saint-Exupéry in *Wind, Sand and Stars*, describing Port-Étienne† on the edge of the then unconquered territories:

[It] could not be called a town. There is a fort, a hangar, and a wooden hut for our crews. Surrounded by absolute

---

* As a chastening case in point, the Bivouac of the Dent Blanche is an actual hut which sits below the north ridge, a stone-built beehive cell that can sleep fifteen and 'contains blankets, mattresses, pillows, utensils and basic cutlery'.
† Port-Étienne is now called Nouadhibou, Islamic Republic of Mauritania, North Africa.

desert, it is practically invincible in spite of its feeble military resources . . . There is no enemy to fight but silence, in the destitution that is our chief protection. And Lucas, the airfield manager, winds his gramophone night and day; so remote from life, it speaks to us in some half-forgotten language, awakening an undefined melancholy which is strangely like thirst.[5]

So remote from life, yet there it is, winding a gramophone night and day . . . the hangar and runway, the lighthouse, the farmstead, the shed: such infrastructure animates the otherwise intractable scape around it with the possibility of discovery, onward travel, or stasis. Each building is a stone dropped from whence ripples spread.

Saint-Exupéry is unequivocal later in the same book that the distance, silence and isolation afforded by time spent in wilderness are a chastening reminder of humanity's place in the grandest scheme. Psychologists have studied this so-called 'overview effect', a cognitive shift following an experience of true awe, and measured its impact on human subjects. It turned out to be transformational. The subjects returned more patient, less materialistic, and more willing to help others.

Anousheh Ansari, the first private female cosmonaut, has said she believes that world leaders should be taken on a spaceflight to experience what she saw and felt. Were this to happen, Ansari contends, they would see the world in a very different light and enact very different policies.

For better or worse *homo sapiens* are a questing, consuming, destructive species. We have now entered the age of Anthropocene – humans are ruining the planet. It might be better for the Earth if we stopped exploring, lest the human litter which now blights the top of Everest and the depths of the sea spread to every part of the world. Or perhaps the wonders of the natural world can yet inspire us to change, and the 'overview effect' can make guardians of consumers. I believe the more we know about our world, the more we see, the more deeply we engage with it, understand its nature, the more likely we are to be good custodians and reverse our most selfish destructive behaviour.

'An amazing thunderstorm last night as I lay listening. Like being inside a kettledrum with a whole symphony going on out there and with thunder in wraparound quadraphonic!' wrote Roger Deakin of a night spent out in the railway wagon where he sometimes wrote and often slept in the grounds of his home, Walnut Tree Farm.[6]

Over the years, as well as the railway wagon, Deakin established a variety of outlying structures, including two shepherd's huts, and an old wooden caravan with a cracked window. Robert Macfarlane has suggested that Deakin was a latter-day Thoreau and, indeed, there seems a strong correlation between writing and refuge dwelling. I don't think it a coincidence that concerted focused work and musical practice is sometimes referred to as 'woodshedding'.

Perhaps a case can also be made for bothy-like sheds with feral animating energy emanating as much from within as without: ascetic creative crucibles.

Ever since Henry David Thoreau described his two years, two months, and two days of cabin life at Walden Pond, Massachusetts, the idea seems to have percolated, stirred and seduced the modern psyche. To dwell within such a place, even for a short space of time, seems to confer a touch of aesthete mysticism, pioneer heroism or, at least, *Boys' Own* derring-do – an uncommon intimacy with nature, embodied so brilliantly by Deakin.

Roald Dahl had a writing cabin in the garden of his home in Great Missenden. Dylan Thomas had a shed above his house in Laugharne – 'my word-splashed hut' – a replica of which toured the UK in 2014 to celebrate the 100th anniversary of the poet's birth. George Bernard Shaw worked for the last twenty years of his life in a remarkably sophisticated writer's hut in the grounds of his property at Ayot St Lawrence, Hertfordshire, built on a turntable so that it could be rotated to follow the sun.

'To write well is to think clearly. That's why it's so hard,'[7] wrote David McCullough, and this seems to me to be at the heart of the cabin's appeal to writers and artists, independent of its practical origins and virtues; it is a cerebral clearing-house. I see a line and lineage running back through Deakin, Dahl, Thomas, Woolf, Shaw and Yeats to Thoreau. Yeats's wish to rise and go to his Lake Isle and build a small cabin of clay and wattles, the better to work and think, epitomises the siren call such spaces seem to sound in creative minds.

There's something undeniably romantic and transcendental about the idea of living and writing in such proximity to the natural world – a thought exemplified by the intimacy of Thoreau's description of his house at Walden Pond:

This frame, so slightly clad, was a sort of crystallization around me, and reacted on the builder. It was suggestive somewhat as a picture in outlines. I did not need to go outdoors to take the air, for the atmosphere within had lost none of its freshness. It was not so much within doors as behind a door where I sat, even in the rainiest weather . . . I found myself suddenly neighbor to the birds; not by having imprisoned one, but having caged myself near them. I was not only nearer to some of those which commonly frequent the garden and the orchard, but to those smaller and more thrilling songsters of the forest which never, or rarely, serenade a villager – the wood thrush, the veery, the scarlet tanager, the field sparrow, the whip-poor-will, and many others.[8]

I once sat for an hour in a shelter resembling an upturned coracle built by land artist David Nash in the four woodland acres where his magical *Ash Dome* lives. The day was clear and a brisk wind mussed the trees so the dappled light shimmered around me. It became so brilliantly obvious that here was a space to clear one's mind and think, invent, imagine – *'the still point of the turning world . . . at the still point, there the dance is'.*[9]

———

This book considers the romantic, exploratory appeal of cabins and isolated stations; utilitarian constructions, pared-back buildings of essential first principles. Astringent architecture attracts me because it seems to represent a longed-for clarity, and in the pages that follow I will examine the importance of dens and eyries as creative spaces – cells containing just enough domestic comfort to allow a person to work, whilst eschewing the usual barriers to the outside world. But outposts are many and various, an idiosyncratic lot, so whilst some may be low-tech interzones made of just enough architecture to keep out the weather like Thoreau's Walden cabin, others will be more robust. Old and new, restored, repurposed; the solid, the decrepit and the brilliantly bizarre. Some will not seem to conform to the outline I've laid out here at all – *Shedboatshed* and Nageire-dō might leave some scratching their heads – but I hope you'll forgive and perhaps join me in celebrating any such apparently aberrant and eccentric detours along the way. I hope you'll be delighted and seduced by such marvels as the belvederes atop Desolation Peak and Phare de Cordouan. This book is not designed to be a definitive tour but rather an odyssey inspired by the world of possibilities and wonder embodied by a polar bear pelvis brought home to South Wales one wet and blustery night.

Every chapter will explore a particular situation or structure, each location a stop in an ongoing narrative, each examining a different facet, perspective and approach to the experience of wilderness. I contend that bothies, depots, silos and beacons form the foundation of many great endeavours; rungs on the ladder, even into outer space.

If the question at the heart of my last book, *Climbing Days*, was 'Why climb mountains?', *Outpost* seeks answers to the question of what draws people to wilderness and the isolated human stations around and within them. What can such places tell us about the human condition? What compels us to go to the ends of the Earth, and what future do these places have?

II

SÆLUHÚS, ICELAND

> I have come to the borders of sleep,
> The unfathomable deep
> Forest where all must lose
> Their way
>
> – Edward Thomas[1]

I n late 2016 I read *Questions of Travel: William Morris in
Iceland*, Lavinia Greenlaw's selection from Morris's 1871
Iceland Journal, a book in which the author weaves Morris's
descriptions of the Icelandic wilderness – 'most romantic of
all deserts' – with her own shadow travelogue of journeys
in his footsteps.

In the book's introduction Greenlaw writes that she
didn't originally go to Iceland because of Morris but was
rather drawn by a dreamlike sense of how the Icelandic landscape *might* be:

> I had seen it at the corner of the map and envisaged
> darkness and emptiness that would help me feel off the
> map altogether. My sense of what to expect was entirely
> abstract: a surface of calm and a depth of wildness, a
> combination of the vague and the absolute.[2]

I too had long been captivated by Iceland's otherworldly
charisma. At school, inspired by landscapes of lava, tundra

and glacier, I dreamt of visiting. I would search through old copies of *National Geographic* for pictures of the islands, and hunt through the library for atlases and books about it, together with its wingmen, Greenland and Svalbard. I found the high North's raw enormity compelling and would stare transfixed at any accounts and photographs I found, transported, always hoping for more. The idea of volcanos in a cold realm thrilled me – the impossible clash of ice and fire.

Later, my Icelandic enthusiasm was further kindled by the music of Múm, Björk and Sigur Rós, whose records came to embody aspects of the Icelandic landscape. Múm's tender glitchy organic music was synonymous with the recoveries from crushing university hangovers – muzzy, communal, celebratory and warm. Björk's world, on the other hand, was emotional and elemental, childlike, inquisitive and questing, each album oscillating between sensual intimacy and uncanny feral wildness. I found and continue to find her work euphoric, cinematic and sensationally *other*.

But perhaps Sigur Rós, most of all, opened up and revealed the landscape, people and sheer size of Iceland to me in their film *Heima*. The film documents a tour the band made around the island in June 2006, playing in ghost towns, outsider art shrines, national parks, cabins, small community halls, and an abandoned herring factory in Djúpavík, before reconvening in Reykjavik to play the largest gig in Icelandic history. The project was about connection and ideas of belonging, home and homeland. I was very taken with the archive footage of the steaming, teeming herring port in the far west of the country, now mouldering rusted and abandoned, reanimated and filled with people and music for a single day in celebration and remembrance.[*]

With all this in mind, Iceland seemed the absolute place to begin my search for outposts and bivouacs.

As a first step, I emailed Dr Katrín Anna Lund, Associate Professor in the Department of Geography and Tourism at the University of Iceland, to ask about bothies unique and peculiar to the island. Katrín put me in touch with a couple of her colleagues who specialised in Icelandic geoscience and wilderness, and the question came back, was I aware of sæluhús?

SÆLUHÚS

Iceland is almost exclusively inhabited around the coast, the interior hardly at all. The original sæluhús (*houses of joy*) were refuge stations for travellers crossing the hinter/highlands. The remains of many structures dating back to Viking times can still be found whilst others, frequented, repaired and rebuilt over the centuries, have become Ships of Theseus, renewed beyond recognition[†] – modern bunkhouses on ancient foundations.

---

[*] On the day of the 2017 summer solstice – shortly after my return from the island – Sigur Rós unveiled a twenty-four-hour 'slow TV' event live on Iceland's national television station – also streamed live globally via YouTube. *Route One* features footage of a 1,332km journey around the whole of Iceland's coastal ring road, set to a constantly evolving soundtrack based around elements of their latest song, '*Óveður*'.

[†] The Ship of Theseus, also known as Theseus's Paradox, is a thought experiment which asks the question whether an object that has had all its components replaced remains fundamentally the same object. The paradox is recorded by the first-century writer Plutarch in *Life of Theseus*. Plutarch asked

Sæluhús are often opened up for the spring and summer hiking season and need to be booked in advance, but retain their original emergency shelter status in the closed season between October and May. The essential generosity of these structures, the ideas of renewal and sanctuary at their heart, appealed to me from the moment I learnt of their existence. I found the idea of cabins animated by joy delightful and immediately set out to find a sæluhús overseer.

Within a fortnight of first contacting Katrín, I was talking to Stefán Jökull Jakobsson, Head Ranger of Ferðafélag Íslands (the Iceland Touring Association, FÍ). A month later I was on a plane to Reykjavik.

———

I met Stefán at his Ferðafélag Íslands HQ. A tall bear-like man with a heavy-duty handshake, he made me a coffee and then led the way upstairs to a large office containing a desk, a phone and a noticeboard on which were pinned maps and photographs.

Such was the spartan nature of the room that I wondered for a moment if it might be a front and I was about to be sent on a secret mission – for the Icelandic Navy Sæluhús perhaps – but no, the office was bare because Stefán was so rarely there. His early summer days usually consist of criss-crossing Iceland in his 4×4 digging isolated huts out of snowdrifts, restocking gas bottles and emergency supplies,

whether a ship that had been restored by replacing every single wooden part remained the same ship. *See also* – Trigger's broom.

fixing infrastructure, supporting wardens and generally troubleshooting the sæluhús network.*

Stefán showed me numbered pictures of the sæluhús in his care, a charming, rather motley collection built to the specifications and whims of whoever took the job. They ranged from big timber barns to pyramidal sheds of a single room, corrugated dens on legs jostling with cricket pavilion-esque gazebos. Some of the largest look like solid schoolhouses, the smallest, modest beach huts, but all in the middle of nowhere – eccentric havens on tundric seas.

The mugshot of #34 showed a tiny shed akin to a boshed-together pigeon loft; the equivalent of a one-man tent in wood.

Ferðafélag Íslands oversee thirty-seven sæluhús scattered around Iceland, but mainly sited in the east and centre. The organisation's mandate remains the same as when it was formed in 1927, to help people travel out from the towns and city into the landscape to see the natural wonders of Iceland. From the 30s on, cabins were built or rebuilt to make particular journeys possible – sæluhús #5–#9 chart a curve around the belly of the Langjökull glacier, for example, whilst #29–#34 allow long-distance trekking beyond the Vatnajökull icecap. 'And there is the Laugavegur Trail,' he smiled ruefully. '*The famous one.*'

A few months before my visit Bradt guides had released a new book raving about the Laugavegur Trail, enthusing about a 'truly invigorating walk across primitive terrain', and

---

* He also showed me photographs of huts that had been broken into during the off-season, ransacked and abandoned open to the elements, shaking his head in sad disbelief.

Stefán was bracing for the impact because such fame and gushing press bring people, more people than Iceland could ever have imagined twenty years ago. 'My job is to make sure the things the people come to see aren't damaged by the people coming to see them,' he explained, equating it to sticking a line of tape to a gallery floor in front of a painting. 'I say, *"Here, look at this, isn't it astonishing?"* And they look and maybe they take a photograph and then they move on down a path and enjoy themselves and look at the next amazing thing.'

His job is to be invisible, he says, to maintain cabins and build and repair paths that people don't notice they're walking; to guide people through a landscape so they have the best time possible and leave no trace. But it isn't easy. In 2009, 464,000 tourists travelled to Iceland. At the time of my visit in 2016, that number had grown to almost 1.8 million and was accelerating. Interviewed in the *Financial Times*, Professor Edward Huijbens of the Icelandic Tourism Research Centre described the graph of tourist numbers as 'currently almost vertical'. Visitors to Iceland for 2017 were expected to reach 2.4 million.[3]

Not all of those people make a beeline for a bunkhouse, but the numbers have hit Ferðafélag Íslands hard.

Once isolated sæluhús often now sit amidst campsites catering for hundreds, such is the popularity and traffic of the trails strung between them. People's expectations have changed since the mid-twentieth century when many of the cabins were built by local volunteers. Back then, the idea was to construct cheap utilitarian lodges to keep the elements at bay a few weekends a year for rambling Icelanders. Now the structures need constant upkeep because they're frail and exhausted, and the delicate wilderness around them is likewise at risk from pollution and over-exposure.

Listening to Stefán, I found myself wondering whether 'destination wilderness' could exist. Can a landscape truly be said to be wild when thousands tromp through it on a hiking superhighway?

And with the clash of culture, people and nature comes a mismatch of expectation. Historically, few cabins had much in the way of amenities, insulation or sanitation, their primary purpose being short-stay shelters rather than destinations in themselves, as some have become. And modern hikers expect, if not chi-chi luxuries, at the least some possibility of heat and a toilet. But Stefán doesn't want to build a shower block and latrine at every Icelandic beauty spot. For one thing it would visually destroy the thing people have come to see and, for another, he can't; the landscape is protected. Which is good. 'But people do not want to carry around bags of their own poo . . . some of them don't even take home their KitKat wrappers.'

I suspect the amount of joy inherent in a sæluhús is apt to fluctuate depending on the amount of excrement and KitKats in the immediate vicinity.

Bad enough pitching up to discover one is not alone in a place, not an original thinker in one's desire to visit and see a Bradt-hymned wonder, but to meet people just like yourself there, to flush hot and feel yourself a charlatan, a caricature, *a tourist*, and – worse! – to find the place strewn with trash . . . It's like 1871 all over again, for these are not new problems as the following extract from William Morris's Icelandic diary attests:

Tuesday, 25 July 1871
IN CAMP AT GEYSIR

We can see the low crater of the big Geysir now quite clearly; some way back on the other side of Tungufljót I had taken it for a big tent, and had bewailed it for the possible Englishmen that I thought we would find there: however go we must, and presently after crossing a small bright river, come right on the beastly place, under the crater of the big Geysir, and ride off the turf on to the sulphurous accretion formed by the overflow, which is even now trickling over it, warm enough to make our horses snort and plunge in terror: so on to the place of turf about twenty yards from the lip of the crater: a nasty lumpy thin piece of turf, all scored with trenches cut by former tourists round their tents: here Eyvindr [Morris's Icelandic guide] calls a halt, and Evans [a fellow English traveller] dismounts, but I am not in such a hurry: the evening is wretched and rainy now; a south wind is drifting the stinking stream of the south-ward lying hot springs full in our faces: the turf the only nasty bit of camping ground we have had yet, all bestrewn with feathers and wings of birds, polished mutton bones, and above all pieces of paper ... So there I sat on my horse, while the guides began to bestir themselves about the unloading, feeling a very heroic disgust gaining on me: Evans seeing that a storm was brewing sang out genially to come help pitch the tents. 'Let's go to Hawkdale,' quoth I, 'we can't camp in this beastly place.'

'What's he saying?' said Eyvindr to Gisli.

'Why, I am not going to camp here,' said I.

'You must,' said Eyvindr, 'All Englishmen do.'

'Blast all Englishmen!' said I in the Icelandic tongue.[4]

Human nature may not have changed but things cannot remain as they are and Stefán has plans. He told me that, the following spring, he intended to substantially repair sæluhús #7 Hvítárnes, built in 1930 – the oldest house owned and operated by Ferðafélag Íslands – and completely rebuild one of their largest cabins, #15 Þórsmörk Skagfjörðsskáli, to bring it up to modern standards by the season's end. His plan was to take the 50s structure apart – a big red tin tabernacle type-affair – then put it back together in such a way that it was still recognisably Þórsmörk Skagfjörðsskáli; 'only insulated and fitted with proper plumbing and electrics'.

'I'll keep the main timbers and reuse all the elements I can,' he told me. 'I want to keep the soul of it. That's very important to me.'

Stefán was a hugely inspiring man, on the quiet. His dual roles as custodian and host conflict him sometimes, he admits, but he has a great belief that a balance can be struck which benefits both Iceland and the tourists who travel to see it. The sæluhús are key to this. No mere means to an end, they embody something of the Icelandic culture and history. The word *soul* jumped out at me when he said it because it seemed on the surface such an un-Stefán word – slightly mystical and woolly – but it's the right word. The sæluhús are not uniform or interchangeable, they're individuals with distinct personalities; monuments to the volunteers who built them. The cabins Stefán oversees have changed the country around them, generous offerings beckoning visitors in, manifestations of the spirit and people behind them . . . and *soul* is the best word we have for that, whatever that emotive cluster of ideas amounts to.

As we parted, I asked if I could return the following summer and help him rebuild #7 and #15. 'Great!' he said, smiling. 'Bring a hammer and a decent pair of boots.'

WHITE WORLD I

A year later I was back. A couple of days after my return, Stefán rolled up outside Kex hostel in his 4×4 – a black beast with thumping great tyres, a matchbox on doughnuts. We were set to drive out to Landmannalaugar in the southern highlands to collect a couple of rangers but first we drove to the Ferðafélag Íslands base to consult a map, drink strong black coffee and eat enormous custard creams with REYKJAVIK embossed on the front – Icelanders have a great interest and liking for coffee and biscuits, an excellent enthusiasm I share. Then we drove east on Route One, the road climbing over the carbuncular lava of the Hellisheiði plateau, wire-wool moss foaming grey-green.

Mountains started to appear. Some stood off in the blue distance, whilst others more immediate and dorsal fringed the road. We began to pass feathers of steam from hot springs, but after half an hour, when the plateau flattened out, I saw a domed complex half obscured by a billowing swoosh of cloud, a massive streaming safety valve. The Hellisheiði geothermal plant, the third largest in the world, sits on the active flank of the volcano Hengill, a mile from the road. The complex screamed super-villainy; futuristic, sci-fi military – a sky plume base amidst miles of zagging pipelines, source of a pylon army marching off to the horizon.

But now we were past the power station and up to the plateau's end where the road began a swift looping spiral down to the glasshouses of Hveragerði, the view opening inland and out to reveal mountains knuckling one side, shimmering silver sea and marshes the other.

Over and off Hellisheiði everything was incredibly green. Looking back, it seemed like we'd spun down an immense emerald cliff with the sun now flaring across us and the road rebalanced. Then we reached Selfoss – a town of early suspension bridge enthusiasts, final resting place of Bobby Fischer, childhood home of Björk – a place which continued the kaleidoscopic mix of concrete prefabs and corrugated self-built homes I'd experienced in Reykjavik. At Selfoss we stopped for food and I added ice cream, wafer-based chocolate bars and hotdogs to my list of 'popular Icelandic things apparently available everywhere'.

Selfoss was the last town. Once we'd swung off the main road, villages and red farms thinned. The loss of the domestic coincided with the landscape hardening and the highlands ramping up. The road was a thick line in soft pencil, glossy and black; a smooth path for heavy hydro plant. The ice blue river to our right raced whiter. The pylons returned, strobing, wires swooping, nodding, keeping time. Here was the hard fix out in the wilds to power everything elsewhere. The river now ran in a deep cut, a trench smashed clean and straight through the rock. Giant workings massed – canals and dam walls holding back glacial lakes, funnels for turbines buried in brutalist Thunderbird boxes.

Every bluff brought new monoliths until we topped out and sped alongside a series of pale reservoirs silvered blind by silt and milky sky. But no people. In the next hour we passed no cars and then the road ran out, ceding to gravel which we bumped along a while until we reached a gate, a chain between two posts, and a sign: *Ófært – IMPASSABLE*. We crunched around and beyond it, up to the top of a hill where black clinker ceded to snow. 'A good time to piss,' announced Stefán. So I walked away from the truck to piss, buffeted by a cold wind. Looking back over our path I saw a black denim world smeared with white and turquoise, an anodised sky fluorescing frosted light. All life and colour seemed beaten back by the wind and the cold but, no, there were lichens and mosses hanging on in the rocks at my feet. It was still a winter world, hardly yet spring. I was early.

Below, a small car stopped at the gate. A couple of miles behind it was another, set to meet it at the end of the road. Meanwhile Stefán had been round the 4×4 and lowered the tyre pressures ready for the next part of our trip, which would be over deep snow. Then we drove up and over the lip of the hill and disappeared out of sight.

For the next couple of hours we bounced and churned in snow holes, edged round hidden hazards and slushed in streams, enveloped in freezing mist. We were totally reliant on a boxy dash sat-nav, our vehicle a dot on its Game Boy screen, ghosting the line of a road buried metres beneath us. I spent a lot of the next hour staring fixedly into the opaque white world wondering what was through and beneath it. Visibility was only a few metres and when a feature did loom out of the haar it often took a moment for it to resolve a clear shape and character – cliffs steepling up, seeming to crest and overhang as moss green breakers; snow slopes shooting away, boulders the size of houses. It was like we were rolling on a frozen sea, almost impossible to know if we were driving along the top of a wave or at the bottom of a trough; although Stefán had a good idea having driven this route a hundred times. 'Most of these are me,' he smiled, pointing at the puffy infilled tracks winding around us, 'or rescue trucks. People shouldn't be out here alone.' After an hour we passed a memorial to a snowmobiler, a pile of rocks poking out of the snow. He was a crazy guy, Stefán told me, known for travelling great distances and going out on his own, but he crashed his ski in a blizzard, was hurt, tried to walk out, fell in icy water and died of cold. 'That's it,' he finished, opening his hand on the wheel slightly, as if to add, *It happens*. But you come out here alone, I ventured. 'Yes, but I've got a truck and I know what I'm doing,' he replied, eyes on the snow sea. 'But you're right, I probably shouldn't . . . but I need to get things done.'

BLACK LAKE I

On my first trip to Iceland Haraldur Jónsson had suggested that I should go and see Kleifarvatn, a black lake in the middle of the Reykjanes Ridge.

Haraldur is an artist who lives in Reykjavik. We were introduced over email by the Icelandic writer Sjón, who said that Haraldur was the absolute best man to show me around. So we arranged to meet the night of my arrival once I'd unpacked and found my feet.

Waiting for my flight to take off, I'd begun to read *The Importance of Being Iceland: Travel Essays in Art* by Eileen

Myles – discovered in a secondhand bookshop the day before and bought on the strength of the title alone. *'Haraldur'* appeared on page 22. It must be *my* Haraldur, I thought, and remembered my childhood bafflement with the amount of crime Bergerac encountered on Jersey. *'But how many banks can there be on Jersey!?'* I used to shout at the television. As crime on Jersey, so art on Iceland: this is a place with two degrees of separation rather than six; everything rapidly triangulated.

Haraldur was described in the book as looking like Christopher Isherwood – another singularly well connected man.

'He's my best friend' says Björk a few lines later.

Sjón himself appears just a few pages on.

Bingo! Full house.

When I met Haraldur, he did look Isherwood-esque, hair parted and swept over to one side. Like most Icelanders I encountered, he was dressed impeccably in natural fibres – wool suit, brogues, a good thick cotton shirt. We sat in the bar at the Kex hostel and had a beer. Icelandic beer is excellent, which is lucky because a pint costs as much as a meal back home. As we talked he waved and nodded to several people in passing, at one point introducing me to his friend Kristín, singer in a local band: Múm.*

---

* Kristín Anna Valtýsdóttir (aka Kría Brekkan, born 5 January 1982) is an Icelandic vocalist and classically trained multi-instrumentalist. She is best known as a former front-woman of Múm – having sung on their first three/ best three albums – *Yesterday Was Dramatic, Today Is OK* (1999), *Finally We Are No One* (2002), and *Summer Make Good* (2004). *Howl*, Kristín's first full-length record under her own name, was released in 2015. Now simply known as Kristín Anna, her new LP, *I Must Be the Devil*, came out in October 2018.

Ecstatic, beaming, I shook her hand, wondering who else might be in the room – Magnus Magnusson and Erik the Red, perhaps.

Later, over a meal of steak tartare and salted cod, I explained to Haraldur how I'd like to find bothies and sheds, and asked if there was anywhere slightly off the beaten track where such things could be found.

He drew me a map of Kleifarvatn, telling me about the black lake as he did so; how it sat on a fissure of the Mid-Atlantic Ridge; how, after an earthquake in 2000, a great deal of it disappeared; how, in some spots, the Earth was liquid and molten, boiling beneath one's feet. There were sheds around there, he said, and he would have driven us out there and shown me himself, but he was leaving for the Atlas Mountains of Morocco next morning. That said, however, in the time we had, would I like a tour of Reykjavik?

For the next hour we criss-crossed the city in Haraldur's battered red car whilst he pointed out landmarks and joined the dots of the city – the parliament, the prime minister's residence, the Opera House, the theatre school, the rocket-ship sweep of the Hallgrímskirkja Lutheran church, the different embassies, the Masonic Hall, the Grótta lighthouse. 'And this,' he said, slowing on a stretch of coastal road to the west of the city, 'is Björk's house. It's a good one, isn't it?' I agreed it was a nice one. 'Right!' he said, pleased, and then began an elaborate eight-point turn in the street outside, by the end of which I'd shrunk down in my seat, ears burning.

WHITE WORLD II

On the flat we drove at a reasonable pace, twenty miles an hour or so, chuffing up ice and chunks of snow, but where the buried road rose or fell sharply, or boulder fields needed to be negotiated, we inched at odd angles. Several areas were clear of snow, dark lava formations to scrape along, orange-dun dunes to churn across, a steaming Christmas pudding tump the size of Silbury Hill to skirt. 'The hills and rocks here are hot,' explained Stefán, 'the snow never settles. The colours you can see are plants and algae enjoying the heat.'

I looked out at the hot rocks and enthusiastic algae all shouting, 'Come on in, the water's lovely!' But were I to open my door, I knew I would not encounter a balmy day.

The road now consisted of two blue grooves. Lava snarls and valleys had merged the many spectral routes into one, so when we nosed and slid down the last incline, dropping out of the mist into a clear day, and drove on to the shingly beach of a wide river system, we knew that we were arrowed right and F208, the one true road, was here, somewhere, buried . . . which was reassuring.

The next part of the journey was across and in the river. The 4×4 may have had a snorkel and tyres the size of Greenland but it was still a very skilful business to negotiate the waterways, find the underwater beds to take our weight and know where to plough into drifts and have a hope of climbing out. Sometimes we drove with the flow and sometimes we forged across to land on one of the many snowy islands in the main stream. Some of the water was deep. It was hard to read it. The sat-nav was no use here and from above it must have looked like we were taking a drunken spidery path, but Stefán clearly knew the stretch of river so well that never once whilst jiving and bucking about did I feel that we'd get stuck. When we pulled up outside a half-buried ranger house, four hours after leaving the great wen of Reykjavik, it felt like a real adventure had come to an end. But this is a normal day for Stefán. 'Okay,' he said, as we unbuckled and climbed out, 'let's get a coffee, collect the women and go back home.'

The women were the wardens who'd been stationed at Landmannalaugar for the last couple of months. Many sæluhús are shut down for the winter but Landmannalaugar opens and closes later due to its position at the start of the Laugavegur Trail, a thirty-five-mile trek down to the towering icecaps and volcanoes of Þórsmörk – *Valley of Thor*. But even in winter people visit and scoot fresh tangles of snowmobile tracks.

This outpost was formed of three buildings – the warden's house, a dormitory and a barn-like washhouse – situated near a hot spring at the head of a valley of multicoloured peaks. In May, these were mostly still covered with snow but the melt was under way and a few flanks were visible, rising rust, rose and amber, luxuriant bright in the sun. Our 4×4 stood level with the roof of the warden's house, atop three metres of snow. A rippling wall ran around the house on two sides – perhaps the building's heat had defrosted the bank about it – but, house hollow aside, the hard-pack filled the valley in every direction. How much water? A boggling amount and it would all be gone in a couple of weeks, I was told, thawed and run away by the time the first hikers arrived ... which astonished me then and boggles me now as I write it down, as it would have astonished me as a child. The idea of all that pent-up power let loose, that water – and even though I knew it wouldn't thaw and 'go' all at once, still, these things always make me feel so small. Which I am, of course.

A few hundred yards to one side was what looked like a large Anderson shelter, half buried – a corrugated stables, I discovered once I'd tromped over, sinking up to my knees in the powder. 'Iceland Horse' said a weather-thumped sign above a smashed window grille. I peered inside to see what could be seen. Very little, as it turned out: a dim floor of earth and tramped straw and what looked vaguely like a small drinks bar. One end of the long shed sported a stubby chimney.

So a hangar-like stable with a hearth and bar. Quite an avant-garde get-up, all told, which, set amidst the sweeping snow-flats, suggested that the horses might be running a small aerodrome.

On the hill behind the main site buildings sat a green-topped shed-like structure – a sheep pen. Sheep are the reason the trail exists, since it was originally a drovers' way, Stefán had told me in the 4×4, a route from the grass of the highlands to the coast, 'because all this will spring green when the snow melts and the world gets moving'; the green and blues breaking out as soon as the sun shouts 'Go!' and the landscape warms.

Visceral, ancient, deep and alive.

'If anything is endemic to Wyoming, it is the wind. The big room of space is swept out daily,' Gretel Ehrlich writes at the start of *The Solace of Open Spaces*,[5] a record of her time and travels in the 44th state. If anything is endemic to Iceland's weather it's force and speed of change. A brief search online for Landmannalaugar turns up several videos of intense sun, rain, wind and thunderstorms; one film of the latter shows it battering, breaking and flooding the campsite until almost everyone has run for cover in the barn. The few tents remaining, weighted down with large rocks, are mere sheets of sopping fabric plastered over the figures of those still huddled inside – slicked in utero campers back-lit by lightning.

It looks cold and ferocious, stair-rod rain strafing the ground, the sky flaring purple, the wind threatening to blow our intrepid YouTuber over. It looks wild, in a word, but the wrong type of wild for most of the people present. 'This isn't what we came for' is writ large on the faces of the barn crowd. 'This is meant to be summer,' someone is heard to say off camera.

But, to return to Gretel Ehrlich, as well as paying tribute to the vast scapes and solitude she experienced whilst immersed in Wyoming's plains and ranges, much of the book deals with hard nature's indifference and the essential fact that even where wilderness is gone, great wildness still remains. 'True wilderness has been gone on this continent since the time of Lewis and Clark's overland journey'[6], she remarks early on, which is to say that we have maps – maps, roads, telephones and satellites – but not to say that humans are now in universal control. We are not. Disorientation and hypothermia can't be eradicated like smallpox. Just because you can physically get somewhere, it does not follow that the place will behave itself once you are there. The Earth may be pegged but the heavens are wild as ever.

To look into a wild place is to stand on a border, to visit wild places is to have crossed their threshold. Sightseers to Iceland's interior are too often unprepared for the untamed reality. There may be snowmobile tracks or a gravel road but these are not guarantees of safety or control, they're just marks left by previous humans. The sort of summer storm recorded at Landmannalaugar is the sort of weather best appreciated indoors, the sort of cloudburst best heard bouncing off a corrugated iron roof above one's head – which is how everyone would have heard it thirty years ago because *everyone*, both of them at most, would have been snug in a sæluhús after a long walk. But now tourists unfamiliar with Icelandic summers bus out here with unfamiliar tents and find themselves maelstromed in a Vango condom.

BLACK LAKE II

I could hear the trucks coming from a long way off, the low hum behind me rising to a roar as they closed, then burst past. The trucks did not stop, would not stop, weren't for me. This had quickly become apparent. So I put away my thumb and stopped trying with the trucks. I dubbed this resigned non-hitching 'saving my energy', as if the act of holding out a thumb was arduous. But, then, it *was* hot, and any economy was welcome.

There were very few cars.

The wind in the wake of the trucks felt cool, the pooled air stirring then settling back. The whole scape simmered. The hot road cooked its way across the mercury plain, rippling liquid as it arrowed to an infinite point.

An hour and a half into my hitch into Haraldur's sketch map, the mountains still seemed no closer.

Shellac black horses hammered away to the horizon – a fissured moor topped by sage froth the texture of scouring pads. A dismantled industrial landscape, coagulated some 100,000 years ago to form a lunar slag plateau.

Dust clouds ahead told of trucks approaching. Seen from the front, head-on, they looked mirrored and implacable as brushed steel trains – the heat haze gave them comet tails.

———

The car that did eventually stop was small and gold. It appeared as an amazing bronze bug in my peripheries, a drone which crunched to a stop. It had three young men inside, two Israelis in the front, an American in the back.

I scrambled in, all thanks and relief, wedging myself to make four. As we pulled away, the car, a small Fiat, seemed to whimper and totter a tad; but it was absolutely faster and cooler than walking, and for that I was thrilled.

The car got up a little speed and the yellow posts at the side of the road began to click past. The mountains grew nearer.

It quickly emerged that the Israelis liked to argue. That was their favourite thing. If a point of conversation could be picked at, questioned and niggled to death, that was what they would do. I was English, yes, of course, but where? London? They had been to London. I wasn't originally from London? They had only been to London. They would prefer that I spoke only of London unless I was going to relate everything back specifically to London, where they had been. Actually, I *was* from London, I decided cheerfully. It seemed the easiest place to be from in the circumstances.

34

I began talking to the American, originally from Massachusetts, who suddenly revealed, apropos of very little, that his parents, not liking the direction he'd been taking as a youth, had paid two ex-Navy Seals to kidnap him and forcibly change his ways. The Seals had dragged him out of bed one night without warning, driven him into the wilds, and there, over a couple of months of hard living in the woods, they'd broken him down and rebuilt him. A change for the better – he was categorical on that point. 'Fuck yeah, I'm a far better guy for that.'

'You are a liar,' said the driver, fixing the Massachusettsan with his eyes in the mirror – a statement which made the little gold Fiat feel suddenly much smaller. 'You're a liar, my friend. Tell the story again.'

The Massachusettsan repeated the main points of his tale.

'Ha!' said the Israeli man, apparently satisfied. 'Ha! Americans!'

'Well . . .' I said, for something to say. 'Blimey . . . I don't think that happens much in London . . .' at which point, luckily, the tarmac stopped, we hit a hill, the road turned to chippings and the car gave up.

We all got out. The Israelis argued, then the driver got back in and drove the empty Fiat up the gravel hill. Then we got back in. I now saw that Route 42 was more literally a truck road than I'd imagined, since the shiny asphalt stopped at the gates of a quarry beyond which the highway was stoney and potholed. Another hire car passed in the opposite direction, peppering us with gravel. Our driver gunned the engine, which groaned, the wheels flailed and we were off again, over the first of the blue hills and down into a green glen. The grit road wound ahead. The Israelis argued about the state of the road and which one was most to blame for hiring this piece-of-shit Fiat. I thought about the Massachusettsan's arranged abduction and wondered how the three had met, but didn't ask.

Once at Kleifarvatn we found the roadsides filled with vans and catering buses. A nice Norwegian man explained that there was filming in the area. 'What is it?' demanded our driver. 'Have I heard of this film or programme?'

I disembarked and made a great show of casualness and wandered off 'to eat my sandwiches'. I had no sandwiches and lost myself in rocks out of sight of the car as quickly as possible.

'That was odd,' I said to myself, to the rocks, to the world at large.

The lake itself was beautiful – the waters a deep blue falling into jet depths unknown. The shore was muscovado. After the black range of the lava field, the territory here was brown. Above the red beach, rocks flaked almond. Serrated mountains reared either side. Two springs exhaled steam in the distance, one beside what looked like a tin chapel. I stared at it across the silent lake, feeling quite alone, the only sound the wind and ink-water shushing on the sand. I could have been the only person for miles around . . . but no. Behind me, I heard a car start up, then it appeared around a cliff – sun bug of doom creeping slowly round the lake. I ducked in case I was being sought.

'Go to Kleifarvatn,' Haraldur had said, 'it's a really strange place . . .'

He was quite correct.

———

Several days later, I met Haraldur again. As we walked around the Marshall House gallery in Reykjavik harbour, a handsome white former fishmeal factory built in 1948, I told him how I'd survived a Kleifarvatn manhunt and escaped from my trouble spot à la Jack Reacher – hitching out, picked up by some jovial Turks – and he smiled as if such things were de rigueur in the Reykjanes.

'But the lake,' he pressed me, still twinkling but suddenly serious, 'the lake is beautiful.'

The lake was awesome, I assured him. Fathoms black, a dark portal.

'To the deep Earth's core,' he nodded. 'You know it disappeared? After earthquakes in 2000 a rift was created in the floor and a great deal drained away.'

He then showed me pictures of an exhibition he'd staged a few months before, a pool of black maps on the gallery floor. He'd had them printed and folded by a famous map maker, black, then laid them out as a sea of ebon butterflies, twitching on the deck, alive to any movement of the air. Maps of void. Maps of night. Less maps of *terra incognita* as maps of terror. Maps of where Kleifarvatn went. Stygian maps in every sense.

'Björk sat with them for an hour, staring through them,' Haraldur smiled.

'She'd recently released a song named "Black Lake" too . . . but that was only chance."

---

* 'Black Lake' was one of the centrepiece songs on Björk's 2015 album *Vulnicura*, a deeply affecting, haunting set of songs which detail the break-up of a relationship, blank despair ceding to cautious optimism. In common with almost all of Björk's music, the lyrical allusions are elemental and rooted in nature – the fractured anguish and ferocious anger tectonic, glacial, visceral

WHITE WORLD III

On the drive back to Reykjavik I sat in the front seat, the two lady wardens behind. There was some whispered worry as we swayed though the river and after a particularly vociferous sotto voce conference Stefán announced that there was only one driver and asked everyone else to please be quiet.

I felt quite guilty about this since my heart had been in my mouth a good deal too on the way to Landmannalaugar – my thoughts full of hmmms, haas, and shitfuckshitfucks – but since it had just been Stefán and me in the cab, I'd kept such angst internal. And after an hour my fears had dissipated since it had become clear that I was driving with an expert off-roader. But I imagined it must be difficult for people who'd been so isolated and self-contained to relax and relinquish responsibility. Of course they were going to be torn to leave their home of several months and the 4×4 was shaking and bouncing around, water slapping at our windows. A couple of times on the journey out, when Stefán seemed to be calmly pitching us into voids white, dark or wet, I'd had to have a word with myself, 'Stop breathing so weirdly, Dan. It's embarrassing.'

Through the river, listing over the marshmallow archipelago, back to the place where the twin tracks fanned, past the Silbury Christmas pudding, across the snow plateau until we were on a black ash track bounded by pylon

---

and earthy. Such songs as 'Black Lake' and 'Quicksand' suggest that the artist finds solace and asylum in nature; that Iceland's wilds can both reflect inner turmoil and provide a vulnerary aid.

walkers, then it was a return to clouds and reliance on the sat-nav dot. Eventually we arrived back at the clinker ridge above *Ófært* and the rebirth of the tarmac. Stefán got out to reinflate the tyres. I walked away a little up the hill with one of the wardens. The black denim view. Unexpectedly we began to talk. I explained that I was there to help with the sæluhús. I wasn't from round here, I joked. She wasn't from round here either, she said. She was from Germany. She'd come here when she was young and never gone home . . . became a nurse – she stopped, then plunged on – and although she felt Icelandic, she knew that it was not true. Now her brother was coming to visit her. Coming for the first time in years. They weren't close any more and they'd once been so, so close . . . and she felt it was her fault. Tears ran into her scarf. 'So close,' she repeated, and I found my face wet also.

'I've never told anybody,' she said in a fierce whisper. 'I've never told anybody.'

'Okay,' Stefán called somewhere behind us. 'Let's go.'

'Okay,' she said quietly, gathering herself with a broad smile. 'Now I cut.' And she put sunglasses on and turned around.

We never spoke again.

HVÍTÁRNES

I spent a week with Stefán and Atli, a young carpenter, working on sæluhús #7 Hvítárnes, which sits beside the ancient Kjolur Route – a Viking road which runs north–south through Iceland's interior highlands, passing the famous Gullfoss waterfalls, Geysir hot springs and the country's founding parliament stone; a pilgrim path for millennia.

Ferðafélag Íslands built Hvítárnes in 1930 on the shore of a glacial lake named Hvítárvatn. The lodge is a two-storey structure, timber framed, clad in corrugated iron. It faces Langjökull, Iceland's second largest glacier, which dominates the horizon of the north, looming opalescent and cavernously cold.

As we drove down towards the lake, towards the glacier's crazed face, sæluhús #7 emerged from the low sepia sweep of grass and marsh: red roof, green gables, white sides banked with turf. A little cabin sat up, hugging its knees.

The first day was spent with Atli operating a mini digger we'd hauled out from town; him shimming the turf in awkward swings and jabs and me carrying the cut sods away, cradling them heavy and cumbersome. Trying not to tear them. Then going back to the newly revealed earth to hammer away at the permafrost with a pickaxe, breaking it up so Atli could get the digger in and excavate the rocks and gravel beneath. Eventually, after a hard day's back and forth-ing, Atli and I walk away from a trench where that morning there'd been a grass rampart.

'You know this place we are going is a very haunted house?' Stefán had announced on the drive out.

'Oh yes?' I'd asked.

'Oh yes!' he'd repeated whilst Atli nodded assent. But that was as far as we got in the 4×4. At dinner the first night he told me the story.

'You notice that this house is built near some old farm ruins?' Stefán began, pointing to a series of hummocks outside. 'Well, there lived a farmer and his wife and they had a girl working too. The farmer tried to sleep with the girl but she said no and so, in revenge, he locked her outside in a snowstorm. So she died, and the farmer was killed by his wife to avenge the poor girl.'

Stefán ended this story with a meaningful look.

'I see,' I said.

Then we all walked round to the room next door where there was a bunk built at ninety degrees from all the others. 'That's the bad bed,' he told me. 'It's built across a doorway. Sleep there and the girl runs through you.'

Atli nodded and so did I.

Strange as it might sound, none of this seemed abnormal. Hvítárnes existed in a land apart, completely other, with its own unique light and gravity.

I remember sitting upstairs shortly after the ghost conversation – upstairs in the loft, gable window open, listening to Doppler geese flying over the flats.

I grew to love and set aside this golden hour around midnight when the sun, skimming low over the glacier snout, coppered the sæluhús front and lit the grass and sedgeland red; *Days of Heaven* light spun gold. Some nights I'd stand in the front door and watch sun surf across the swells of grass, a leopard-print sea rolling out to the white mountains and glass of the horizon. The river banks before the house were soft as soot. The glacier face implacable enamel; beaming a hypnotic Cheshire cat charisma; pearly cruel. The panorama spread vast and cold; wind skimmed, assailed – Gretel Ehrlich's big room of space sweeping past and whistling as it went; buffeting the cabin and the river in front, whipping the water into sharp little waves, backing it up, slowing the flow. To watch it happen was to see time turn around.

In terms of work, we rebuilt one side of the sæluhús. The frozen turf ramparts having been dug away, we levered off the cabin's tin cladding to reveal the timbers underneath, then set about replacing rotten planking and posts, burning scrap and offcuts in the kitchen stove.* One afternoon we had the little burner running full blast in a room with no walls and I thought of Phileas Fogg on the steamboat *Henrietta,* burning all the wooden parts of his ship to keep up steam having run out of coal mid-Atlantic. And us, puffing away on the shining marshes – our little crew renewing the good ship Hvítárnes for voyagers to come.

———

Next morning I descended the stair-ladder from the loft to find Atli cooking breakfast and Stefán sitting red-eyed on his bunk. He looked a washed-out wreck. 'The ghost,' he said, flatly, massaging his nose. 'I had a long night with the ghost.'

He described his haunting as a series of dreams; dreams within a dream, none of them good. He'd been woken by a weight on his chest, something pinning him, pressing so that he could not breathe. He tried not to panic. He asked it to please get off him; he was polite. Unnatural silence. Not quiet: a total lack of sound – apart from his breathing, shallow and creaking.

He was not sleeping in the bad bunk, but a lower bunk in the front room where we ate. Still held fast, the slats of the bed above a few inches from his nose, he began to talk, as best he

* The stove was a handsome dark green Jøtul NR507 with a horse cast on the front. Stefán told me this was the second such stove Hvítárnes had had in its lifetime. The first was stolen in the middle of winter about twenty years ago. 'A hell of a thing to do,' Stefán said, shrugging. 'A really bad winter. These stoves weigh a ton. Crazy robbers! I've never known another such theft.'

could, about the work we were doing on the cabin; the fact he was repairing the building, respecting the fabric of the place and landscape; explaining that he meant no harm. Then it was gone, the ghost, the presence, the weight, and he closed his wet eyes and filled his pained lungs and turned to sit sideways out of the bunk, head in hands, aware that oily twilight was pooling in the room. After an indeterminate time, minutes or hours, he climbed the stair-ladder to Atli's room and got into bed with him. Atli woke and turned, wide-eyed, and Stefán opened his mouth to explain and woke downstairs with an apparition pressing on his chest. He couldn't breathe . . .

This happened a number of times.

'I'm part troll so I can deal with it,' he told me with a wry smile but he looked utterly knackered, like a man who'd fought his way out of a supernatural tumble-drier.

All the time we'd been talking the gas burners had been flaming and the windows were now misted opaque. Large tears had began to run down the glass, pooling on the bunkhouse floor.

Hvítárnes's guestbooks are filled with sightings, phenomena, feelings, uncanny goings on. Recurrent elements of hauntings include parties approaching a lit cabin with a figure visible inside but entering to find the house empty, dark and cold. Others record meetings with the silent figure of a woman in either the cabin's entrance hall or around the single bed built across a former doorway nearest the stairs.* Encounters with a 'ghostly force' whilst in bed and drifting between wakefulness and dream – the fraying borders of

---

* Notably the ghost seems to appear mostly to men, although that may be due to that fact that historically it has been mostly men who've stayed at Hvítárnes.

sleep, the mouth of that deep unfathomable forest. Unaccountable sounds and lights emanating from upstairs when guests were downstairs and vice versa and, very occasionally, there is mention of 'a horrible black face in the east window of the house', assumed to be that of the farmer.

The first log of the ghost occurred in July 1938. 'Got the Ghost' wrote an anonymous hand who only identified as 'coming from Hveravöllur and going to Reykjavik'. The following year (August 1939) Francis Gordon Reid, an English dentist, wrote 'ghosts'. I love the formidable pith of these notes and smile again to read them now. *Here be laconic monsters.*

Later travellers were more explicit about ghostly goings on. Here is the note from a group of friends from Europe who visited Hvítárnes in August 1979:

This was a terrible night.

At 11:30 we have been awakened by a most peculiar noise upstairs. Dieter wanted to go upstairs to investigate the noise but was thrown backwards down the stairs by some inexplicable blow. After this Jeanine tried the same, now imagine: she was lifted up by some invisible hand. This happened in front of all of us. When Jeanine came back to consciousness, she found herself right on the top of the roof. We all climbed on the roof in order to rescue Jeanine. At this exact moment, we heard a feminine voice downstairs in the cabin whimpering something that sounded like 'HELWITIS KATLIN' which does not make any sense to us. Coming back we were terrified by a supernatural light flickering over the bed which is located under the staircase. At this moment we just lost our nerves and ran outside ... where we spent the rest of the night shivering and trembling in bracken.

It was only in the morning that we dared to come back to this haunted house, just to fetch our belongings and to testify to this very strange experience.

21 September 1996 – two anonymous companions planned to stay the night:

Arrived at 6:30 pm. Had dinner and went to bed.

Woke up at 3:30 [downstairs at the front of the house] – heavy footsteps in the attic, doors slamming and furniture moving back and forth.

Fled just after 4:30 [and spent the] night out in a car.

Strange light was seen in a window of the house sometimes.

When we left, we turned back to see the house and saw light surrounding everything inside.

PS: Never come back here.

Reading these accounts back in Reykjavik, my mind retraced the road out to Hvítárnes – the miles out past Geysir and Gullfoss to where the tourist coaches could go no further and the road had become compressed snow; on to the place where we'd encountered a bulldozer, massive yellow tank-tracked wedge: the leading edge of the road; and on another hour or two over vestal drifts, forging our own path until

---

* The logbooks of Hvítárnes 1938–2003 are kept in the Manuscript Collection at the National and University Library of Iceland in Reykjavík, whilst Stefán

we reached a bridge across Hvítárvatn's steely meltwaters. There snow ended and the mousey marshes began, the 4×4 sloshing through waist-high swims surrounded by bare dwarf bushes beaten down wyrd by the wind. Finally, framed by the glacier, rising charged and singularly lonely from the levels, our preoccupied haunt.

'Solitude in the city is about the lack of other people or rather their distance beyond a door or wall,' wrote Rebecca Solnit, 'but in remote places it isn't an absence but the presence of something else, a kind of humming silence . . . words strange rocks you may or may not turn over.'[7]

In Hvítárnes the silence hums whilst turning the rocks over for you. Some places invite you to engage and be changed and some give you no choice at all.

———

On our final day Atli told me about a week he'd spent alone on the Ross Ice Shelf in Antarctica – completely alone in

---

and Ferðafélag Íslands currently hold the books from 2004–12. I'm very grateful to Halldór Óli Gunnarsson, Icelandic folklorist and author of *Draugasögur úr Hvítárnesskál / Ghost Stories of Hvítárnes Bowl* (University of Iceland, 2012) – a fascinating and hugely useful document and compilation of hauntings and ghostly happenings at Hvítárnes. Halldór spent many hours carefully looking through old guestbooks and kindly let me quote some of his findings here. 'But remember,' he told me, 'those guestbooks only date from 1938 to 2003. I'm pretty sure there are more stories in the books from 2003 to 2012 that are kept by the FÍ.' He also reckons that a great many people might have experienced strange events at the sæluhús but left no written record; so much so that he could easily imagine a thesis or book being written about Hvítárnes based on oral history alone – 'because I do think there are many people who have experienced something out of the ordinary in that cabin . . . it would [be] a massive project to interview every single person with a story to tell.'

the featureless white with only far distant mountains for company; how it had been fine, really good, actually; he'd been part of an expedition; how in fact he'd been to Antarctica twice . . . He broke this news so lightly, so kindly, perhaps concerned about hurting my feelings and bursting my bubble as a would-be trailblazer. 'Wow,' I said, stunned. 'Amazing stuff, Atli. You kept that quiet!' And he grinned. And I thought of his skills and capability – this gentle twenty-something man out here on the digger, hefting a pick, showing me the best way to tackle the hard earth; the way he'd set about de-nailing the tongue and groove inside the cabin – all smooth practised movements and efficiency, clear eyes and calm manner; the warmth in his demeanour; the happy bonhomie he and Stefán shared. Expedient people. Eminently tough, good-humoured and able.

Atli told me how he and Stefán once moved a couple of rundown Ferðafélag Íslands buildings out to his farm with a view to repairing and reusing them somewhere down the line. They'd dug them new foundations and patched them up a bit, meaning to see to them properly once winter was over and the days drew out again. But the winter storms that year were spectacularly bad and the buildings were torn from their foundations – in the case of one, picked up and dragged several hundred metres together *with* its foundations – before exploding in the monster gales; torn to shreds. 'Yeah,' said Atli cheerfully. 'It was a bad one. The buildings were completely blown up and away. The largest bit I found which wasn't made of concrete was a wood panel about a foot square. Bad weather. Really bad. Really not good.'

Stefán had just got on with his job the morning after his haunting; put on his padded boiler-suit and carried on with the work; wasn't put off by it, took it in his stride. That's just how Icelandic people are, I think. It's just the sort of thing they say: 'Luckily I'm part troll'; 'It was a bad one. The buildings were completely blown up and away. The largest bit I found which wasn't made of concrete was a wood panel about a foot square'; 'You have writer's hands, Dan. You need to toughen up.'

———

The morning I flew home from Iceland, as the plane's silhouette fell away and sped green-grey over Keflavik – a spectral cross flickering ever smaller over scrub, black rocks and deepening blues – I imagined a shadow self left behind, an offering to the land, now stowed unseen beneath the sea.

Iceland: black and white, gold and blue; fire and ice; a supernatural state where the line between dream and reality feels gossamer thin. To negotiate such a territory one needs a grounding, a guide – Icelandic nous.

I was very lucky to have met Stefán and Atli because they allowed me insight into Iceland as Icelanders behold it. Their practical intelligence and environmental outlook is balanced, perhaps *founded* is a better word, on Iceland's ancient myths and folktales – stories passed down and taught to each new generation, most dealing with man's relationship with the powerful natural world. Respect for nature and the spirits of the land – the trolls and huldufólk, hidden people – is central to all such stories and rather than being an eccentric anachronism, such narratives have created a deep connection with the land and a national character steeped in sustainability.

In a recent article, Ólina Thorvarðardóttir, a specialist in Icelandic literature and cultural anthropology at the

National Museum in Reykjavik, explained the existence and importance of an elemental respect culture, stressing how many ancient and apposite messages are delivered through the supernatural beings* of Iceland's super-nature:

> The fate of humans depends on how they interact with these spirits. We are not speaking here of pretty fairies with magic wands, but rather the *huldufólk* [who] cast spells upon people, blessing or cursing them according to how they judge their behavior . . . The stories have served a meaningful role in raising children. What child would dare to climb the rock believed to be the habitation of the *huldufólk*? The *huldufólk* took grim vengeance upon children who caused a disturbance near their dwellings, and likewise they punished farmers who strained the resources of their estates. Environmental concerns, thus, have been one of the motifs of Icelandic oral tradition since ancient times.[8]

---

*   In the prologue to his beautiful book, *The Earth Is Only a Little Dust Under Our Feet*, Bego Antón provides a more fulsome résumé of Iceland's magical bestiary:

There are elves in Iceland. Also fairies, unicorns, huldufólk, trolls, beach dwarfs, water sprites, mountain spirits and ghosts. Icelanders don't throw stones in the air for fear of hitting one of these mysterious beings. They don't jump on stones, in case a huldufólk might be living inside. And someone once told me:

> 'If the president
> claimed he didn't believe in these
> magical creatures
> he would never be re-elected.'

— *The Earth Is Only a Little Dust Under Our Feet*, Bego Antón, Overlapse, London, 2018, p.iii.

Having spoken to Icelanders like Haraldur and Stefán, and worked in such a remarkable place as Hvítárnes, I think belief and respect for the huldufólk is perfectly reasonable, logical even; an Arctic animism akin to the Shinto of another island beset by tectonic Sturm und Drang: Japan.

In a 2015 interview, Terry Gunnell, professor of folklore at the University of Iceland, told the *Guardian*:

> When your house can be destroyed by an earthquake, when you can be blown over by the wind, when boiling water from your taps tells you there's lava not far beneath your feet – then you don't mess with nature.[9]

To live in a country as potent and metamorphic as Iceland is to be constantly reminded, made acutely aware, that the land is both ancient and new. Bolshie, raw, evolving geology; a territory as likely to mushroom a volcano as to disappear a lake overnight. Here, mighty maelstroms habitually tear buildings apart and vanish the debris as you might brush crumbs from your lap.

In such a situation a charge of pareidolia might be made – the psychological phenomenon by which the mind perceives familiar patterns and shapes where none exist; as the Man in the Moon so the trolls in the mountains around Hvítárnes and Þórsmörk – phantasms engendered by an eldritch scape, spectres of a terror firma. But to do so would be to misunderstand the respect and connection Icelanders feel for their world.

Rather than the negative associations of pareidolia – a word with its roots in illusion, of thoughts beside the truth, as paranoia stems from 'irregular' + 'mind' – I suggest that many Icelanders possess an almost extrasensory perception, an imaginative facility which affords a better understanding of their isle. William Blake wrote of twofold vision – the world seen 'not with but through the eye'* – a doubling of sight which enables a person to see beyond the concrete to behold contexts, associations and emotional meanings. The huldufólk embody this doubling, an empathic insight which has helped foster an elemental solidarity between people and place.

Flying out of Iceland I thought of my great-gran, an implacable Scots voice echoing down the ages; 'the spectator sees more of the game' she used to say – she had many maxims – another favourite being 'Don't come all yea with me, Sonny Jim, or you'll get your head in your hands to play with.' I sense she and the huldufólk would have got on like a house on fire. 'Don't come all yea with me,' warn the Icelandic wilds, 'or I will respond in kind . . .' And with that my mind flew back to Rebecca Solnit, a brilliant chronicler of the modern human condition, political and environmental drama and upheaval, who often deploys parables and allegoric essays to better unpack the stories, unpick the people and speak truth to power. Here she is regarding America's forty-fifth President:

---

* The EYE . . . 'not with but through the eye', a phrase which Blake may have taken from Plato's *Theaetetus*. This ability consists in the spontaneous translating of the visible into human qualities, the process now called 'empathy'. – *A Blake Dictionary: The Ideas and Symbols of William Blake*, S. Foster Damon, Brown University Press, New England, 1988, p.134.

'He who does not imagine in stronger and better lineaments, and in stronger and better light than his perishing, mortal eye can see, does not imagine at all.' – *Life of William Blake*, Vol. 2, Alexander Gilchrist, Harper Perennial, London, 2011, p.153.

He was supposed to be a great maker of things, but he was mostly a breaker. He acquired buildings and women and enterprises and treated them all alike, promoting and deserting them, running into bankruptcies and divorces, treading on lawsuits the way a lumberjack of old walked across the logs floating on their way to the mill, but as long as he moved in his underworld of dealmakers the rules were wobbly and the enforcement was wobblier and he could stay afloat.[10]

An ancient story. The tale of a tyrant – an anti-huldufólk. The cap fits and so does the form of the telling. Far from anachronisms, the environmental morals and message of Iceland's ancient fables remain resonant and relevant. Deeply strange and supernatural, compelling, clearsighted and wise.

The original sæluhús were refuge stations for travellers crossing the interior hinter/highlands. The remains of many structures dating back to the Norse can still be found, whilst others have become modern bunkhouses, new buildings on ancient foundations.

New visitors arrive – drop in.

Not all of them esteem the environment as they should.

Some 'get the ghosts'.

So it goes.

Much has changed since the first sæluhús were built but the wilful earth and ice, and the stories they stir – the maxims, counsel and cautions of old, the novels, music and dreams of now; the essential questing unrest and respect that exist between Icelanders and their nature – are thriving; potent and apt as ever.

Hvítárnes, Iceland. Photographs: Dan Richards

III

SIMON STARLING – *SHEDBOATSHED*

Clear? Ha! Why a four-year-old child could understand
this! Run out and find me a four-year-old child ...

– Groucho Marx[1]

SAILHOUSE

I caught a train to Copenhagen to see the artist Simon
Starling. I wanted to talk to him about his Turner Prize-
winning installation, *Shedboatshed (Mobile Architecture
No. 2)* – a work described, a little erroneously, on his gallery's
website as a 'Wooden shed, 390 × 600 × 340 cm, 2005'.

Yes, *now*, I want to say; *now* it's a shed of the proportions
you suggest, *at the moment*. The brilliance of *Shedboatshed*
is that it is an evolving roving work – the sort of work land
artist David Nash might describe as 'becoming'. It is
currently a shed ... again. But it was once a boat. Shed is
the bread of its sandwich life, the middle is filled with
travel, rivers and derring-do. It is a shed with stories to tell.
A shed that's been on a great adventure. Its timbers dream
of the river.

In the run-up to my trip I began to see the world in
sandwich terms. Days became sleepwakesleeps, my cat was
a napeatnap, this book a teawritetea.

An hour out of Hamburg, I travelled on a trainboattrain when we rolled on to the rail-ferry which links Puttgarden and Rødby, crossing the Vogelfluglinie or Fugleflugtslinjen – the *bird flight line*, a wonderful compound name which alludes to both the 'as the crow flies' course of the ferry and the transport corridor's importance to birds migrating between Central Europe and the Scandinavian Arctic.

I was not flying as a crow. I'd taken the train to experience the distance and landscape between London and Copenhagen, stopping off in Brussels where I made friends with the owner of a record shop who introduced me to sour beer as gravy; Köln, where between connections I saw an unsettling Gerhard Richter exhibition at Museum Ludwig in the twin spire shadows of the high gothic cathedral; and Hamburg, where I got confused and ended up in a Tesla showroom being shown electric cars by somebody who for some reason thought I was solvent and able to drive. Then I was back on another train with a winningly square flat face and rolling north to the ferry where, near dusk, we clacked on to the car deck, snug beside lorries. Upstairs in the observation lounge I saw that the first thing seasoned Fugleflugtslinjeners do is form a snaking queue around the closed canteen. This seemed quite a passive-aggressive display until the moment the ferry, with a hoot, left the slip and, as one, the shutters shot open and a school-dinner supper was served. The system, the shutters, the singing men on the next table over: all were clearly very well oiled.

---

*   Tesla: famous exponents of the carcarcar – driverless cars which take people out of the equation.

I bought a coffee and sat back down amongst the diners, all of us gazing at the dark waters and red outlined horizons whilst the ship trembled beneath us. Eventually the windows welled into mirrors and the formica diner fanned out either side like wings spreading into the night.

All that way on rails and water to see a man about a shed. It might sound like a shaggy dog story but it was actually something of a pilgrimage. *Shedboatshed* is an artwork which I like lot. I liked it the moment I saw it as a shed at Tate Britain and took an even greater pleasure in it once I'd learnt its backstory. But even at face-value it has an excellent face: a porch-mouth of cubicles, four little chalets, above which a single paddle is fixed. The roof is angled like a jaunty hat with a fringe of corrugated iron. The boards of its face are wide, old boards from big trees. It's mostly creosoted but some planks seem to have missed the brush. Some are mellow chestnut, others tangerine, some new wood and some leathered grey. In pictures it looks soft, like a shed which has been worked quite hard and had its corners knocked off in the process, but in person a lot of it was quite knotty, gnarly-grained, a mix of silky and splintered wood – an expedient assemblage. And once that mongrel aspect is noted the chalet-mouth seems to take on a panting aspect and, with that, the shed reveals itself as rather canine.

Dogs like a river. They like to stand above water and look down past their front paws, examining the rippling ribbons of sun or brown silty shallows. I've seen them. Sometimes they jump in with abandon and sometimes they lower themselves with minute care. *Shedboatshed* looks like the sort of dog-shed which, having yolloped in a river, has just hauled its joyfully quivering back-end out, spira-shaken itself dry and is now having a rest, panting at the scene with more than half a mind to lunge in again – launch itself off the bank as Simon Starling launched it on a trip down the Rhine in 2005 in the temporary form of a boat.

In short, a shed of agency; a transportive space of imagination. As children build dens which are infinitely more than the sum of their parts, so *Shedboatshed* is both infinitely more and *exactly* the sum of its parts; nothing added or taken away. Somewhere beside the Rhine there's a flat piece of ground, the spot where Starling discovered the shed, saw its potential, beheld its charismatic raw material and, shortly afterwards, set about rebuilding it as a flat bottomed weidling punt. Shortly after *that* he poled it several miles down the river to a Basel gallery where he returned it to its original form.

I've always been drawn to simple structures – garden sheds, hay barns, line-side shelters glimpsed from passing trains. As a child, every door in a whitewashed wall held the promise of a secret garden, every cupboard was a possible gateway to Narnia, every cellar stair or crypt a portal to the underworld. A great many stories I loved involved passing through doors with unexpected worlds the other side. Each week Mr Benn would walk along Festive Road in his black suit and bowler hat to try on a new costume at his local

---

* A weidling is a flat-bottomed boat – a type of flat-bottomed punt that can be tracked back to Celtic boats built more than 2,000 years ago. The weidling is traditionally constructed from solid wood, although today some boats are also made from plywood, plastic or aluminium. It is usually around 9 or 10 metres (30 or 33ft) in length. In the Middle Ages, the weidling was used for river transportation and fishing. Today, the boat is primarily used in Switzerland, on the Rhine and its tributaries. It is used as a leisure and pleasure craft, and as a passenger ferry. The sport of Wasserfahren in Switzerland is conducted almost exclusively with weidlings.

fancy dress shop. He chose an outfit with the help of the owner – a befezed man with a sphinxy smile – before dressing up and walking out of the changing room door and into an adventure. The Batcave was accessed down the Batpoles which were situated behind a perfectly ordinary-looking sliding bookcase. The TARDIS is a spacecraft and time machine, bigger on the inside and disguised as a police box.

My closest encounter with a TARDIS occurred as a child in the dunes above Porthcurno beach. We were on a family holiday to Cornwall, perhaps we'd gone to see the Minack Theatre or Land's End; either way, whilst exploring the sand and marram grass I found a small concrete hut emitting the kind of wavering singsong sound of a radio set between stations. The walls inside were lined with apparatus akin to elderly gas meters plumbed in to wires and hoses emerging from the oxblood floor. A brief notice informed me that this, the Porthcurno Telegraphy Station, had once been the landing point for a web of intercontinental submarine cables. A map showed massed lines eeling out from the cove below. The original network had long been retired, their current of morse and voices cut off, but the wires did not fall silent. They began to sing. Today they broadcast the sound of sun-flares and lightning around the world; electromagnetic music bubbling up from the bottom of the sea. The siren which had drawn me into the hut had been a mix of deep tectonic tunes, elemental airs and the cosmic songs of stars.

I think of Porthcurno and Hvítárnes sæluhús as kindred transmitters.

The first time I walked into Simon's studio, I felt that here was a workshop where new outposts and adventures might be created – a long light room a little like a drawing office with desks at one end and a big table at the other. Hidden in a courtyard behind a high blond-brick tenement, a low-key inner-city ideas factory from which stories and artworks might be loosed into the world. The first works I saw were two silver photographic prints pinned to the back wall. They were of a canoe on a beach, no people. Just the canoe, the beach and the horizon, below which water, above which sky. Some clouds. Odd marbled mounds on the beach to the right of the canoe gave a clue to the canoe's location: the salt shores of the Dead Sea.

Such was the crisp clarity of the prints that the grains of the beach seemed to stand proud like the flaking foil of an antique mirror and the boat appeared to float, levitating hard ellipse, scalpel-prowed.

It was the opposite sort of craft to *Shedboatshed*, all sharp lines, hard edges and efficiency. Simon, turning to greet me, tall, slightly shaggy, smiling, bearded, glasses, seemed to have more in common with weathered wood than alkali metals, although the V of his cardigan was neat and his shirt underneath was ironed.

He looked academic. He offered coffee. His voice was speedy but precise; driven by ideas rather than angst; gently amused – he reminded me of a letterpress printer I know. His voice had the song of a Heidelberg in it.

'You put it through a transformation and it comes out the other side and it's the same thing that you started with but it's in a different place. There's a certain economy to that, I suppose,' he told me a few minutes later when we were settled with our drinks at the table in the sun. He wasn't talking about *Shedboatshed* but rather the magnesium canoe on the wall – a work named *Rift Valley Crossing* which he described as 'a kind of walking on water; turning the road into a vehicle'.

The canoe was made of magnesium extracted from Dead Sea water, 'the most concentrated source of magnesium in the world'. Simon described the project to me as 'another super simple idea', that of taking some sea water, making some metal, casting a boat, and then paddling across the sea in a boat made from its water – something from nothing. Alchemy. 'But then, in doing that, you begin to think, "Ah, the Dead Sea is in Israel, and it's in Jordan, and the West Bank . . ." so the project grows.'[†]

The simply plotted projects that he makes are very open to interpretation, he tells me, but 'leave no trace' is an idea that runs through a lot of his work; the transformation of materials from one state to another then back again, or not.

The artist's statement for *Rift Valley Crossing* states that 'circular journeys both real and metaphorical form a large part of Simon Starling's work' whilst he describes them as 'the physical manifestation of a thought process'.

His art as a vehicle for stories, I suggest, and he agrees, pointing to the urge to travel and the desire to tell stories as being the two driving motivations behind a great deal of his work.

---

* *Project for a Rift Valley Crossing*, Simon Starling, 2015. Artwork details: 53 × 474 × 85cm. Material description: Canoe cast in Dead Sea magnesium, two paddles, two canvas seats, Dead Sea water, tanks, wooden welding jig, two silver gelatin prints.

† After exhibiting the canoe in Nottingham in 2016, Simon returned it to source and paddled the tricky, potentially treacherous crossing from Israel to Jordan.

'In a way I'm taking objects on journeys, putting them through something. At times it's almost like a prototyping process or crash-testing – like when you take a chair and put it into a machine which pummels it for a week. The work may be made in a studio but, for me, it only gets interesting when it gets out in the world; when it's being tested. Out there, in the world, it accrues narratives. I often talk about detours, where you start somewhere and somehow end up back where you began but you only get there by making a ridiculous circuitous journey and *Shedboatshed* is a very good example of that; we start with a shed and end with a shed, but we've basically gone ten, twelve kilometres downstream from one location to another; from a riverbank to a museum, and in doing that the object has accrued this new story, this new history which is now readable in its structure, you know?'

———

The week before I travelled to Copenhagen, I went to see Roald Dahl's writing hut in Great Missenden, Buckinghamshire. Dahl moved to the village in 1954 and had a shed built in his garden after a visit to see Dylan Thomas's boathouse and 'word-splashed hut' in Laugharne. A space away from

---

* 'Eighteen months ago, British artist Simon Starling dropped a replica of a sculpture by Henry Moore into Lake Ontario. This weekend, visitors to the Power Plant gallery in Toronto will see the result as part of a retrospective of work by Turner Prize-winner Starling ... The work he's created in *Infestation Piece (Musselled Moore)* is partly the story of a Henry Moore sculpture, but also the story of the zebra mussel, an invasive species that will cover any object that sits long enough in Great Lakes water.' – 'British artist pulls sculpture from bottom of Lake Ontario', CBC Arts News, 29 February 2008.

children seemed to be the driving idea – a 'work-hole' to bunker down and write.

Rachel White, collections manager & archivist, kindly gave me a copy of a talk Dahl wrote about his hut and process. The original typewritten sheets are titled 'For Children' and dated 13/10/75. In it he describes his daily routine, beginning around 10 a.m.

> So I go up to what everyone calls my 'Wendy house', which is simply a small brick shed up in our orchard, well away from the house. It is heated with an Aladdin paraffin stove and in the winter it gets perishing cold. So all through the winter I work in a sleeping bag. I step into the sleeping bag and pull it right up to my chest, then I sit down in an old leather armchair. Then I put my feet up on a trunk that is filled with wooden blocks to make it solid.

The trunk is wired to the legs of the chair so it won't push away, he continues. Then he puts a roll of cardboard across his knees to support his writing board which is covered with green billiard cloth, 'a nice restful colour'. The curtains in the hut are permanently drawn shut so he won't become distracted and 'sit staring out at the squirrels messing about on the apple trees outside'. Cows have been known to poke their heads in though the window and try to eat the curtain. Once one leant in and pulled it right off its rod – you can imagine the audiences' smiles of delight at that detail.

He switches on a lamp and puts a yellow pad on the green board, then begins the ritual of his Dixon Ticonderoga pencils:

I use six pencils, the kind with rubbers on one end. I have these sent from America by the gross, I don't know why except they are what I started with and it would worry me enormously to change the colour after 30 years. Now, because I am actually afraid to start work – most writers are – I employ a lot of delaying tactics. I reach for a clothes brush and brush the previous day's rubber shavings off my board. Then I clean my glasses. Then I start sharpening the six pencils. This is a very lengthy affair. I have an electric sharpener, made in Japan and bought in California, and first I sharpen each of the six pencils in there. It makes a lovely whizzing noise when you put a pencil in the hole. But it doesn't make the points nearly sharp enough for me.

So he sharpens each pencil again with his pocket knife, having first sharpened the pocket-knife on a little grindstone 'to make it sharp enough to sharpen the pencils which the pencil-sharpener hasn't sharpened properly'.

Having trimmed up six lead points with great care and concentration so that they're 'sharper than needles . . . so sharp, in fact, that the point always breaks off the moment I press it against the paper', he'd place them in a toby jug on a table by his side and pour himself a cup of coffee from a thermos he'd brought down from the house. Then he'd light a cigarette 'and look around for something else to do so that I won't have to start writing. There is nothing else to do. The yellow pad with blue lines on it is watching me and waiting to be written upon. So I settle down and become quiet and at last begin to write the story.'

When Dahl died, the contents of the hut were left undisturbed for around twenty years. In 2011 the interior was transferred to the museum and reconstructed in a new shed of the same dimensions as the original but with a glass wall instead of the end with the original yellow door. Everything is in there, down to the original scuffed linoleum. There is Dahl's chair, the peg boards, photographs, ashtrays full of his cigarette butts and ash.

Rachel was kind enough to open up the display shed for me and as soon as I stepped in I was surrounded by smells – coffee, tobacco smoke and Marlboro stubs, pencil shavings, feathers from the sleeping bag and stuffing from the writing chair. The smells tell of the work. I think of a line in Alice Oswald's *Dart*: 'he makes a den of himself – smells and small thoughts',[2] that's what went on here and that's why the family and museum were so keen to preserve and celebrate this hut – the manifestation of Roald Dahl's mind – his writing life condensed, his denspace.

There are the exposed squares of padding he cut out to better support his cronky frame – so beaten up in the Second World War when his fighter plane crashed into the Libyan desert. The table of totems and trinkets: a unique rock from Babylon, an opal from Australia – but the interesting thing about the chair, this cut-about expedient tool, is that it's become a recognisable character in its own right. It appears in Wes Anderson's stop-motion *Fantastic Mr Fox* film, there's a reproduction of it in the museum's activity area for children to sit in and write. The original chair sits at the centre of the museum – revered seat, cockpit, talisman. The modifications, smell, patina, they're all canon now.

I described the hut and chair to Simon, the holes, the angular high armrests, the Heath-Robinson heating system Dahl strung up above it on wires – an electric heater he pulled forwards or pushed away with his walking stick. 'It sounds like some sort of invalid chair,' noted Simon, laughing. 'It's almost like he had to trap himself.'

I think that's spot on. This enormous man of six foot five, the proto-BFG, traps himself in a shed each morning, and straps himself into his cockpit to go to work. I don't think it was a particularly curated or romantic space during Dahl's lifetime. It was a spartan means to an end, a space away from the family home where he could write undisturbed. 'When I am up here I see only the paper I am writing on, and my mind is far away with Willy Wonka or James or Mr Fox or Danny or whatever else I am trying to cook up,' he once told an interviewer. 'The room itself is of no consequence. It is out of focus, a place for dreaming and floating and whistling in the wind, as soft and silent and murky as a womb . . .'

But such disavowals only added to the myth.

The pencil moves across the yellow pad, back and forth in a circle of lamplight. The cigarette trails in the ashtray. The writer huffs, he shifts his rump, scratches his temple and dives back in, cosy in his peach-stone cave born aloft by 500 seagulls; safe in his foxhole whilst, somewhere else, three crazed farmers dig and gnash their teeth; smiling to himself as the glass hut spins and drifts far out in space, Buckinghamshire light years away, the yellow door a million miles.

'I write the first sentence and I rub it out,' he wrote in his talk 'For Children'.

I write it again, and again, many times, trying to get it short and clear and clean and easily understood. The first page of any book or short story always takes me at least three weeks to do, working four hours a day. I think that is because when you are writing and erasing so endlessly, you are also working out, though you don't know it, the whole of the rest of the story in your subconscious mind. So after the first draft is at last finished, then things go a little quicker. A book like *Charlie* or *James* with about 150 pages, will take roughly a year to write. It's a long business, and you have to be patient, and above all you have to stick at it.

———

Whilst aboard my several trains to Copenhagen I'd reread some of the press written around the time that *Shedboatshed* won the Turner Prize. The general view of the critics seemed to be that this was difficult modern art – was it even art? – labyrinthine and postmodern; the sort of thing you'd need to read a book about before it made any sense. Yet it was also reported that the visiting public were quite taken with the work. Young people were approaching Starling between interviews to say how much they liked the work, asking if he'd sign their tickets.

The Tate website still carries a quote from Starling at the time:

Art for me is a free space to explore things. The things I do don't always come out looking like conventional works of art. But then I'm like any artist these days working in relation to a long history of art. I think the press is a long way behind understanding this or responding to art in a sympathetic way. I got a lovely poem from a lady in St Albans about sheds.[3]

Now, at a distance of twelve years, he describes the experience of 'the whole Turner Prize thing' as quite brutal. 'The guy from the newspaper, the *Daily Mail* or somewhere, going to B&Q and buying a garden shed and trying to build a boat out of it . . . I kind of loved it in a way but, for me, there was this complete disconnect from how I felt the public were enjoying and understanding the work and the way that the press portrayed it. They made out that it was super-difficult and convoluted and remote and, actually, from my experience people got it straight away.'

Was that because the public engaged and properly looked? I wonder. The press seemed to bypass the shed to focus on the shyster artist who'd had the nerve to present it as art; the shed was almost in the way of the story – *Contrary 'artist' puts shed in a gallery.* Nobody seemed to comment on the fact it was such an interesting, beautiful shed, they didn't look for the marks of its metamorphosis, ignoring the shed's patina and story in favour of their own hatchet jobs.

——

I want to ask you about the shed, Simon.

'Okay. Good!'

It was originally on the Swiss border, is that right?

'Yes. Even when I found the shed it had a great history – a history as an object that had already been moved. It was originally a guard post on the Swiss border and then I guess it reached a point where it was getting a bit dilapidated so they replaced it and the boat club in Muttenz, Switzerland, the Wasserfahrverein Muttenz, who race weidlings on the river, they heard of the shed and thought "we need a shed" so they put it on the back of a truck and moved it to the club. Bits of it had been rebuilt because they had gone rotten – so it was already something that had had a real life as an object; you could read it in the object. In a way I was just trying to add one more layer to that history by cutting it up in weird ways and making holes in it so it could be joined together . . . and when I exhibited the rebuilt shed I perhaps naïvely thought that people would be able to walk around and start to piece the boat back together in their minds – which some people did but the press seemed unable to make that leap, or *want* to make that leap.'

It sounds very straightforward.

'Super-simple.'

You gave a shed that's had many lives another life.

'Yes.'

And then you returned it to the state you'd discovered it in.

'And it's so logical as well – you find a thing with a paddle on it so you use the paddle.'

I'm struck that you could have made your life so much harder. 'I found this brick wall by the side of the river . . .'

'I think if I showed *Shedboatshed* again now, if it went back to the Tate, I think the reception would be utterly different because works accrue history, they interact with the world and change. You know, this time it would be "Ah! The shed!"'

How do you feel about the work now?

'Well, I mean, it's an okay work but it's certainly not the most interesting thing I've ever done. It was what I was doing . . . basically I got the call to be in the Turner Prize when I was standing on the bank of the river, working on the project, and it was what was current and what I had to show so that's what ended up there. I don't know . . . yeah, it's odd. But that's the work that defines me now and . . . I like it. It has a simple, lyrical, elegant logic to it – because I'd so wanted to use the river. The river is so impressive in Basel, this huge, cold force that runs through the city, and everything about that city is defined by it. I think I'd been with Henriette, my wife, to see the beautiful Roskilde Viking museum for the first time just beforehand – the idea that the Vikings took their boats out of the water in the winter and turned them upside down, so suddenly you had a nice shelter . . . a simple building. In Basel I borrowed the curator's bicycle and cycled along the river and found this shed. It was completely ridiculous. Completely ridiculous! I had half an idea of what I was looking for and there was this shed and it was a weird moment where the project just fell into place in a matter of seconds. I saw the shed and the paddle nailed to it, the paddle was for a weidling – and that was that. Then it was just a question of realising the potential of that found scenario – following its internal logic.'

How big was the weidling you built?

'Ten metres long! A weidling's like a gondola in a way, really big. And then we were back and forth. It was a ferry to transport the rest of the shed from one place to the other. When the Wasserfahrverein launch a new boat, they traditionally roast a suckling pig by the river and fire a cannon so they fired the cannon and then we launched the boat and barbecued. One of the guys who was on the installation crew at the museum turned out to have been a youth champion weidling oarsman – he was completely into the idea.'

Did you build it on your own?

'No, I worked with a guy named Haimo Ganz, who was an artist but had trained as a carpenter; like many Swiss people do. And then there was another artist – an art student, Christian Felber was his name. So we worked together on it. It was a wonderful process, the sailing club had a beautiful open shed where they keep boats in the winter and they gave us free rein so that became our workshop. So there were lots of boats on hand to measure.'

Did you have to add new material?

'A few screws and we had rope in the joints and things like that, just to make it all watertight, but it worked a treat, actually. The best timber was in the roof and the floor. Because that was actually the most recent addition to the shed. A lot of the side material was rather ropey.'

And the people who owned it, the weidling club, they were happy for you to take the shed away?

Simon shook his head and laughed, still delighted and bemused at the memory. 'Yes! The curator called them and said, "I've got this artist, he's interested in your shed," and they said, "Oh good! We've been trying to get rid of that for ages!" It was absolutely perfect.'

Shedboatshed (Mobile Architecture No. 2), Production Stills, 2005.
Photographs: Simon Starling; courtesy: the artist

IV

DESOLATION PEAK, WA, USA

'I'm afraid you'll have to take up art. Art is the only work
open to people who can't get along with others and still
want to be special.'

– Alasdair Gray[1]

My flight from London to Seattle was at 09:50 GMT
on Monday 18 September. At check-in I was asked
when I would be returning and I said early October-ish since
I was not sure. I haven't actually booked a ticket home, I
explained. 'Ah, then you cannot fly!' said the Norwegian Air
lady brightly. Oh dear, I said. But I need to fly. What do I
need to do so I can fly?

Book a ticket home, it turned out. So I lugged my duffel
and rucksack back into the mêlée of the south terminal,
found a seat, sat down, booked a flight home with my phone
and then, as instructed, walked back to the Norwegian Air
desk, past the angry side-eye queue, and the smiling lady,
having made sure my there-and-back-again itinerary was
solid, cheerfully checked me in and wished me well.

This was all rather more harum-scarum than I'd have liked
and in retrospect I was probably cutting things a bit fine, but
the fact was that my US plans were in tatters and I was
waiting on news from an unresponsive Mars base in Utah.

Ten days earlier my itinerary had looked fairly solid –

- *DY7131 – 09:50 GMT London Gatwick – Seattle 11:45 EST –* 18 September
- *Big Creek Baldy Lookout, Kootenai National Forest, Montana –* 21–25 September
- *Mars Desert Research Station – 2200 Cow Dung Road, Hanksville, Utah –* ?

Setting aside that I don't drive and had no real plan for getting from Seattle to the lookout tower I'd rented in Kootenai National Forest, Montana – or the 900 miles south to Utah as the crow flies after that – things were in reasonable shape. All I needed was a 'Yes' from Mars, Utah – a green light to pitch up in their red desert. But then, a week before I was due to go, an email arrived from the National Park Service:

Dear Mr Richards,

This is an important message from Recreation.gov regarding your reservation at Big Creek Baldy Lookout Rental. We regret to inform you, that due to a fire in the area, the lookout will be closed from September 18th, through September 30th, 2017.

Your reservation has been cancelled, and a full refund has been issued.

. . . We apologize for the inconvenience this has caused.

Sincerely,

Blair
Customer Support Representative

Which was a bit of bugger, really, because that was one of the main reasons for my trip. So I was flying out to Seattle to see what happened and maybe trace Jack Kerouac's 1956 journey north to Desolation Peak. This, ironically enough, had been my original intention at the start of the project, since I'd researched and written about some of Kerouac's mountaintop experiences in *Climbing Days* – specifically his run-in with a bear – but then, fearing that the path to Desolation Peak was perhaps too well trodden, my sights moved towards Big Creek Baldy, partly because it was a tower-style lookout, raised on stilts like the fire-watch cabins of my imagination, partly for the name, but mainly because it was in the area of the Idaho Panhandle where the writer Denis Johnson lived* – a literary hero and the author of a book named *Train Dreams*.

I was first put on to Denis Johnson by the staff at Mr B's Bookshop in Bath. I was in the early planning stages of this book, a blank panicked state of mooching – browsing with a terrible furrowed intent – scouring the shelves for miraculous mulch to germinate vague ideas.

In retrospect it was here that this book was really born – a realisation that my enthusiasm for the Alpine cabins I'd visited whilst climbing and writing my last could accumulate and meld with stories of other eyries and spartan architectures on the edge; a continuation of the more tangential reading I'd done for *Climbing Days* – *Consolations of the Forest* by Sylvain Tessen, Rebecca Solnit's *Field Guide to Getting Lost*, *The Dead Mountaineer's*

---

* Specifically the small city of Bonners Ferry, a gold-rush and lumber hub on the Kootenai River – population 2,543, c.2010.

Inn by Arkady and Boris Strugatsky, *The Solace of Open Spaces* by Gretel Ehrlich. I told this to Nick and Ed behind the Mr B's counter and they set about racking up a reading list.

I mentioned Kerouac's *Lonesome Traveler* as the sort of book I had in mind, since I'd enjoyed his tales of a season fire-watching in the high Cascades, a summer spent eyespeeled for smoke and bears. Kerouac had been inspired to become a lookout by his friends Gary Snyder and Philip Whalen, fellow Beat writers and belvedere vedettes, and the idea of a link from one book to the next – an echo of familiar mountain huts, the recommendation of friends – felt like a good place to begin.

I left Mr B's with several books, *Train Dreams* by Denis Johnson amongst them. Several things about it impressed me straight away, chiefly Bookseller Ed's wild-eyed, almost manic passion for the author.

The cover showed pale trees on a rusted steep overlaid with solid typography, white capitals akin to film titles –

DENIS
JOHNSON

TRAIN
DREAMS

[THUNK.]

'[A] love story, a hermit's story . . . a small masterpiece.
You will look up from the thing dazed, slightly changed.'
NEW YORK TIMES

It was also the shortest of the lot at 116 pages. I read it first, in one sitting. Then again immediately afterwards to check I was correct that it was the work of staggering brilliance I thought it was. Then again a week later to try to work out how he'd done it.

In retrospect the clues were there even before I began reading – the filmic cover, the novella length reminiscent of catnip Simenon, the fact the *New York Times* had used the word *thing* to describe it – the myriad universal noun, manifestly more than just *any old book* – 'You will look up from the *thing* dazed, slightly changed.'

In short, *Train Dreams* is an epic in miniature and tells the story of a man, Robert Grainier, birth to death, a man born at the end of the nineteenth century who 'had one lover . . . one acre of property, two horses, and a wagon . . . [had] never been drunk . . . never purchased a firearm or spoken into a telephone'.[2]

Robert works in the American West, cutting timber for railroad tracks and then, when he's too old for that, carting people's possessions around the countryside. The book's chronology is loose, or rather – as the writer Jonathan McAloon puts it – 'Grainier's whole life comes at us all at once.'[3]

A life concentrated but effortlessly airy, panoramic in sweep but deeply personal and concerned with the specific – this man, this life, this cabin, these woods; specific tragedy, recovery and transformation.

I was utterly smitten.

It made me want to light out after this America, these wilds, this author and so, hoping to immerse myself in the wildfire flood of *Train Dreams*, I found the nearest lookout to Grainier and Johnson's world and booked a stay in Big Creek Baldy, a white cabin on stilts in a forest.*

Then, having dreamt of my crow's nest week for five and a half months, I received that email ten days before my flight out – *We regret to inform you that, due to a fire in the area, the lookout will be closed . . .* – all of which perhaps begs the question whether the tower should have been decommissioned in the first place, but even before the veto I'd had the sense that I was chasing a shadow because Denis Johnson died in May. There would be no yatra down to Bonners Ferry with a vague address and a hopeful grin. He was nowhere to find now but in his books, so I packed my foxed copy of *Train Dreams* along with *Lonesome Traveler* and flew out of London with a hastily booked return ticket leaving New York on 6 October and no plan as to how I'd get to Desolation or Utah.

I had nineteen days.

———

* The current Big Creek Baldy lookout is the third on the site. The first was built in 1929, a log cabin which still stands in a rather dishevelled state at the foot of the current campanile. In 1934 a 30ft tower with a small 7 × 7ft cabin akin to a garden shed was erected on a cat's cradle-like pylon to better peer over the forest. In 1966 the current lookout went up – a 41ft tower with a positively palatial 15 x 15ft box atop it – *BCB (III)* as I came to think of it. Retired around 1990, the lookout can now be booked for up to two weeks at $40 a night – the 15 x 15ft room sleeps four and confers uninterrupted views over Kootenai's blue chevron pelt to the Purcell Range, Lake Koocanusa and the Yaak River valley. The tower comes with propane lights, a stove, heater, one double bed, one twin bed with mattresses, a shovel and some cooking utensils. There is a pit toilet in the woods a little way away – hence the shovel. There is no electricity or water supply. Residents are asked to bring their own. I reserved Baldy in March 2017, having scoured the US Recreation.gov site for a suitable perch. Retired lookouts can be booked six months in advance and it's advisable to do so, since berths sell out with remarkable speed.

The immediate omens weren't great.

Shortly after take-off the screen in front of my seat began to tell me about Knud Rasmussen (7 June 1879 – 21 December 1933) – a fresh-faced Greenlandic/Danish polar explorer and anthropologist, the first European to cross the Northwest Passage by dog-sled: 'father of Eskimology'.

'Hero in focus' ran the final screen of the series:

> Rasmussen died of pneumonia in 1933, contracted after
> he suffered a bout of food poisoning on the seventh Thule
> expedition.*

Righto, I thought, tucking into my inflight elevenses. Seventh time unlucky. Best avoid that then. No Thule tuck for me.

A little later in the flight I drank a Spitsbergen pilsner, reassured that this was Arctic fare of a safer nature and buoyed by the cheerful story of the brewers, Robert and Oddvor, who, the can told me, started their friendship working together in Svalbard's Mine 3 in 1982, have explored and shared adventures of many kinds through the years, and become friends for life. I found the fact that both Robert and Oddvor are still alive very cheering and enjoyed my beer

---

* Thule was a far-northern location in classical European literature and cartography – often surrounded by enormous illuminated script and sea monsters. Though often considered to be an island in antiquity, modern interpretations of what was meant by Thule often identify it as Norway, an identification supported by modern calculations. Other interpretations include Orkney, Shetland, and Scandinavia more generally. In the Late Middle Ages and Renaissance, Thule was often identified as Iceland and/or Greenland.

all the better for that. Here's to staying alive, I toasted them, then fell fast asleep.

———

The queues at Seattle airport were two hours long. Several planes seemed to have landed at once so we all shuffled and snaked along together, oscillating between sullen silence and forced cheerfulness. At passport check I was inspected by an enormous border security guard who silently scanned my passport before asking why I'd come.

'I'm a writer,' I said. 'I've come here to write.'

'What sort of writer?'

'Travel?' Realising that sounded a bit woolly, I added, 'I write books. I'm here to write about your fire lookouts.'

'Oh really?' said the guard, raising his eyes and brightening slightly. 'You can rent those, you know.'

'Yes,' I said, rallying also, 'I'm planning to head up . . .'

'Yeah, I've always wanted to do that, rent a place up in the mountains, but none of my friends want to . . . not a one . . .' he gloomed back down at this point and I was half minded to assure him that I was bound to have a terrible time but by that point he'd returned my passport with an 'Enjoy your stay' so neutral as to be aggressively vicarious, and turned to frown at the next hopeful.

———

I was boarding in a neighbourhood named Fremont in the north of the city, rising beside the ship canal which connects lakes Union and Washington to the Puget Sound. I checked into a hostel, crammed my bags into a dorm locker and went for a walk to find coffee. The area is dominated by water and bridges – at the bottom of the hill is the deep blue double leaf Fremont Bridge which spans the Fremont Cut. Striding over everything is the massive Meccano of Aurora Bridge, cantilevering State Route 99 through the sky; the air full of engines. I found coffee and the barista topped my flat white unbidden with a milk froth skull. I felt confused and slightly hipstered* as I sat and began texting everyone I knew in Seattle. This did not take long because there were two people I knew in Seattle and one of them turned out to actually live in Portland. Luckily my one Seattleite hope, Colin, was at a loose end and agreed to drive around Washington State and gallivant up a few mountains, so that was excellent.

We arranged to meet at the hostel next morning and, emboldened, I began to email everyone I knew at the unresponsive Mars base in Utah . . .

That evening, too wired to sleep, body-clock bewildered, but delighted to have Colin on board, I paused before the secondhand bookshop opposite my hostel. In the centre of the display was a book named *Continental Divide: A History of American Mountaineering*.[4] On the cover was a photograph of my great-great-aunt, Dorothy Pilley, climbing in the Montana Rockies in 1926.[†]

---

* Fremont is a free-thinking, quirky neighbourhood, I was to discover. If the statue of Lenin at a central crossroads wasn't already a clue, the area's motto is *De Libertas Quirkas* – 'Freedom to be peculiar'.

† *Mountaineers Dorothy Pilley, Count Rinkie Donnersmark of Germany and Hans Russ of Norway climbing Grinnell Point in Glacier National Park*, Ray Bell, 1926. Dorothy is in the midst of scaling twenty-five peaks in nineteen days – another nineteen-day dash, ninety-one years before my own. I bought the book next morning and carried it with me for the rest of the trip.

I stood on the sidewalk regarding the book for several minutes before crossing the street to go to bed. I couldn't begin to fathom the chances of her being here to meet me – the subject of my last book encouraging me on to the adventures of the next. This surely augurs incredibly well, I remember thinking in my bunk. I must be on the right track.

———

Two nights later and I'm walking with Colin in the Snoqualmie National Forest. It's pitch black and raining. We're both drenched and Colin's phone has died. Actually it's wrong to say we're *in* the forest because we're actually above it, above the tree-line but zig-zagging down towards its deep mass having visited a stumpy tower-style lookout as a dry run for Desolation Peak.

That morning we'd hired a Jeep and driven to Colin's storage locker in Newcastle, south of Seattle, to dig out his walking boots, waterproofs and sleeping bag. That afternoon we headed southeast down Highway 90 towards North Bend, arriving at the foot of Granite Mountain in pallid sunshine shortly after 3 p.m. – or maybe 4. We started up it, first a gentle well-trodden path in the shadow of giant cedars, then a smaller stony switchbacking track covered in the gnarled roots of tenacious trees and shrubs keyed into the mountain now growing sparse and steep, the path cliff-edged so one side was thin air.

Since we'd agreed that this would be a proper 'practice climb' for the real thing later in the week, we pressed on into the thickening drizzle. This obviously makes no sense *now*, but at the time it felt like the right thing to do. My map, like most else, was sodden but definitely suggested that there wasn't much further to go. It was now five or maybe six. We met a lady on her way down who was wearing shorts and enormous socks rolled down so they resembled rubber quoits. She said it wasn't far and warned us about the wind on the ridge. We thanked her and carried on up. Later, having experienced not a jot of wind, I would remember the lady in the doughnut socks and wonder why she hadn't mentioned the knee-deep snow I was tromping through, but hey ho. Later – let's say it was seven o'clock – we stood below the dark shuttered tower of the Granite Mountain Lookout in silence. Dusk was falling, as were large flakes of snow. Summit visibility was minimal. The few trees around us were hunched blueish. A sign on the tower informed us that we were on camera. *Well, lah-di-dah*, I thought, and took a picture of Colin, who flashed a weary smile – strained but still game. Then we began the crunch back down.

A couple of hours later, who really knows when, the night was loud with water.

Trees streamed unseen beyond my phone's halo, my hood was drumming, the trail was awash, our boots were slurping. It had become clear that Colin and I could walk for hours in relative silence – always a good thing and often the best way of avoiding unpleasantness. I don't know what Colin was thinking as we tramped in step but I was musing on the thin line between climbing Granite Mountain and everything going well and climbing Granite Mountain and it being a Stygian shower. Everything would have been okay had we started an hour or two earlier and brought some chocolate and a torch. As it was we were descending at a fair lick through a precipitous forest in the dark by the light of my iPhone,

It all had an irksome feeling of déjà vu. This had happened to me in a fashion before – but at least *this time* I had a working phone and we were below the snow-line. I'm getting better at this, I rallied, this is not entirely awful. Thank goodness I'd cack-handedly smashed my phone en route to Iceland and had to buy a weatherproof cover to hold the screen together, so I now had a rubberised torch to guide us down this mountain. Excellent slice of luck. I felt quite chipper. But other misgivings about the situation now crept in – the main being whether Colin's silence behind me might be due to rage; had the fact that I'd written a book about mountaineering lulled him into a false sense of security . . . Had he read the book? Had he seen the cover quote which said it was a miracle I lived to tell the tale? Was he aware that its two recurrent refrains were 'Bad in life, good in the book' and 'Still not dead!'?

He hadn't read the book, I decided.

His silence was a mix of hypothermia, confusion, and betrayal.

But as preparation for Desolation Peak this had been worthwhile. We would not do this sort of thing this way again, if Colin agreed to do any such thing again at all.

Reminded of the Cascades, I began to mull an article I'd recently read on the *New York Times* website about a writer who'd hiked up Desolation and met the lookout there – a Marine reservist who'd served two tours of duty in Iraq. The watchman is frank about the fact he hasn't read any Kerouac, he's tried a couple of times – the cabin had a shelf of his books left by Beat pilgrims, apparently – but no, he can't get on with him: 'Me and that guy just don't see eye-to-eye.' Then the article's author lays into Kerouac a bit to boot – I mean, fair enough, we've all done it; I'm going to do it in a few pages' time – but it raised the question of who we'd encounter when we reached the top of the mountain because, of all the places I was going for this book, Desolation Peak was perhaps the riskiest in terms of who I'd meet when I got there – the big difference between Big Creek Baldy and Desolation Peak being that the latter observation post was still manned and in service. I knew there would be one person sat on top of the mountain. We were going to hike up to their cabin and it would be complete pot-luck whether they'd be an enthusiast and welcome us or a taciturn jobsworth and, well . . . We'll see, I thought, in the streaming woods as we neared our Jeep and the sounds of the highway swelled.

———

That evening, back at the Fremont hostel, we hoisted ourselves up into our bunks and went straight to sleep. At least, I did. Colin, poor fellow, woke repeatedly with loud terrors. Next morning he explained that he tends to have a nightcap before he goes to bed to stave his nightmares off . . . But he was looking forward to our trip into the mountains, he enthused, because . . . to be honest I can't remember why. The rest of the conversation is a blank because I'd become distracted by a thought, a thought which began to cycle around my mind to the tune of 'The Wheels on the Bus': 'Sleeping in a tent with a screaming man, screaming man, screaming man; Sleeping in a tent with a screaming man . . . up a mountain surrounded by bears.'

———

We approached the Cascade mountains on Highway 99, the same route as Jack Kerouac hitched in June 1956. His description of the drive in 'Alone on a Mountaintop' is windshield filmic and the dreamy panoramic excitement he relates – the flow of the landscape past and through you, melting molten, bunched and abstract at the edges – was very much our ride too. Kerouac was following the lead of his friend Gary Snyder – a well-liked former Cascades lookout of several seasons' experience on Sourdough mountain – who had written him a long and detailed letter explaining what to expect and look out for en route, at the Forest Service HQ at Marblemount and once ensconced on Desolation Peak.[5]

I felt an escalating thrill as we left the main highway and sped east along SR 20, the Cascades rising on the northeast horizon as the sun began to sink in the west. Kerouac hails Mount Baker by its indigenous Lummi name of Komo Kulshan, which roughly translates to 'white sentinel with puncture wound' – a reference to its volcanic crater which gives its head a twin summit look.*

> At Burlington you turn right and head for the heart of the mountains along a rural valley road through sleepy little towns and one bustling agricultural market center known as Sedro Woolley with hundreds of cars parked aslant on a typical country-town Main Street of hardware stores, grain-and-feed stores and five-and-tens.[6]

---

* Mount Baker – a family note – First Ascent △ by a woman, Dorothy Pilley, (w/ I. A. Richards) 1926. Elevation △ 10,781 ft (3,286 m), it is the third-highest mountain in Washington State.

Again, the time-lapsed comparison – Kerouac's then, ours now. For us it was dusk and warm. We stopped in Sedro Woolley, parked aslant in a quiet street to use a cash machine – there was no bustle a block back from the fluorescent junctions of State Routes 9 and 20. We left the town in early evening and the great peaks which were covered with trackless white for Kerouac loomed grey green for us, seeming to hesitate and recede as twilight knocked them back blue until, as the sun set behind us, they caught and kindled into alpenglow so red, so hot and vivid that the mountains looked ablaze.

I'd always pictured Kerouac's approach as being an assured swoop to his lookout post, arrowing up the timbered valleys, the Skagit River, over the Ross Dam and up the lake to Desolation, but read again on the drive it seemed more of a slog achieved in fits and starts. I'd thought of it as an opening out but now I saw it first hand as a tapering down; barns and fields both becoming less frequent and valleys V'ed, the roads becoming *the road*, route options dwindling as the formerly loaf-like mountains became more numerous and began piling in – not so massive in height as massive in mass – huge green brutes, each on the shoulder of the next; the river faster, whiter. Nature taking over, the landscape beginning to bite.

———

Which brings me back to bears.

I think that I must first have read about Kerouac's Desolation Peak stint whilst at school, or maybe art school. I definitely knew he'd had a run-in with a bear because when a Swiss fox rifled my tent in the Alps and sloped off with my milk – I thought, *Hello, this rings a bell* . . . and so I went back and compared the dairy-based larceny of 'Alone on a Mountaintop' with my own:

> One morning I found bear stool and signs of where the monster had taken a can of frozen milk and squeezed it in his paws and bit into it with one sharp tooth trying to suck out the paste.

Kerouac stared down into the foggy dawn, down the mysterious Ridge of Starvation 'with its fog-lost firs and its hills humping into invisibility', aware that somewhere in that fog there stalked a bear. He imagined all the attributes and stories of the bear, its life and times: 'He was Avalokiteśvara the Bear, and his sign was the grey wind of autumn.'

He waits for the bear's return. It never comes.[7]

I enjoyed all that and the image of writing at the top of a fairly accessible mountain appealed to me, since the book I was then writing involved climbing to the top of several famously inaccessible mountains and then getting back down and writing about them later. If nothing else, I reckoned, this could be a time-saving exercise.

—

Kerouac had dreamt of writing in a backwoods shack for years, the idea becoming entwined whilst a teenager with notions of what it meant to be a writer. *Get to Thy Hermitage!* he scribbled in his journal on Thanksgiving night, New York, 1954. But no such thing happened until he met Snyder and Whalen, for, as well as constantly oscillating between a desire for companionship and an equal and opposite need for solitude, he seems to have lacked the practical application to turn his ideas into a reality. A plan to build a shed behind his sister's house came to nothing, in fact he seems to have grown rather panicked by his own idea – 'What do I know about deserts? Water? – Where shall I go to escape this civilisation which at any moment may thrust me in jail or war or madhouse? A shack in the woods outside Rocky Mount, be near family? – what of the gnats, heat, tics, mosquitoes, disapproval?'[8]

So he kept roving, pitching up and moving on, until October 1955 when, back in San Francisco after a time writing down in Mexico, he became enthused and persuaded of the paid possibilities a couple of months fire-watching might afford him. John Suiter's book *Poets on the Peaks: Gary Snyder, Philip Whalen & Jack Kerouac in the North Cascades*[9] is a great primer for the way these pre-eminent Beats came to inhabit and chronicle their roosts, the boondock dais of the fire lookouts forging them as nature writers almost by default.

On Friday, 7 October 1955, at 3119 Fillmore Street, San Francisco, five poets – Allen Ginsberg, Philip Lamantia, Michael McClure, Gary Snyder and Philip Whalen – gave a reading of new work. The Gallery Six Reading, as it would become known, is mainly celebrated as the first time Ginsberg performed 'Howl' – which he began carefully, slowly, before picking up locomotion and momentum, his lines spilling out and striving the length of a breath:

> I saw the best minds of my generation destroyed by
>   madness, starving hysterical naked,
> dragging themselves through the negro streets at dawn
>   looking for an angry fix,

angelheaded hipsters burning for the ancient heavenly
    connection to the starry dynamo in the machinery
    of night . . .'[10]

Kerouac was in the audience – having been invited but
declining to read – fortified, mesmerised and urging
Ginsberg on – *Yeah! Go! Go! Go!* – in the manner of a
saucer-eyed fan in the bleachers.

In the aftermath of 'Howl', audience and poets giddy
alike, Snyder read 'A Berry Feast', a poem in praise of Coyote,
a Native American trickster myth infused with Buddhist
ideas of impermanence. The poem traces the destruction of
forests to build suburban houses – 'boxes to catch the biped
in'. It looks forward to a time when people are gone, and
ends with the image of Coyote surveying an abandoned city
gone back to seed – 'Dead city in dry summer, / Where
berries grow.'

After the readings Kerouac quizzed Snyder and Whalen
about their time in the mountain wilds, asking how he
could follow in their footsteps. Recently met, all three were
practising Buddhists at various stages in their literary and
spiritual journeys, with Snyder shortly to depart for Japan
to undergo formal training as a Zen monk. In a letter to
Jack, a few months after Gallery Six, he describes lookout
life in the sort of elliptical aphoristic terms which define so
many of the Buddhist sutras – fire-watching, he writes,
requires 'physical and mental toughness' whilst also allowing 'vast leisure' – words that would come back to haunt
Jack during his sixty-three days alone as he became pretty
crazed pretty quickly with too much time to think and only
himself for company.

By the tenth day of his stay in the Desolation eyrie he'd run out of tobacco and was smoking coffee grounds; by the end of his tour he had rooted out and read every single piece of mouse-chewed paper in the attic, invented several imaginary friends and begun playing poker with them.

Where Snyder and Whalen had been the big eyes and big ears, opened out, looking, listening, meditating, Kerouac struggled to live in the moment and felt strangely strained and afraid.

In the middle of the night I woke up suddenly and my hair was standing on end – I saw a huge black shadow in my window. – Then I saw that it had a star above it, and realized that this was Mt Hozomeen (8080 feet) looking in my window from miles away near Canada. – I got up from the forlorn bunk with the mice scattering underneath and went outside and gasped to see black mountain shapes gianting all around, and not only that but the billowing curtains of the northern lights shifting behind the clouds. – It was a little too much for a city boy – the fear that the Abominable Snowman might be breathing behind me in the dark sent me back to bed where I buried my head inside my sleeping bag.[11]

This is played for laughs of course, but the mystic loner is a central figure and theme in almost all of Kerouac's books; Zen bebop man-cub hobo exploring the great beyond.* But

---

* 'This was what Charlie Parker said when he played: all is well. You had the feeling of early-in-the-morning. Like a hermit's joy.'— *Charlie Parker* (3:43) from *Poetry for the Beat Generation*, Jack Kerouac's debut album of spoken word poetry released in 1959. (Hanover LP #5000.)

the hermit's joy he later hymned wasn't his experience on Desolation, at least not very often. He had flashes of it but his notebooks and letters of the time make plain that he suffered, pined and gnawed his way through the sixty-three days in a way reminiscent of one of Denis Johnson's addicts attempting cold turkey – fumbling at the monastic, striving for the ascetic, trying to remake himself closer to heaven – but writing a lot, albeit crazed and haunted by the void.

In *Fire Season,* Philip Connors lists the enduring qualifications and qualities needed to be a wilderness lookout based on his own experience and the writings and reminiscences of 'Jack Kerouac, Gary Snyder, Edward Abbey, and Norman Maclean' –

- Not blind, deaf, or mute – must be able to see fires, hear the radio, respond when called
- Capability for extreme patience while waiting for smokes
- One good arm to cut wood
- Two good legs for hiking to a remote post
- Ability to keep oneself amused
- Tolerance for living in proximity to rodents
- A touch of pyromania, though only of the nonparticipatory variety[12]

Jack Kerouac's name tops Connors's roll-call. Kerouac: the fire-watch poster boy who ticks about half of that list. Kerouac who, in Connors's words, *mined* Desolation for two novels, *The Dharma Bums* and *Desolation Angels*, but I don't think he ever really let it go. He reworked the experience repeatedly in retrospect, trying to make it right, anxious to retrofit resolution and significance.

I imagine him sat up there at night, sadly bemused that he wasn't enjoying his post; that he seemed so temperamentally unsuited to his task; this pillar-saint position he felt he *ought* to be owning. Gazing over the dark gulf at the horned shadow of Hozomeen, rubbing his eyes, refocusing on his own face in the black mirrors of the glass. Very much alone on his mountaintop, his cross – less sage than martyr. A still night and cold. Hard cold. Stars unknown. The radio is silent; no fire or light for miles but his own – the potbelly stove all purr and tick. He's wrapped up, hunched over his desk, pencil scratching, mice skittering, bugs tapping at the lamp, cigarette smoke pooling in the green cabin eaves – the cigarettes he radioed a plea for two weeks in, hangdog and sheepish. Talking to himself as he walked down the trail past all the trees and plants he couldn't name, a couple of hours back to the lake where the Ross Dam ranger boat was waiting with coffee and cigarettes – company and conversation. They took him round the lake with them, a night back on the float, a ham steak dinner, then they dropped him back to the trail head, one pound tin of Prince Albert tobacco under his arm, feeling better but also like he'd failed, been humoured. Back up to the summit. City boy. Couldn't do without smokes, couldn't do on his own. He'd dreamt of this for years and he was fucking it up . . . 'no liquor, no drugs, no chance of faking it but face to face with ole Hateful Duluoz Me.'[13]*

---

* Sylvain Tesson makes the point in his marvellous *Consolations of the Forest* when he's left alone for six months in a cabin in the middle Taiga: 'It's −27° F.

But the bit with the bear was good so here we were, the latest pilgrims to follow Kerouac up the road to Diablo; driving in the dark towards Marblemount, the mountains rearing around and above us having long since faded from red embers to charcoal silhouettes. After Concrete, a town Kerouac pegged as the last in the Skagit Valley with a bank and a five-and-ten, the Cascades closed to hang in our peripheries; monstering from the wings.

———

We arrived at Marblemount in darkness. The gas station was lit up like a close encounter. Opposite was a diner named The Buffalo. Dazzled, we slowed and pulled into the lot. A mile before we'd passed a green sign, LAST SERVICES FOR 74 MILES. This was the last place to eat and find a room. We hadn't booked anywhere nor eaten since breakfast. The Buffalo looked a good bet. We went in.

'Evening, boys,' said the man behind the counter. An old guy with a mass of bristly hair. He was tall and wearing dungarees – just the sort of guy to run a brass tacks diner named The Buffalo. 'You eating?' he asked. At his elbow was a glass cabinet full of different pies. Behind him a grill was sizzling. Several tables of silent men were busy eating down the way. Roy Orbison was playing, 'Oh, Pretty Woman'.

The truck has dissolved into the fog. Silence falls from the sky in little white shavings. To be alone is to hear silence. A blast of wind, sleet muddles the view. I let out a scream. I open my arms, raise my face to the icy emptiness, and go back inside where it's warm . . . I will finally find out if I have an inner life.'— *Consolations of the Forest – Alone in a Cabin in the Middle Taiga*, Sylvain Tesson, Penguin, London, 2013, p.16.

We would like to eat, we said, could he sort us out with a room as well? He could! This guy would do us a deal. He was a deal-making kinda guy. He quoted us a price then did us a deal on that, knocking a few bucks off. One night, sure, no problem, he'd beds. He ran the motel too, he told us, beyond the arc-eye garage. He'd take us over in a bit, sign here, and *this guy* would fix up the wifi as soon as he was done eating. He was the wifi guy. One of the silent men looked up and nodded greeting.

Blindsided by this blunderbuss hospitality, grateful but suddenly dog tired, we signed and paid. It all sounded very good, particularly the bed bit. 'Now food!' said the owner of the town. 'Better order quick, boys, because it's 8.45 and at nine this place is dead. D.E.D. Ded.'

That's verbatim. The most American thing ever said. I wrote it down as soon as we were sat at a table. Shortly after that some drinks arrived and then some burgers too. We'd been pressed to have the burgers. The burgers were good. 'Damn fine burgers and big!' My God, the bristly man could talk. And sell. And we'd been sold. But numb nodding had got us a bed and a buffalo burger . . . and possibly wifi as well.

———

Next morning we drove to the Wilderness Information Center, handily located down Ranger Station Road, to sort out backcountry permits and collect a bear canister; not, as my mother thought, a canister for the bears – as if the plan was to beckon them over then buy them off with buns and honey – but a sturdy drum to store food *away* from our tent so hangry bears wouldn't come a'sniffing after dark.

Colin asked the ranger whether we needed bear repellent. The ranger said probably not. My attitude was to get up there and see what happened. The idea of pepper spraying a bear didn't really appeal, it seemed a surefire way of making an inquisitive bear angry and an already angry bear apoplectic . . . but I respected the fact that Colin was worried about the bears and, again, wondered whether cajoling him into Twin Peaks territory and dark forests at night where, apparently, mountain lions as well as bears were known to pad was a good idea conducive to sound sleep. My friend Stanley has a theory that all our deepest fears stem from the dark forests and caves inhabited by early man. Our motel stay the night before had been all right – no shouting, just a bit of muffled howling – but we weren't up in the dark woods yet . . . All the same, I was glad we weren't packing pepper spray. I didn't mention the lions.

We gave the duty ranger our planned itinerary and booked ourselves a tent berth atop Desolation – the only people due up there that night. He gave us a couple of useful maps of Ross Lake trails and suggested spots where we might camp on the walk back – Devil's Creek, Lightning and Rainbow Point; the sort of places where mysterious things happen in Enid Blyton novels. A burn ban was in effect so we couldn't light campfires; no problem we said, of course.

Kerouac spent a week at the Marblemount Ranger Station in 1956 attending fire school before moving up to Ross Lake. At night, after dinner, he took to sitting alone down by the swift swirling Skagit with a bottle of wine, writing in his notebook – 'drinking to the sizzle of the stars'.[14]

We followed the Skagit up to Newhalem – a company town owned by Seattle City Light and populated entirely by employees of either the hydroelectric company or government agencies so, unless you work for the Dam Man or The Man, you can't stay. Until 1940 the town was only accessible by train, an outpost born of the necessity to build dams to slake Seattle's growing thirst for electricity. The first, Gorge Dam, was up and running by 1924, and the grand grey powerhouse – solid, industrial Deco – still stands over the Skagit, spun water foaming out from underneath, 500 kV three-phase electric power flowing back over our heads on lines carried high by pylons.

The Diablo Dam followed Gorge in 1927, four miles back up the green walled pass. The railway was pushed further into the Cascades, ending at the foot of Sourdough Mountain against which the gigantic new bulwark was to be set. So steep was the gorge at this point that a massive inclined plane was built to lift loaded freight cars broadside up the mountain to where they could be shunted along a short level track and unloaded at the head of what was then the tallest dam in the world.

In the 30s thousands of summer sightseers from Seattle and beyond rode the trains and incline up to see the great works at Diablo. Seattle City Light built accommodation, canteens and exotic gardens, ran tours of the powerhouse control rooms and boat trips on the new Diablo Lake. No expense was spared, so keen were the company to show the mammoth public works off to the full. My favourite discovery whilst researching the tourist dam boom was that J.D.

Ross, the famously charismatic superintendent of the Skagit River Project, convinced Seattle City Zoo to lend him all their monkeys to, in his words, 'stock an island' on the lake to further dazzle day trippers.

By 1956 the tourists and monkeys were gone. There was a road up the Skagit but it ended at Diablo, the last train having run in 1954. Kerouac was carried up the incline sideways to the brimful lake, then half an hour on by boat to the newly built Ross Dam, completed in 1953. His description of the scene in *Lonesome Traveler* carries a sense of looking out from castle ramparts:

> Here for the first time you're high enough really to begin to see the Cascades. Dazzles of light to the north show where Ross Lake sweeps back all the way to Canada, opening a view of the Mt Baker National Forest as spectacular as any vista in the Colorado Rockies.[15]

———

There's a short story that I love by Richard Brautigan called 'I Was Trying to Describe You to Someone' in which, having tried and failed to describe his beloved in terms of other people – 'I couldn't say "Well she looks just like Jane Fonda . . ." I couldn't say that because you don't look like Jane Fonda at all' – the narrator instead likens her to a movie about rural electrification, 'a perfect 1930's New Deal morality kind of movie' which he saw as a child in Tacoma, Washington, making it quite possible that it was a film about these very Skagit dams. A movie about farmers living and working without electricity until a new dam is built and electricity flows, appearing to the farmer like a young Greek god, to take away for ever the dark days of his life: 'Suddenly, religiously, with the throwing of a switch, the farmer had electric lights to see by when he milked his cows in the early black winter mornings. The farmer's family got to listen to the radio and have a toaster . . .'

'That's how you look to me,' he ends.[16]

But the power and light generated from the Cascades flowed away from the mountains for many decades before it began to illuminate the wilds themselves. It would be another sixteen years before the Cross Cascades Highway connected Newhalem and the Skagit River Valley to Eastern Washington over Rainy Pass and the headlamps of trucks and cars cut through country only ever previously explored by foot, horse and boat.* So – as John Suiter points out in *Poets on the Peaks* – when Snyder, Whalen and Kerouac stared out from their lookouts the landscape around and beneath was lightless, deep dark in a way not possible today.†

———

* Funding for a possible route through the Cascade range was appropriated in 1895 but the road was not completed until September 1972. Today it forms part of State Route 20 (SR 20), also known as the North Cascades Highway, a road which traverses the Washington State, travelling 436 miles (702 km) from Discovery Bay on the Olympic Peninsula, merging with US 2 near the Idaho State border in Newport then running on to Bonners Ferry – Denis Johnson country.

† In 1792, only 180 years before Kerouac & Co. took up their Cascade positions, the British navigator George Vancouver had arrived on HMS *Discovery* in the Puget Sound and given English names to the mountains he saw – all of which already had excellent titles of course, the indigenous people who'd inhabited the area for millennia having developed myriad names,

From the top of Diablo Dam, Kerouac took a boat north to Ross Dam with a company of power employees, hunters fishermen and forestry workers. At Ross he climbed a trail one thousand feet up to the dam top where the vast lake opened out, 'disclosing small resort floats offering rooms and boats for vacationists, and just beyond, the floats of the U.S. Forestry Service. From this point on, if you're lucky enough to be a rich man or a forest-fire lookout, you can get packed into the North Cascade Primitive Area by horse and mule and spend a summer of complete solitude.'[17]

We drove through Newhalem past the handsome power-house, up the canyon to Diablo, through tunnels dug and blasted through the stretched granite of the cliffs, then, leaving the path of the railroad, we turned right on to the new road on the south side of the gorge. The road was a corridor cut into hemlock firs so it wasn't possible to see much of the dam bar the occasional grey flash until we'd passed it, when we pulled over to look back from the Diablo Lake Overlook with its picnic benches, pay-telescopes and

---

myths and legends about the Cascades: 'Tahoma', the Lushootseed name for Mount Rainier, 'Koma Kulshan / Kulshan' whom we've already met as Mount Baker, and 'Louwala-Clough', meaning 'smoking mountain', for fellow volcano Mount St Helen's. Thirteen years later, the Lewis and Clark Expedition passed through the middle Cascades, which they named the Western Mountains, on the Columbia River – becoming quite possibly the first non-indigenous people to see Mount Adams, which they misidentified as Mount St Helen's.

In 1814, Alexander Ross, a fur trader with the North West Company and possibly an ancestor of J.D., *might* have used Cascade Pass to reach the Skagit River whilst seeking a viable route across the northern Cascades – his reports of the journey were very vague. So perhaps just under 160 years passed from the discovery of the Skagit by non-indigenous men and the Ross Dam's turbines coming online.

entitled sparrows. The sickle of the dam top away down below, a thin rib checking the lake which was an oddly milky aquamarine* that day – as if the real water had been hidden beneath a plastic pool cover, winched across by heirs of J.D. Ross to keep the lake nice for when the taxpaying folks of the 30s returned.[†]

———

A while later we left the car in a lay-by, repacked our bags to include the bear canister – now stuffed with sleeping bags – and walked down a rocky path to Ross Lake.

Earlier in the day we'd phoned ahead to ask about a boat up the lake. The people with the monopoly on boats up the lake had told us that, yes, they could take us on their boat up the lake and we had agreed a price – inasmuch as they

---

* The lake's queer colour was caused by glacial flour, which is made up of fine-grained, silty particles of rock, generated when bedrock is ground by glacial erosion. Because the material is very small, it becomes suspended in water, making it appear cloudy – sometimes called glacial milk.

† At the top of the dam, on the right-hand side, a pale track can be seen heading back to the head of the incline lift, the solum of the old railroad. The lift was still used to carry boats and materials up to Diablo Lake until 2001, when it was mothballed after 9/11 for security reasons.

'Diablo Dam – Skagit Incline (1920–2001)

Due to heightened security, Seattle City Light has restricted access to certain areas of the Skagit River Hydroelectric Project.

There is no public access to Ross and Diablo Powerhouses and the Incline Railway. Other seasonal attractions including the Gorge Powerhouse Visitors' Gallery and Ladder Creek Falls are open May through September. The Trail of the Cedars and the Gorge Dam Overlook Trail remain open year-round for public use.'

– www.seattle.gov/light/history/inclineRR.asp

had told me the price for the boat up the lake and I'd winced, agreed, hung up and felt sick. But, as Colin later pointed out on the drive, this was a once in a lifetime trip so money didn't matter so much. 'But it's not your money,' I may have muttered, gracelessly . . . 'I could have *bought* a bloody boat for that. I could have had a boat *made* for that,' I conceivably carped to my generous upbeat friend without whom I'd have been completely stuffed.

The instructions from the boat people – who I imagined all had fur coats and crowns – was to get down to the lake shore and phone them on 'the lake phone'. We found the lake phone easily enough. It was housed in a tin box strapped to a single telegraph pole by the water's edge.

Colin, who reached it first, stood regarding the Heath Robinson assemblage a moment before unhooking the latch, opening the box door and lifting out a pink receiver. I heard him click the cradle a couple of times but I was watching his grin grow larger with each development. Above him a transformer hugged the pole, trailing wires which disappeared down into the lake further on. He held the phone up to his ear and set his features in a furrow to listen for a dial tone. Over Colin's shoulder arched the bony brow and roadway of Ross Dam. Across on the far bank were a line of wooden chalets with a pier in front, whilst behind trees shot sheer up Sourdough and I thought how different these mountains were to Swiss Alps and English fells, the mountains I knew best and had visited most recently. The Cascades were so green . . . and suddenly I had an image of sea glass, weathered smooth and rounded, slightly chipped, those were the Cascades. In mountainous measure the Alps were freshly broken shards, the fells ground amber and the Cascades tumbled green nuggets pushed into the sky.

Meanwhile Colin had dialled a number and was speaking on the pink phone to one of the boat plutocrats over the way; he then replaced the receiver and told me that they were on their way. I nodded but it was hard to credit that a normal conversation had taken place because the lake phone was so jerry-built and madly odd, incongruous as a Narnian lamppost. Walking round to look at the phone from his perspective I found a pair of large alarm bells nailed to the post above the locker-box like big black bosoms or googly eyes.

Talk done, the telephone tump returned to birdsong and lapping water.

We waited.

———

A couple of minutes later I saw a boat curving a lazy arc around a boom line, making for a concrete jetty to our right. When it arrived we stepped on, shaking hands with the skipper, Malachi. He had a beard and a trucker's cap and was wearing a plaid shirt. The only way he could have been any more *slacker backwoods American boat skipper* was if his CB radio had been fuzzing Neil Young or Grandaddy. We nosed out on to the crystal lake and started zooming remarkably fast. This was our ride, I had cash – of course it was a cash transaction – and I was reminded of times I'd climbed in the Alps: you carry all you need or else you don't have it. Nothing is going to come from the sky. No card transactions here. My phone had blipped to NO SIGNAL somewhere around Newhalem and it would stay there for the rest of the trip. The only reason I didn't turn it off, turn it off and metaphorically throw it overboard, was that I'd be using it as a camera and occasional watch. Would we be coming back this way? Malachi later asked us, because if so we should book ourselves in with him now. Analogue rules – headlamps may have invaded the wilds in 1972 but 3G is yet to make its presence felt.

How should you behave on a speedboat you've hired to race up a lake? Almost as soon as we left the little jetty the boat had sat firmly down in the water and we'd gone like a dart. I didn't really talk to Malachi much because he was cabbed up front and the open back where we were was roaring loud with engines, air and water spray and, well, the mountains either side were just *there*, beasty big – the lake like the water in a pair of cupped hands – the green flanks rising either side, the mountains opening up and folding out ahead, our churned wakes crossing behind. We hung on happy; buffeted, enthralled. I'd had no idea how long the trip would be so the question of what to do in the event never occurred; I hadn't really considered the boat.

I knew that Kerouac had taken a couple of hours to make the trip on a small blue tugboat 'lashed to a large corral float bearing four mules and three horses, groceries, feed, batteries and equipment'. He'd left the dam head at 6 a.m. in lashing rain with a muleskinner named Andy who 'wore the same old floppy cowboy hat he'd worn in Wyoming twenty years before' and who told Jack they were gonna put him away where he couldn't be reached: 'It's just what I want, Andy, to be alone for three solid months nobody to bother me.'

'It's what you're sayin' now but you'll change your tune after a week,' responded Andy with excellent clairvoyance. He'd probably had Kerouac pegged as a coffee grounds smoker from the off.

Andy, King of Schadenfreude, then regales our man with miserable weather forecasts and worst case scenarios – one day it'll be so hot he'll boil and there'll be too many bugs to count, the next day 'a li'l', ole summer blizzard come hit you around the corner of Hozomeen' and he won't be able to stick logs in his potbelly stove fast enough . . . – Andy is up there with the bear for me as 'Alone on a Mountaintop' highlights go. He's the weather-eyed voice of the wilds, and you can feel Jack's angst as he splutters that he's got a ruck-sack full of turtlenecks, flannel shirts, thick pants, 'long wool socks bought on the Seattle water front', gloves, an earmuffed cap 'and a ton of instant soup and coffee'.

'Shoulda brought yourself a quart of brandy, boy,' says Andy shaking his head.

When Jack later asks where Desolation Peak sits in the torrential shadows which hem the lake, he's told, 'You ain't gonna see it today till we're practically on top it and by that time you'll be so soakin' wet you won't care.'

'Nobody seemed to envy Desolation Peak except me,' mopes kicked puppy Kerouac as, after two hours pushing through the storming waves with misty timber rising sharply either side, patient mules and horses chomping on their feed-bags all the while, they arrive at the foot of the Desolation Trail and the tugman eases her over and settles the float against a steep muddy slope full of bushes and fallen trees.

Had I expected a similar journey? Perhaps I'd imagined us making the trip on a similar tug or a small wooden fishing boat, intimate, old-fangled and sedate – a means to the peak – but this was a modern motor boat with a thwacking great outboard on the back and so it was that we were leant out, grinning, hanging on. This was the boat and here we were on our way, blasting up the lake like a rocket – *What a ride! What a ride!*

There was snow and glacial ice on the high cleft summit of Jack Mountain. There were inlets and suspension bridges, cliffs and small beaches along the far shore. Our day was the brilliant opposite of Kerouac's dousing. The sky was clear blue and the sun bounced up from the fizzing water so it felt as if we were skimming in a halo of light. We shot on. Minutes passed and a small voice told me we'd shortly be walking walking walking back the way we'd come. No lifts home. But then we got our first sight of Desolation Peak, the boat tracing the slightest of crescents up the kidney-shaped lake so it emerged in increments, seeming to crane slowly over to watch our approach, our 1,860-metre climb to come. Turning towards a rocky strand overhung with pines the boat's pitch changed and then we were skating in neutral, shaking hands and jumping off the bow, no trip home, no, but thank you, and he backed up, turned then dwindled, engine noise a hum, then a distant echo, then . . . gone. And we, having watched him go, turned ourselves and headed up into the trees.

———

We found a faint track and walked it north through pale grass and scorched firs with fissured scaly bark. It was hot. The air smelt sweet and waxy, slightly oily like old hemp rope. To our left the open slope fell away to the lake whilst above us, hidden by the waves of forest, rose the peaks. We walked our arid line for an hour. Grasshoppers clicked, stones skittered, pine-cones splintered underfoot and our packs, now settled, began to weigh and our skin began to prickle. Occasionally the path would descend into lusher shaded gullies with enthusiastic streams racing down from on high and the air would freshen and we'd meet stepping stones and balance pole bridges. Some parts of the trail were damp and fuggy but mostly the woods were tinder dry. As the trees grew thicker the path became a rich and bouncy humus of mossy soil, rotted wood and fallen needles bronzing the ground – a tawny road to follow up through ferns, pines and cedars rising straight into vapour, green vaults or a maze of massive pick-up sticks. And when we reached the Desolation Peak trail proper – the spot where Kerouac landed – and turned up and away from the lake, the needle bed was like a rainbow of basmati thick and springy, dusted with rot wood powdered by termites and innumerable similar saw-toothed beasties unseen. Here we met the big trees, Western red cedars and Ponderosa pines with huge trunks a couple of metres across, trees so high that the Pacific silvers below were mere ankle-biters and we were good as ants. And here began the gentle switchback slaloms which would steepen and snake us up the mountain for the rest of the day. The area hadn't seen rain for months and the air was close and perfumed vanilla and sap.

Back at the Marblemount station, we'd been run through the pyro-prohibitions of a total burn ban – no wood camp-fires though gas and meths stoves were allowed, we'd been told, but, like the long walk back along the lake, the idea of a fire whilst we stumped up the mountain – sweating in T-shirts, shouldering our bags, panting a bit – seemed something far off that we could do without.

The track was long and inclined to hurt us. At one point we had a close call with some bees who'd made their home in a dry bank and took umbrage with being walked near. As we zig-zagged up, I began to look more closely at the map and suspect that the line we were following hid or ignored hairpins so the path was actually twice the length advertised.* Colin was minded to look on the bright side, suggesting we'd soon be there and eventually we were, arriving on Starvation Ridge before sunset, having ascended at a reasonable pace with regular stops to turn and see the view whenever the forest allowed, appreciate the size and profile of the peaks around us and take in the lake which, after several hours hiking, now resembled a silver lightning bolt. The Nohokomeen Glacier atop Jack Mountain flashed cold but there was still warmth in the air and fire in my calves as we pitched our tent in the campsite on the mountain's south shoulder and decanted our food into the bear canister, which I then placed a distance away. Screwing the lid back on, it struck me that it was just the sort of childproof twist-cap used to keep toddlers from

---

* The Desolation Peak lookout is officially measured at twenty-three miles from the nearest road by foot or twelve to thirteen miles up Ross Lake by boat and then seven or eight more on trails – which is what we did. Whilst it may be 'one of the most remote active lookouts in the US', I think there are some much further flung. Philip Connors's lookout in *Fire Season* sounds far more out of the way.

eating aspirin, only scaled up for bears. So the bears here have mastered regular screwtop lids, I thought. Interesting.

Underfoot, the ground was stubbled. There were papery lichens all over the rocks as well as delicate bulbous seaweed-like plants which my pocket flora guide told me were related to the caribou moss of the Arctic tundra.

Red blueberry bushes waggled in the breeze – the woods having ceded to tuft-grass meadows and small stands of subalpine firs which all looked to be heading towards the as yet unsighted cabin; climbing back up the mountain in the wake of historic fires, off to have a word with the lookout responsible.*

Having set up camp, we followed them up past boulders and spinneys and into firn snow, a granular crust on a rise which turned out to be a false summit but from where we could see the low pyramid roof of the true summit cabin. It was a wonderful moment, only slightly undercut by the realisation that we'd have to descend a little way before we could climb the final stretch. Then we saw a figure, a tall man, walking down from the cabin. He saw us at the same moment. He waved. We waved back and met on the path a few minutes later. Hello, he said, I was just going out for a stroll around. He hadn't expected to meet anyone. Would we like to come up and see the cabin? He was Jim Henterly, the Desolation Peak fire lookout.

We followed him up the slope and suddenly the light was back, the hot pink honeyed alpenglow flaring up once more. It had been dim in the dip and Jim had looked forbidding

---

* The ridge last burned over in 1926. The lookout was packed in and built in 1932.

as he strode down towards us. I'd had the thought then, the split second after he'd seen us but before he waved, that here was the watchman to tell us to piss off, piss off back down the mountain, no you can't see the cabin. But he was all smiles and welcome and the sun now lit the rounded summit so the belvedere glowed pink and looked, with its window shutters raised all round, a little like Leonardo's whirling sketch of a helicopter.

We went in and Jim set to making us tea, telling us about the cabin as he lit the stove and got the silver kettle going. The late sun cut gold across the panelled room and flared on the central fire-finding turntable, the washing-up drying on top of the fridge, the delicate window frames; the books on the desk and the sleeping bag neatly doubled on the mattress. The huge panorama of the windows – the spectacular mountains all round us either shadowed blue or saturated red – you could see it all from this glass pagoda on top of the world. 'You can see right into Canada,' Jim gestured with his mug once we were all settled with a drink.

It really did feel like a station suitable for pilgrimage; the view was sublime. This was the place to be and here we were.

—

Jim was encyclopaedic about the cabin. In the time it had taken to make the tea he'd told us some wonderful details: that this cabin was an L-4 built in 1932;* that the circular apparatus in the middle of the room was called an Osborne

---

* The L-4 were 14 × 14ft frame cabs which could be placed atop tall fire-towers. The earliest models had a gabled shingle roof and heavy shutters.

Fire-Finder, invented by William Osborne; that the turntable crosshairs were horse tail – nothing else does the job so well. He showed us how the finder worked, swivelling the sights to zero in on prominent peaks – Prophet, Terror, Challenger, Fury, Ruby, Baker way off yonder in the glowing haze – beckoning us over to have a go, close one eye and focus on steeps of our own. This was the 'ubiquitous' 1934 Osborne model, he told us, still here, still working – just as the cab was still painted in its original willowy green, a shade named 'Irish Meadow'. When the National Park Service came to restore the structure, some time around 1998, they discovered that 'Irish Meadow' was no longer in production so they had to recreate it – so somewhere they've a shed with the global reserve. He showed us how the windows opened, pivoting halfway up, described how the whole thing would have been carried up as a kit by pack horses and mules. And then, quite suddenly, it was dark and we realised night was here. How long had we been talking? 'I guess I'm a kind of evangelist for the historical lookout experience,' he said, turning on a central light.

The sky was filling inky blue. Jim advised us to get back to our tent before it got properly dark and cold but invited us back for coffee next morning. We thanked him, bade him goodnight, and descended the four stairs down to the ground. The cold air thumped me in the chest after the warmth of the room. The evening was still and silent. Freezing. The little light house, warm beacon, receded, Jim's

---

Those built in 1933–53 had hip roofs, which used bolts from extended ceiling joists to hold the shutters open. From 1936 these bolts were superseded by 2 × 2 inch pine struts.

shadow stood in the open door. As we walked away I could feel the frost form and the earth begin to crisp.

———

We crunched back down the dark ridge delighted at our luck to have met somebody so full of enthusiasm and story, delighted also to be the only people camped up on the mountain that night. We went to bed immediately, mainly to warm back up, looking forward to breakfast coffee with Jim.

I woke around 1 a.m and sat up. Colin was asleep. Two thoughts occurred in rapid succession:

Colin is asleep! Well done, Colin.

Colin is asleep! That noise is not Colin.

The noise was a snuffly sniffing, something big snuffly sniffing and shuffling about. On large paddy feet. It was dark and there was no moon so there was no shadow on the tent but had there been any light I was pretty certain the shadow would have been a colossal black bear.

Colin woke up and turned on a torch.

Hello! he said, what's going on?

No, Colin, I said, with exaggerated calm. No, Colin. Please turn the torch off.

The moment of silence and darkness that followed, the sound of three nervous souls holding their breath, was long. Then the probably-a-bear moved away.

Blimey, I said. Well, there we are. Then I lay down and went back to sleep.

I think Colin remained acutely awake for some time.

———

Next morning we returned to Jim's green house. White cloud filled the gulf on every side of the mountain so the peak was an island. The air was chilly, the sun a pale disc, but Jim had coffee on the go when we arrived and presented us both with an improvised heater – Colin got the kettle wrapped in a tea towel and I was given a kettle bell hot from the hob. Again I was struck by the light in the cabin, the windows so big; a view with a roof.

It became clear that the radio was the real focal point of Jim's Desolation day-to-day. A crackling creature, a bulky walkie-talkie, which needed regular attention. Now was the time for all the trail crews and stations in the vast area of the park to check-in and be told the news and weather, all delivered in reassuring stylised shorthand akin to the Shipping Forecast:

'. . . *north of Park Creek Pass and Cascade Pass. Break . . . CHHHHHP . . . The burn ban remains in effect for Lake Chelan National Recreation Area and the area of North Cascades National Park located in Chelan County, which includes campfires or the ignition of wood, briquettes, or any fuel in fire pits, fire pans, and barbecue grills . . .*'

'That's over in a drier section,' explained Jim.

'. . . *North Cascades Park Service land southeast of Cascade Pass, Park Creek Pass and Rainy Pass as well as the entire Stehekin Valley . . .*'

'Pretty much everything east of that crest over there. This report's real brief. The Forest Service give a much more detailed broadcast later in the day, about ten o'clock, and then again about four when there's a fire weather forecast.'

'*All units on McGregor, stand by for more reports . . . today, Saturday . . .*'

'At the moment he's restating the bulletin on another repeater for the east side of the park,' said Jim, turning the set down. 'He's in Marblemount. Our primary dispatcher. I can't tell if he's been cut off there . . .'

'*CHHHHHP.*'

'I usually try to jump in and sign on just before he starts. I missed it this morning. Nine o'clock's my usual time.'

'*CHHHHHP.*'

The radio broke back in but sounded phased, as if turning away. Then the sound came back thicker, slurred, the crackling louder, all clear sense gone out of it – the shadow of a voice in white noise. '*CHHH-CHHP. National Park CHHP. Break.*"

The silence whenever a broadcast ceased was deep. I made a recording in the cabin at the time and hear it on the tape now whilst transcribing; a deep calm, a sudden peace in the cabin as if a banging door had been shut, the abrupt crunch of call-end like a boot on icy snow.

'Due to the elevation here, I'm the only one who receives traffic from several repeaters,' said Jim. 'No one else gets this crossover. I'm in the centre of it all. The fire crew out there, the trail crew down in Lightning Creek right now, they won't be hearing this. Sometimes I'll call crews up later in the day and see if they want the weather repeated, especially the fire weather forecast, particularly if things are changing or a red-flag alert is posted since they can rarely hear it at their locations and are often out in the field for a week at a time.

---

* 'Break' is used when the message is getting long and allows another unit with potentially more important traffic to 'break in', explained Jim. 'When you say "break" you momentarily let off the transmit button to allow for that. Not everyone uses it properly.'

Funny how paternal I start to feel about crews out and about who I know only have me for a link with dispatch to check-in and check-out, especially if something goes dramatically side-ways and help is needed. So I am always listening and crank up my radio full volume next to my bed all night. I've had to relay emergency traffic in the middle of the night in the past; traffic from remote people in trouble that only I could hear . . .'

'. . . *Sunrise 0649. Sunset 1855. Today: mostly cloudy. Isolated showers in the morning, low level: 6,500 feet, Highs: mid to upper 60s. Tonight, mostly cloudy. Lows . . . Sunday Highs: in the lower 70s. Break.*'

'Okay, I'm going to sign on, let them know I exist before they start worrying about me.'

He picked up the radio and turned round in his seat to face Mount Hozomeen.

'Comm Center, Desolation Peak on Ruby.'

'*Desolation, Comm Center CHHP.*'

'Desolation is in service.'

'*0911.*'

'Okay,' said Jim, 'that's done.'

Jim was economic with his words, to the point. I imagined that he'd been in the military, he had that sense about him. He was reading Fridtjof Nansen's chronicle of his 1893–6 North Pole odyssey when we met him and spoke with great alacrity and enthusiasm about the Norwegian explorer's journey on *Fram*.* A professional illustrator for many years, deft pencil sketches of faces,

---

* *Fram* ('Forward') is a ship that was used in expeditions of the Arctic and Antarctic regions by the Norwegian explorers Fridtjof Nansen, Otto Sverdrup, Oscar Wisting and Roald Amundsen between 1893 and 1912. It was designed and built by the Scottish-Norwegian shipwright Colin Archer

figures and landscapes were pinned up around the cab, along with quotes from Joseph Conrad, Cormac McCarthy and Herman Melville. Next to the desk was a shelf of books and I noticed *Tree of Smoke* by Denis Johnson in the mix, along with McCarthy and Kerouac – *The Road* side by side with *On The Road*.

Jim told us about the amount of the visitors he meets – 'a lot' – who've made the trip specifically 'because of the Kerouac aura'.

'I try to be very careful to respect that and in no way stifle. They come with expectations of feeling some essence of what they got personally from Jack's writing, and I fully get that worshipful quality the pilgrims come with – maybe because I was raised Catholic,' he laughed.

He had three young men show up one day last year dressed for a gentlemen's club, 'down to little leather flat bottom dress shoes, having come all the way from Europe, explaining in their broken English that they came to America to chase the ghost of Kerouac across the country and up this mountain in the wilderness . . .'

Ever since we'd met the night before I'd been trying to place his face. Then when he was speaking to the Marblemount dispatcher I had it, he had something of Matt Smith about him – the look of a young man made by old men from memory. Kindly, craggy, lean and tall – his head almost brushing the cabin ceiling. Yes, there was something

---

for Nansen's 1893 Arctic expedition, for which he planned to freeze *Fram* into the Arctic ice sheet and float with it over the North Pole. *Fram* is said to have sailed further north (85° 57' N.) and farther south (78° 41' S.) than any other wooden ship. *Fram* is preserved at the Fram Museum in Oslo, Norway.
* *Doctor Who* showrunner Steven Moffat once described Smith in these terms.

of the Timelord about Jim, alone up in his 'Irish Meadow' TARDIS bathed in static and radiophonics, materialised here on the mountain.

I asked him how he'd ended up here and he reeled off a biography of such economy and grace that I've transcribed it below almost verbatim from my notes:

'I grew up in northeast Ohio, suburban kid, the nearest city was Akron with Cleveland to the north on Lake Erie. Large Catholic family, 8 kids, across the street from Immaculate Heart of Mary. Twelve years of Catholic schools. Went into the army – a completely absurd, radical thing for a seeming hippie kid from my liberal college prep high school to do in the summer of 1972. I thought I was going to Vietnam, but signed up for the storied 101st Airborne, which was already back [from Vietnam], so I had basic training in California and jump school in Georgia. I was initially an infantryman/paratrooper, but qualified to go to medic school as a rare individual who hadn't been to jail and had taken high school Chemistry. I trained in Texas the next summer and came back to my unit as a field medic. I was anxious to get out and go to college, where I figured I should have been all along, although I did get a lot of time to read and draw [in the army] and a taste for helping folks in a medical sort of way. I worked in urban free clinics as a college student – so I was out of army and into college in 1975. In 1977 I joined US Forest Service fire crew; I did that for three years, ending up in northeast Oregon; my wife, Ann Marie, got hired early that season as a fire look-out there – a 90ft tower near the Snake River in the Wallowas. She was anxious after being our only radio link on a fire in remote Idaho and talked me into quitting fire crew early and joining her on the lookout. Bosses talked us into coming back as a team on a remote lookout for the next season, and we did that from 1980 to 87, on four different lookouts in the Wallowa-Whitman National Forest Burnt Powder Fire Zone with a small child with us for some of those years – she first went up to a lookout at two weeks old. After our second daughter was born in mid fire season– first was starting school – we quit lookouts for 14 years but we had always had fond memories of lookouts and felt a special connection. In those years we were raising two daughters, I had a rather busy career as an illustrator and teacher and Ann Marie was teaching too.

'Then a call came out of the blue from a forest in northeast Oregon looking for a fire lookout, somehow they had gotten our names. And I said no, we didn't do that any more but then had a conversation with Ann Marie and the idea that forests were still staffing lookouts – which was a surprise – and I'd turned one down led to my calling our old forest who said they'd love to have me and/or us back, so I was back on Summit Point – a 30ft tower on the southern edge of the Wallowas above little Halfway, Oregon. It was great; I got to lead incoming fire crews to fires like the old days. But when I learned Alpine was free, a lookout much closer to home, I applied and got assigned that up on the Cascade Crest. I spent the next decade on Alpine, 2004 to 15. Then Alpine was closed, defunded, and I was hired by the National Park Service to man Desolation Peak in 2016 and 17.'

As he told us about his life I lost myself in the story. The world of this man and his history of lookouts, sat up alone above the timber-line for months on end, then helping to fight fires and patch people up at lower altitudes when a spell was over and he was back down in the world of people, electricity and roads; and before that he'd been jumping out of aircraft . . . what an interesting uncommon life he'd had – still airborne, watching, listening, looking out, jumping in to sort things out when situations called.* Perhaps the discipline of his time as a soldier, medic and teacher gave him the skillset to enjoy lookout life; exacting on the radio, happy alone, good with people. He certainly seemed to be a man who lived in the absolute now – as any watchman must, reappraising the world moment to moment – but the nostalgia and mystique associated with this position, 'that Kerouac aura', clouds and fudges its purpose. This was never a hermitage shack, the Zen Buddhist 'do nothing hut' of Kerouac's imagination and later panegyrics. Possibly the most surprising aspect of Desolation to me was the realisation of just how connected and engaged it was with the world around it – an outward-facing signal box interacting with people otherwise cut off, as well as performing its original function of fire-spotting and guiding first responders; a historic monument still pulling its weight – neither the lightning nor the lookout having retired.

Jim pointed to a tool leant against the wall which combined a wood axe and ice adze in one head, like an axe wearing a Davy Crockett hat. A tool to cut and dig with, a Swiss Army axe.

'That's a Pulaski tool, named after its creator who was a

---

* 'The motto of my division in the army was "Rendezvous with destiny",' Jim told us. 'The motto of my battalion was *Ne desit virtus* – Let valor not fail.'

hero ranger of the 1910 Idaho fires. He died neglected, near blind, in pain and poverty but, hey, they named the tool after him! I make sure one is always at hand in any lookout, tool of choice for initial attack. Because I'd been on the fire crew on the Wallowa-Whitman, I sometimes got to go out solo with fire tools to do an initial attack on small lightning strikes – pretty cool, just like in the olden days! Some seasons I called in over a hundred fires, and often spent long periods monitoring and relaying for fires all around us; on a few occasions I was the only person someone in dire straits could reach on the radio in the middle of the night for rescue or assistance. Evenings, the Wallowa-Whitman lookouts would talk with each other over the radio. No phones, imagine that . . .'

———

We left him around 11 a.m. I have a photograph of us standing in front of the lookout with the chert iced gem of Hozomeen behind. We're talking about something, Jim's making me laugh. He'd got the measure of us fairly quickly – enthusiastic fellows, bit wet behind the ears. 'Now,' he'd asked, 'how much water do you have for the walk back? . . . No, that's not enough. Here. Now, what have you got to eat?' We walked back to the campsite with several packets of jelly babies, an extra tin of salmon, and a couple of bottles of water in our hands. Tent and bear canister (untouched) repacked, we retraced our steps back down to the lake but at more than twice the speed, then on along the shore, over those bridges, those side creeks, through dark woods and open meadows, the tracks flatter, stopping to talk with several massive toads en route who gave themselves away by crashing about trackside. As always, Colin was excellent company and we spoke about Jim, what we'd do when we got back to Marblemount – coffee and pie was the general consensus – our various aches and pains, our feet particularly, and that bear. Oh yes, the bear got a mention too.* We made May Creek and pitched camp at dusk – an eighteen-mile day. The burn ban now lifted, we made a fire as the evening grew chill around us, our circle of trees lit a flickering red. The night before I'd seen a couple of lakeside lights whilst walking back to camp, now we were one of them. I wondered if our fire was visible to Jim.

The next day we walked on to Ruby Creek and down to a stock landing spot named Hidden Hand where we tried hailing an elderly couple in a fishing skiff and were totally ignored. 'They definitely heard us!' I complained to Colin. 'They absolutely did, I saw them laugh.'

So we walked a few miles extra up the trail round Ruby Arm and reached Highway 20 by lunch. We were both rather tired by this point and didn't really want to hike the last six miles back to the car, so we waited about and eventually found favour with a lady named Peggy on her way home from a square dance championship upstate. 'I'm actually glad I met you boys,' she told us, shifting iceboxes and polythene-wrapped dresses around to make room on the backseat, 'Do you mind having that on your lap, dear?' she asked Colin, hefting a microwave towards him. 'Yes, I'm actually glad I met you boys because I was feeling a little

---

* Jim later sent me pictures of two neighbourhood bears – one on Sourdough which looked irate and big as a bus, another, possibly ours, standing in the meadow below Desolation's false summit. It had a kind face.

bit sleepy back there on the road and I'd only got my baby here' – a small Scots terrier in the passenger footwell – 'and my piece'a pie to keep me going here' – a large bowl of apple pie and ice cream rested half eaten on the driver's seat.

Well, I'm glad we could help, I told her, watching Colin contort himself around the microwave and dog. How long have you been square dancing?

———

When we arrived back at the hire Jeep, Colin's gloves were still on the roof where he'd apparently left them. We gave Peggy a big hug and promised to stay in touch. I knew a lot more about square dancing now – a strange union of barn-dance and bingo, performed whilst dressed like Dorothy from *The Wizard of Oz* to judge from the costumes I'd had across my knees.

Then we drove back to Marblemount, down past the dams, and the pie *was* fine and the filter coffee too, the bristly man in the dungarees nowhere to be seen. Then on through Concrete and back to Seattle, the journey passing like a song playing out, something like the end of 'Went To See The Gypsy', the final thirty seconds – the singing is finished and the band rally, you can feel the joy in the room, hear the delight; something great has just happened, now all you have to do is play on; jam merrily on to fade.*

———

* 'Went To See The Gypsy', *New Morning*, Bob Dylan, Columbia Records, 1970. Jim later suggested that 'All Along The Watchtower' would have been a

Jim Henterly and Dan Richards, Desolation Peak LO, WA, USA.
Photograph: Colin Cady

On the Road was published on 5 September 1957, a year to the day that Kerouac left Desolation Peak. His life changed overnight.

The outsider became a sensation, perhaps the first superstar writer of the television age. A celebrity, hailed as the voice of a generation, a seer, a sage, a guru – he received the sort of frenzied attention and scrutiny which would later drive Dylan off the road.

More books followed, thrashed out to sate the demand for new words and the man himself. Everyone wanted a piece of him; the writer who a year previously couldn't get arrested was suddenly a household name.

He repurposed diaries, letters, conversation, dug out

---

fitting Dylan song to have been playing en route to the lookout – 'but the best version by Jimi Hendrix; a fellow paratrooper of the 101st, strangely enough!'

previously rejected manuscripts, rejigged fragments for novels, short stories, records, radio – and at the heart of it all, those sixty-three days – a shambles retooled in the course of three books – *The Dharma Bums*, *Desolation Angels*, 'Alone on a Mountaintop' in *Lonesome Traveler* – into an iconic posting of *Nirvanic Bliss*. The final three pages of the latter account are a rapturous hymn to serenity, acceptance, peace – all the things he lacked.

Lines like 'silence itself is the sound of diamonds which can cut through anything'[18] replaced the spasmodic primal screams of his contemporaneous notes.

But it says a huge amount about Kerouac's gifts of graft and grift, his mercurial flair, that readers and believers still come to climb *his* mountain and see *his* glass pagoda to pay their respects.

Desolation has become a Beat Sinai. In the final edit, Kerouac pulled it out of the fire and reframed his martyry as a font.

But I wonder now, a little time having passed, if he kept returning to his time in the Cascades simply for the raw material, the need to set his record straight for shame, or because the experience genuinely grew in significance as time passed.

As he became public property and his distance from friends like Snyder grew, as his life began to accelerate out of control, did he look back to his firewatch stint as a halcyon time? Did it come to haunt him?

'Sometimes I'd yell questions at the rocks and trees, and across gorges, or yodel – "What is the meaning of the void?"' he wrote in *Lonesome Traveler* – that famous line. 'The answer was perfect silence, so I knew.'[19]

He would never know that silence again.

V

MARS, UTAH

It was as hollow and empty as the spaces between
stars.

– Raymond Chandler[1]

Kate met me at LAX in a brown Range Rover belonging
to her dad, alienly British in the neon underpass of
Arrivals. It was dark, the sun having set as I'd flown over
Sacramento, the horizon a smudge of fire above dark earth,
the sky's visor tint rising blue to black.

LA at night lived up to the hype – it was a great big
freeway – myriad ramps, trucks and lights. The roads were
a maze of spillway chutes like those of Diablo and Ross, a
torrent of cars fluming off each. We drove southeast down
405, the San Diego Freeway, six peroxide lanes flashing past
In-N-Outs and over the Los Angeles river in its concrete
sluice; ghost white and lime dry.

I was moving south to Utah. At least, I was in the process
of doing so. When we'd left Jim in the watchtower, the Mars
Desert Research Station (MDRS) had still not responded
with a definite date and I didn't want to arrive at 2200 Cow
Dung Road, Hanksville, and find nobody home, so I decided
to fly down to see my friend Kate in Long Beach and await
the call there.

'Remind me why you're here,' her mother asked me when

we arrived. 'It's an artist's residency, is that right? A space station in the desert. I'm sure Kate's told me but –'

'I don't really know what it is,' I told her. 'It's an experimental Mars Base in Utah.'

'But you've been there before?'

'No . . . but I've seen pictures.'

And it was true. I had seen pictures, but this was a stranger quest than Desolation Peak and had no central figure at its heart – no Johnson or Kerouac to follow. Nothing as specific as that. In fact almost the opposite. I was drawn to Utah because of absence, the vacuum of space.

In early 2016 I saw a picture of MDRS on the front of a magazine named *Avaunt*, a picture of an astronaut walking into a red world of rock and ice, a skyline of blue mountains, and I thought, 'Mars! Now there is the ultimate outpost, the final frontier of exploration and cabins . . . because we'll have to live somewhere when we get there . . . which we haven't yet – so where was this photograph taken?' And I determined to go to the place where that amazing picture had been shot and see what was going on with prospective life on Mars – human life on Mars.

Much of this book examines emptiness, the way particular spaces affect people and vice versa in a creative and explorative sense, but 'space' itself, *outer space*, mankind's fascination with the heavens, the mechanisms, mysteries and beauty of vaults and worlds unknown, explode such thoughts to a dazzling degree.

I'd been fascinated with space travel and exploration in childhood and these enthusiasms evolved as I grew older and an element of the mesmeric existential terror of *2001: A Space*

Odyssey and *Alien* overtook the naïve wonder of *The Clangers* and *Button Moon*. So many of my touchstone artists and writers were similarly obsessed by dreams and images of a life beyond Earth; a future of spacecraft and great leaps in technology, alien races, worlds of uncanny symmetry and unimaginable difference.

H.G. Wells, Ray Bradbury, Philip K. Dick, Stanislaw Lem, Douglas Adams, Dr Who and David Bowie informed my picture of Mars. Particularly the latter – Bowie as Ziggy singing 'Starman' on *Top of the Pops,* as the ashen cadaverous proto-Thin White Duke of Nicolas Roeg's movie *The Man Who Fell to Earth* – goat-eyed visitor, multi-screened prospector; wax-skinned addict, flame-haired in a duffel coat, profile honed by a flashing blue light, frozen in the anechoic egg-box of *Station to Station* – and before that 'Life On Mars?' itself, and *before all that*, 'Space Oddity'.[*]

I discovered that *Avaunt*'s photograph had been taken in a Utah desert. So, in the great American tradition, *I determined to go to Utah! I chose to go to Utah in the next couple of years and do the other things (involved with writing this book), not because they were easy, but because they were hard; because that goal would serve to organise and measure the best of my energies and skills, because that challenge was one that I was willing to accept, one I (and*

---

[*] A well crafted but ultimately opportunistic 'cheap shot' at the impending *Apollo 11* mission (according to Tony Visconti), 'Space Oddity' was David Bowie's first single to chart in the UK, reaching the top five on initial release and receiving the 1970 Ivor Novello Special Award for Originality. Bowie sang the song at the televised ceremony, dressed in an amazing pair of salmon-pink flares.

my publishers) were unwilling to postpone, and one I intended to win ... And so, to that end, I'd spent the past few months trying to persuade a Mars station in Utah to let me visit and see Mars on Earth. Just to see. To try and better understand my own fascinations and motivations, to journey to the heart of it. Because of that photograph, Lem, Bowie et al.

But explaining all that to Kate's mother in a Long Beach sitting room was beyond me that night so I asked where I might put my bags and was led to my bedroom, bathroom and towels.

———

Colin and I had stayed in Seattle for a couple of days after leaving the Cascades. One night I met an old guy outside a bar in Ballard, a man with a face like a crumpled paper bag. He had told me about how he'd worked in a London brewery in the early 70s and tagged along with a group of lads with crowbars who he'd initially thought were going to attack him in a back alley in Chelsea but were instead set on breaking into Earls Court to watch Pink Floyd. So this guy, legs unbroken, joined the mob who called him 'Yank' and heard *Dark Side of the Moon*.

When I got back inside the bar Colin asked me if my new friend had tried to sell me drugs. I said no, we'd been talking about Pink Floyd.

---

* With apologies to President Kennedy and his 'We choose to go to the Moon' speech of 1962.

'Wow,' said Colin, 'that surprises me. You must be the first person he hasn't tried to shake down or sell dope.'

But I wasn't that surprised. The further from home I am, the more people seem to tell me things. It's easier to talk to strangers maybe, or perhaps I have the sort of face that invites confessional conversation.

Two days later, on the flight down from Seattle to LA, I got talking to a lawyer in the next seat who worked for Amazon. She asked what I did. I said I was an author. She seemed sad and concerned by this. 'Oh dear,' she said, 'I'm sorry.'

'I know,' I said. 'There we are . . .'

But it turned out she'd misheard and thought I'd said I was an orphan; a professional orphan. She was delighted when she realised her mistake and her smile returned full-beam. 'You write books!? That's wonderful.'

'I think you can buy them on Amazon,' I told her.

'I'll bet you can! Amazon sell books. That is absolutely something we do.'

But the company is constantly expanding and evolving, she told me. In fact they were currently busy looking for a new base beyond Seattle. She paused, wanting me to ask why.

I said, 'Why?'

The move had been spurred by North Korea's development of ballistic missiles capable of reaching the west coast, she said.

'I guess we'll all need new "stuff" post-nuclear apocalypse,' I replied, trying to keep it light.

She enthusiastically agreed – Amazon would be vital post-World War III. 'And also we want to give back,' she told me. 'We want to give back to the American public.

When we build HQ2 it'll be so great for whichever lucky city we choose.'

In the following months I thought about that conversation often – the jump from the analogue Cascade mountains to an unexpected briefing about Seattle's likely ballistic demise delivered several thousand feet above Oregon. It might seem simplistic to say that the America I visited felt edgy and paranoiac – half the country primed to wince and condemn the Twitter President's latest braggadocious hot take or fractious small-hours text-speak screed, the other set to cheer it – not a land of peacemakers; *the other thing* . . . But of all I experienced as I travelled down and across the US – the conversations about flags and civil war history, the rise of the emboldened far right, guns, Russia, immigration, the stripping of environmental protections, the people who told me point blank that Obama had been the worst POTUS ever – it was that conversation about the fact that World War III figured so highly in the thinking and agenda of a billion-dollar company like Amazon which best summed it up.

But maybe I was being overly dramatic, the result of too much time spent in airports – oscillating between isolated wilderness, high-security cities and transport hubs, whilst jet-lagged, with no workaday normality in between. Perhaps I hadn't seen the real America at all. Perhaps the fact that I was en route to a Mars Base had put me in a slightly apocalyptic state of mind. Imagine serious people using World War III to justify billion-dollar projects, that would just be ridiculous. Imagine a world like that, I frowned, glancing briefly at the *Guardian*'s website whilst fact-checking Pink Floyd's 1973 tour dates:

ELON MUSK: WE MUST COLONISE MARS TO PRESERVE OUR SPECIES IN A THIRD WORLD WAR[3]

Humans must prioritise the colonisation of Mars so the species can be conserved in the event of a third world war, SpaceX and Tesla founder Elon Musk said on Sunday.

'It's important to get a self-sustaining base on Mars because it's far enough away from Earth that [in the event of a war] it's more likely to survive than a Moon base,' Musk said on stage at SXSW – just days after Donald Trump announced plans to meet the North Korean leader, Kim Jong-un, in an attempt to defuse rising nuclear tension.

'If there's a third world war we want to make sure there's enough of a seed of human civilisation somewhere else to bring it back and shorten the length of the dark ages,' Musk said, responding to questions from his friend Jonah Nolan, co-creator of TV show *Westworld*.* [. . .] But building a colony would require 'tremendous entrepreneurial resources', Musk said.

The next logical step must surely be for Amazon to build HQ2 on Mars.

———

* *Westworld*: a sci-fi programme about Wild West robots. Later in the article we're told that SpaceX are working on a vehicle to take humans to Mars, a 100-metre ship codenamed the BFR (Big Fucking Rocket) . . . what a wag.

When I'd left Colin in end-times Seattle it had been raining. When I landed in the neo-noir of LA there was a dry
wind blowing fit to strip paint and my skin strobed ashen
the half hour it took to reach Long Beach. The heavens
burnt orange, the air was filled with fuel and engines.
Switching yards snaking silver under tungsten gantries –
everything and everyone routed elsewhere, peeling away
from an automotive city where to be mobile was to be
automobile and I imagined the only wildlife to be lizards
and nighthawks. LA: newly extruded, thrumming talcy
and hot. The oldest things I saw on the drive were fellow
motorists; over- and under-taking pensioners.

Bath felt impossibly quaint and far away.

Kate is a native Long Beacher and her house was a 50s
suburban dream – a craftsman home on an avenue lined
with magnolia and jacaranda trees in a neighbourhood set
back from Los Coyotes Diagonal. The air was full of sweet
pollen. Everything was dusted with blossom. We'd been
talking about America since LAX – family, Colin,
Desolation, Bath, Kate's life here, her Hollywood childhood – anybody who got taken along to meet Harrison Ford
on set as a birthday treat had *A Hollywood Childhood* as far
as I'm concerned – but everyone here is involved with films
in some way, she told me; everyone knew *someone* and everyone was working on a screenplay, including Kate. So that
was all right.

I'd met Kate and Colin the year before when they'd been
in the UK to study. They'd been to Bath, now I was in the
US. I'd shown them the classical ropes at the Royal Crescent,
Jane Austen museum and Roman baths, and now I was
learning all about bears, Beats, Tinseltown and Armageddon.

Kate met my saucer-eyed angst about the *Mad Max* traffic with easy, teasing Californian charm. This was her patch and she was the perfect company and guide; graceful, glamorous and assured – hair flowing, walk languid, sunglasses habitually worn indoors and out. She was a local. I was not. Snapshots from the next few days show me looking panicked and shifty at various LA landmarks having apparently forgotten how to stand in a relaxed human way; crumpled and shifty at the Walk of Fame, clammy and crazed outside the Hollywood Masonic Temple, slowly pitching over outside Grauman's Chinese Theatre . . . But there's a lovely shot of us up at the Griffith Observatory in gold-pink light one afternoon where I managed to raise my game and we look happy, normal. Inside the grand domed space was a Tesla Coil whose orb of purple lightning recalled the electric storms which heralded the Terminator's arrival on the lawn in 1984 – as James Dean had rolled up three decades before and the stars of *La La Land* danced a few later. The Observatory is so keyed into LA's film and television history, the backdrop and setting for so many movies, that you probably know it even if you've never heard the name – the *sci* behind a great deal of *fi*. But then LA is a dreamlike zone where roles and lines of reference blur. On the afternoon of 25 May 2008, an audience in the Observatory's Leonard Nimoy Event Horizon Theater watched live pictures of the NASA Phoenix rover's touchdown on Mars* – the data feed from Mars, fifteen minutes delayed at the speed of light,

---

* Radio signals received at 4:53:44 p.m. 25/05/08 Pacific Time confirmed the Phoenix Mars Lander had survived its difficult final descent and touchdown fifteen minutes earlier.

playing out across tense faces at Pasadena mission control, beamed into a room named after the man who played Mr Spock; a sci-fi TV funded TV science seance.

Later that day I was handed a free bottle of chilled chocolate shake by a smiling girl on a downtown street. The drink was named Soylent. 'It's made of soy,' the girl explained. 'Is it though?' I asked her. 'Is it really? Nothing in this town seems to be exactly what it claims and this would seem a worst case scenario.' She laughed and told me yes, it was really made of soy. 'It says so on the bottle, you see?' She was charming. The drink was cold and tasted good. LA might consume beautiful people but the beautiful people didn't consume each other.

Soylent Cacao – Ready-to-drink meal – Natural and artificial flavours – 20% daily nutrition – 20g protein – 14 FL OZ – tasting of chocolate milk but actually soy. Not people, silly, *soy*. The bottle said so.

———

On the sixth day of my stay, Dr Shannon Rupert emailed to invite me down to the Mars Desert Research Station outside Hanksville, Utah. I booked a flight out to Salt Lake City and a train, the *California Zephyr*, down to a town named Green River, the nearest stop to Mars. That left me with a little under sixty-five miles of scrub and desert to negotiate. I sat for a long time scrolling across it on Google Earth, zooming in and zooming out of the rust and tan expanse. Any way you spun it, it was sixty-five miles.

Kate drove me back to LAX.

I emailed MDRS to tell them I was on my way, explaining that I did not drive and asking if there was any chance of a lift from Green River. Before leaving LA I had an answer: I should rent a car in Salt Lake City and drive down to Hanksville. Dr Rupert knew of no way to get from Green River to MDRS. This was the true West, she told me, and there was no public transportation in such rural areas, but if I drove down from Salt Lake City on Highway 6 through Price, the fall colours were currently really pretty.

I arrived in Salt Lake City to news of a mass shooting in Las Vegas. The attack grew more horrific with each news cycle. My train was at 4:30 a.m. so I sat for five hours in the empty terminal, a huge deserted glasshouse echoing with escalators, air-con, rolling news and hand-driers which sounded like blenders.

A small-hours taxi took me to the Amtrak station. There were no other cars on the road. The frosted blacktop shone. The sky was clear. There were stars. The air was freezing. My breath steamed.

Our off-ramp snaked through a freight yard full of pitched tarps and polythene; shadowed avenues stretching line on line.

'Tent city,' noted the driver.

'How long has that been here?' I asked him. 'It must be so . . . cold.'

'They move them about. Bus them around,' he told me. 'We've had a lot come in from all over Utah. Troubled folks, my man. A lot of pain.'

At the silent station, I shook the driver's hand. 'Good night,' he said. 'God bless.'

My train turned out to be a bus – *Temporary substitute service for train* – 'It's been like this for months.'

As we crunched towards another freeway the ghostly camp flickered through the window. On and on and on. Then gone.

We were due into Green River at 8:15 a.m.

———

The rest of the night passed as a set of strange dreams. I slept only lightly, waking often, face close to the window, glimpsing a town, some lights, blurred raindrops, striated mountain passes, always vaguely wondering where we were, where I was. The city of Provo passed me by but I was awake for the fifteen-mile crawl up Price Canyon and over Soldier Summit to Helper, a town named after the banking engines stationed there to help the coal and freight trains climb the steep and prolonged grade of the Wasatch Plateau.

There was no dawn as such, the night just paled until, an hour out of Helper, there seemed no point denying that it was another day.

I focused on the layer cake of sandstone cliffs which had been a constant for a while – a 2,000-foot wall, peach with sooty feet – and noted that its current flank and profile resembled the sort of proud silver-orange locomotive I'd romantically imagined piloting me down to Green River in warm sunshine.

I checked my phone. There was an email from Dr Rupert at MDRS:

Hi, Dan – Just wanted to let you know it has been raining heavily here all night, which makes moving around a bit sticky. The clay soils swell when it rains and I don't know if you will even be able to get in here unless it stops very soon.

Please give me a call when you arrive in Hanksville and I'll come to town and get you if the roads are passable.

Best,
Shannon

I leaned into the aisle to look down the bus. The road ahead ran dead straight, blacktop on xeric. The sky was putty-coloured, equal parts water and spite.

———

Green River was a rainstorm. Whereas everyone else, both of them, hopped into waiting cars, I shouldered my bag and walked up to the main road, then a mile further on to a gas station. There were two; I chose the one with an Arby's diner in the direction of Hanksville but a little questioning revealed that hardly anybody had heard of it. It's not really a place, someone told me. I bought a lousy coffee. Whilst muzzily spilling cream at it in a doomed attempt to improve its essential evil, I felt a tug on my arm.

You a hitchhiker too? asked the tugger. He was a short beaverish man who smelled like he ate and washed in cigarettes as well as smoking them. The word 'too' immediately struck me as dangerous, not in terms of peril but association.

Where are you headed? I asked him.

Vegas, he said.

Ah, I said.

Lucky place, he said.

There was a pause.

Always been lucky for me, he said.

Good. I said. Good luck! I'm trying to get down to Hanksville.

It's not really a place, you know, he told me, and went outside to smoke and try to get lucky with a truck.

An hour later I had scared a dozen upright citizens with my polite requests for a lift. I was Hugh Grant stumbled onto the set of *No Country for Old Men*. I was also wet and tiring of being asked if I was okay and being offered cell phones to call for help.

I have a phone, I explained. I don't drive, you see.

You should have hired a car, they said.

Everyone was incredibly kind and concerned but nobody gave me a ride.

The beaver man was having no luck either and now sat in a diner cubicle smashing his mobile to bits on a table whilst swearing high and hissy through his teeth. I took my third horror coffee back out into the rain, huddled under an Arby's awning and began emailing everyone I knew who might know someone in Utah, anyone who might know an American who drove, then I phoned my mother in Bath just to, you know, say hi, pretend everything was okay and ask if she knew any Utahans. She didn't.

I rang my friend Roz in Shanghai where it was midnight.

Hello, I said, I'm in a bit of jam. Do we know any Americans?

We did.

We'd gone to university with Katy Corneli.

Katy lives in Price, Utah, Facebook told me once I'd rung off from Shanghai.

I called her up. She was working as a palaeontologist at the USU Eastern Prehistoric Museum. She sounded surprised to hear from me after fifteen years and her surprise became incredulity when I explained that I was holed up in Green River and needed a lift to Hanksville. *She* knew all about MDRS, 'That's actually a prime spot for Utahraptor fossils,' she told me . . .

Katy couldn't help immediately, she couldn't drop her dinosaurs and drive me down herself, but she asked around and her friend Amber volunteered to take me. So, four hours after arriving into Green River, I was on my way down to Hanksville with Amber.

In the time it had taken her to reach me I had read up on the Utahraptor or 'Super-slasher' as it's charmingly nicknamed; a three-metre-high Jurassic beast with big death-dealing claws and knife-like teeth, 'one of the most ferocious killers ever to walk the Earth', my phone told me. And the desert surrounding MDRS was full of them, apparently.

As soon as Amber arrived on the forecourt I'd broken cover and jumped into her car to avoid attracting the attention of 'super-smasher beaver man' and within an hour we'd made it the sixty miles down through Hanksville – a town that was almost actually a place if you squinted – and up to the spot where my map said Cow Dung Road began.

My gateway to Mars was an actual gate with a Snoopy style mailbox on a post. Dr Rupert's phone went straight to voicemail. Amber peered mistrustfully at the red track which wound sharply down into an umber gulch. Beyond and all around us strange rock-forms reared, hoodoos, hillocks, tumps and scarps, with massive mesas further off; a land of towering fists and fingers. Is this it? Amber asked. I reckoned so. Climbing out, my boots sank an inch into claggy clay. I told her I could walk from here, I didn't want her getting stuck. We shook hands; another amazing auto-Samaritan, Amber gingerly did a three-point turn and drove away.

———

Perhaps it was apt that I'd spent several hours in a service station. The month before, I'd spoken to Lucinda Offer, Executive Director of the Mars Society as well as Education & Outreach Officer at the Royal Astronomical Society, at a TGI Friday in Berkshire, UK – a similarly nondescript identikit space to the Green River Arby's. Over daft cocktails we'd discussed Mars and the several science expeditions Lucinda had undertaken with the NASA Ames Research Center and their Spaceward Bound programme.*

'We're always looking for extreme lifeforms,' she told me enthusiastically. 'You're probably familiar with tardigrades?'

I wasn't, so got a crash course. Tardigrades are minute animals – aka water bears / moss piglets – resembling

---

* NASA Ames Research Center is located in the heart of California's Silicon Valley, one of ten NASA field centres. For more than seventy-five years, Ames has conducted research and development in aeronautics, exploration technology and science. It was established on 20 December 1939, as part of the National Advisory Committee for Aeronautics (NACA), in 1958 absorbed into the National Aeronautics and Space Administration (NASA).

eight-legged sumo beavers with faces like crushed Coke cans. They are found all over the world, incredibly resilient and capable of lying dormant for eons until conditions improve. If anything might have stuck it out on Mars and made a go of it whilst being baked, swamped or frozen in an atmosphere of carbon dioxide, tardigrade-like critters would seem a solid bet.

Microscopic moss piglets: the happier alternative to Martian super-slashers.

Lucinda told me how she'd gone looking for tardigrade in the Mojave. That involved scooping up a bit of brackish desert pond water and looking for life under a microscope. The same team then went to Abu Dhabi for about a month to look at Martian analogues in Empty Quarter salt flats, exploring the low parts of the dunes where flats had been exposed by the wind's constant shifting and sculpting of the sands.

'We dug down to get a nice fresh sample about three or four inches thick and were astonished to find very distinctly coloured layers, each a different set of micro-organisms or algae. There was a top layer of white salt that you would typically see on a salt flat. Under that there's maybe a green layer forming, and then a pink layer, and then a brown layer – different organisms living at different depths depending upon how much light they were getting.'

The whole salty sandwich resembled a hamburger with special sauce, apparently. Yum.

Lucinda also told me about how NASA Ames had recently been out in New Zealand investigating geothermal vents similar to the geysers and hot springs I'd seen in Iceland and Bath, looking at life in bio-mats in areas of

scaldingly hot percolating water. On the same trip they scru-
tinised some three-and-a-half-billion-year-old stromatolites
in Australia.*

So that's the sort of thing the first Mars explorers will
look for? I asked. Water bears and stromatolites?

Yes, she said. It's an exciting time to be a Martian tardigrade enthusiast. The idea of sending humans to Mars is
being taken seriously again: 'The Mars Society used to be
the ones screaming in the crowd but now it's all over the
world and we're really excited about that. India has ISRO[†]
starting their own mission, China is about to go to the
Moon and they're also interested in going to Mars, UAE is
interested in going to Mars – the whole world is taking part
so I think that it is going to be a team of people and not
just the United States – although I think they're all waiting
for the US to make the first move because that's what we've
done in the past . . . and that's the whole idea of Dr Zubrin's
book: that we could all get on and do it within a decade if
we have the same energy focus as JFK had when he said "go
make it happen".'

Dr Robert Zubrin, aerospace engineer, nuclear physicist
and all-round polymath, is President of the Mars Society and
his book *The Case for Mars: The Plan to Settle the Red Planet
and Why We Must* details the Mars Direct scheme to get
humans to Mars in the near future. It covers risks, costings,

---

*   stromatolite *noun*
    plural noun: stromatolites
    1. a calcareous mound built up of layers of lime-secreting cyanobacteria
       and trapped sediment, found in Precambrian rocks as the earliest known
       fossils, and still being formed in lagoons in Australasia.
†   Indian Space Research Organisation.

timelines, crew makeups, mission imperatives, vehicle and base designs, terraforming – all in a confident, accessible way, reading at times like a marvellous How To / Can Do manual for yer average Martian frontiersman or woman – which isn't actually as far-fetched or glib as it might sound because the idea of prospecting is one of the main Martian draws for those immune to tardigrade charms.

It's notable that whilst both Musk and Zubrin talk about Mars as a great adventure, the next step in essential human nature – to go, quest, dream, and learn – and both extol the science and trickle-down of advanced technologies from any research and development programme, neither SpaceX nor Mars Direct are altruistic enterprises – they mean business. 'Because it's there' will not cut it regarding Mars; 'because it has untapped mineral, metal and gas deposits' plays better with investors, and *The Case for Mars* suggests that Mars colonisation may be a highly profitable enterprise for two reasons: a high concentration of precious metals and deuterium, the heavy isotope of hydrogen:

> Mars will enjoy a power-rich economy based upon exploitation of its large domestic resources of deuterium fuel for fusion reactors ... Deuterium is five times more common on Mars than it is on Earth, and tens of thousands of times more common on Mars than on the Moon.[4]

I was thinking about the gold rush ruins I'd seen up in Skagit Gorge and Ruby Creek as I walked down my red road; thinking about how we'd driven through Helper this morning, 'Hub of Carbon County', wondering whether the people of

Utah, communities who still dreamt of King Coal's return, might feel any enthusiasm for Martian deuterium.

When I'd spoken to Lucinda she'd been doubtful about Trump's interest in space. 'He's no JFK,' she'd told me. 'We [at The Mars Society] were hoping that Elon Musk was *it* for a long time and we're very appreciative of all the work he has done but he seems to have pulled back [from Mars] and he's now focusing on the Moon and I've heard it's because he didn't get any funding from NASA for the heavy lift launcher that he wants to build.'

Utah is staunchly Republican. When Trump won the presidency in 2016 it was the thirteenth consecutive time the GOP presidential candidate had also won the state. Trump campaigned in Utah on a pro-coal ticket. Two months after my visit, on 4 December 2017, President Trump reduced the size of the Bears Ears National Monument* in southeastern Utah by 85 per cent, potentially opening up 1.3 million acres of public land to energy companies with mining leases for coal and uranium deposits.†

Then, a week later, on 11 December, the 45th anniversary of the *Apollo 17* lunar landing, Trump signed a policy directive telling NASA to focus efforts on human exploration, with an eye towards returning to the Moon.

---

* A US national monument is a protected area similar to a national park, created from land owned or controlled by the federal government by presidential proclamation. Bears Ears National Monument was established by President Barack Obama on 28 December 2016.

† The move was celebrated in the Trump White House as a rollback and rejection of Obama-era environmental policy and Native American land protections – casting them as anti-coal, anti-jobs measures; out-of-touch meddling by arrogant Big Government.

The announcement drew support from NASA and Republican Congressman Lamar Smith, Chair of the House Science, Space and Technology Committee, who praised the Trump administration's 'dedication to space' – sounding a mite grandiose and premature.

However, *New Scientist* reported that many aerospace proponents were cautiously supportive – 'Even SpaceX CEO Elon Musk, who parted ways with Trump last summer over climate change, tweeted his approval. "It's high time that humanity went beyond Earth," he wrote.'[5]

Dr Robert Zubrin is quoted in the same article, pointing out that when John F. Kennedy announced his dream of putting a human on the Moon, he did so in a speech before a joint session of Congress, not in a lightly attended press conference. 'There's no evidence whatsoever of any serious commitment,' Zubrin told *Cosmos* magazine, suggesting that it was far too early to know if Congress would fund the plan or even take it seriously.

However, should the Trump administration and Congress follow through with the idea, Zubrin said he would support the initiative, pointing to the Moon as a useful test-bed for spacecraft and other technology ultimately designed to reach *beyond*: 'It's only possible to launch for Mars once every two years so [in the interim] you'd be idle, so you really want to do the Moon and Mars in parallel.'[6]

Then Elon Musk and SpaceX conducted the maiden launch of *Falcon Heavy* on 6 February 2018 – a massively impressive and powerful rocket with only slightly less oomph than the *Saturn V*. The showmanship and technical brilliance of the event – the fact they sent a Tesla Roadster with David Bowie on the radio off round the Sun on a journey into the neighbourhood of Mars; the fact two of the boosters landed safely back on Earth in unison plié – dominated front pages worldwide . . . but read the small print and you'll see that as well as being designed to carry humans to the Moon and Mars, *Falcon Heavy* has the potential to go to 'asteroids for mining'.

They won't be digging for tardigrades.

I think Elon Musk, Dr Zubrin and the Trump administration may be rather more ore-inspired by the Red Planet's metal and deuterium prospects – the opportunity to plant a flag and shout 'Mine!' – than the starry-eyed public are aware.

———

By this point I was walking in old jeep tracks, slip-sliding down twin red ruts – tired but curious to see what I'd find when I finally got to Mars, Utah. I was thinking of the Wild West; blood and rust, earth and rocks; thinking that the massive flat-topped mesas in the distance looked like they'd had their heads blown off. I thought again of Jim on Desolation Peak and wondered if he was now packed up and back home, fishing. We'd spoken about fishing the morning I left; he'd told me he caught salmon in the river behind his house. I pictured his lookout so green in the sky, the Cormac McCarthy quotes pinned on the window frames.

'I think we're going to the moon because it's in the nature of the human being to face challenges', Neil Armstrong told an Apollo mission press conference in May 1969. 'It's by the nature of his *inner soul* – we're required to do these things just as salmon swim upstream.'[7]

That same year Gary Snyder published the essay 'Four Changes' in a collection that would go on to win a Pulitzer Prize. Salmon also feature:

> Goal: clean air, clean clear-running rivers, the presence of Pelican and Osprey and Gray Whale in our lives; salmon and trout in our streams; unmuddied language and good dreams.[8]

Armstrong was home and hosed by the end of July. Snyder's terrestrial hopes are still a work in progress.

Half an hour into my walk I was overtaken by Dr Shannon Rupert in a pickup truck. A white-haired lady in a *Star Wars* T-shirt. 'Dan!' she said. 'Hop in! You made it. Yeah, phones don't work out here. Green River's quite a place, isn't it!?'

I climbed up into the cab and the 4×4 bounced forward and we reeled and meandered through tumulus desert formations for something like fifteen minutes until, rounding a vermilion hummock, the landscape opened out and I saw a Mars base, pill-white in the red ahead. From that moment everything turned around.

———

The base was a series of flasks and domes; it shone even on that murky day. There was a central cylinder and orbiting pods set amidst maroon undulations. The buildings were connected by radial covered walkways. It all looked new, landed, alien even in that uncanny panorama, and here we were driving up to it in a pickup, slaloming on to a gigantic film set, an undeniably theatrical experience.

The rain had fallen here and puckered the ground and formed wormcast-like lugs. The sand and mud were veined with powder-pink rivulets. Everything was peppered with round little rocks.

The scale of it struck me, not just of the scene, which in the first moment looked a whole world in itself. The brilliant hab, as Dr Rupert called it, surrounded by desert – salmon through ruby and beetroot rising to lavender where it met a horizon of inselberg and mesa. Nothing in view spoke of human presence apart from the base and even then one double-took. We might be on Mars.

'We could be on Mars,' Dr Rupert agreed. 'We have two habs, MDRS here in Utah and Flashline Mars Arctic Research Station (F-MARS)* on Devon Island in the High Canadian Arctic. When the Mars Society was formed in the late 90s, we knew we wanted a hab in the Arctic and we knew we wanted one in the US so we sent teams out in aeroplanes flying all over the world and they narrowed it down to three sites – this being remarkably Martian-looking – and then things worked out in terms of leasing the land and so the hab was placed here. So we put it here because it looked like Mars and since then the rovers that have done work on Mars since we established MDRS have, in effect, shown that this is a true Mars analogue – the same processes just on different scales. So we're really lucky that we picked this place because it looked like the hab should be here because, in the end, it truly should be here. Now, if you look at the search for life, micro-organically, there are other places on Earth that better resemble where we think

* fmars.marssociety.org/

we'll find life on Mars but as a whole, to do field-work, this is the best geological analogue.'

We got out of the truck and climbed into the largest hab structure, a teapot in the midst of cups. To get up to the door we climbed a set of wooden stairs and once inside, past some thick airlock doors, we climbed a further staircase to the first-floor lounge where we sat on what appeared to be regulation Earth sofas and drank Earth coffee and Dr Rupert, who by now had asked me to call her Shannon, told me about what goes on at MDRS and how it all started.

The nature of the venture has changed from the early days, she said. At the start the goal of this station was to provide a more fully realistic immersive experience of a Martian posting and in that the Mars Society were pioneering. 'Nobody did that. And, yes, some people thought we were playing spaceman and all of that stuff but as time's passed I think the value of this hab has been shown to be in the people who've been through it and are going to go to Mars. Those of us who started this project are all old now and so, when people tell me that we don't have a real research programme, don't have this or that – or a lot of times people will say "your station's just rough, there's no technology" – I think that absolutely misses the point. The UK Space Agency comes out here for three and a half weeks a year and they spend two million dollars.'

What do they do when they're here?

'They bring their rover. And we've actually collaborated with them and done some human/robotic studies and they've been so friendly – the German Space Agency, the Canadian Space Agency and the UK Space Agency all come out here. We communicate with all of them but the only one we actually collaborate with is the UK – probably because the guy who's the lead on the project is very open to humans on Mars. So they bring their instruments for robotic studies and we ... play! [Laughs.] We took their instruments and compared them with our human instrument and compared how long it took to drill a rock: find the right rock and drill a rock. It took their instrument six hours to drill the rock. It took our guy six minutes. The Germans brought the two most beautiful rovers you've ever seen. One was orange. It was adorable. But they spend millions of dollars and we don't have millions of dollars so we do operational studies. We don't do technology ...'

It's serious play. People travel here from all over the world to inquire into how human life on Mars might go, and in so doing many discover problems with extant human life and behaviour on Earth.

Would it be fair to say you're as much a sociological experiment as hard science? I asked Shannon early on.

'I think so. If the goal here is a simulated mission to Mars then yes. This is the analogue. This is as close as humans can get to a Mars environment. The hab may have wooden stairs and IKEA door handles and an airlock which requires people to use their imagination slightly, but this is where you come to experience Mars desert conditions on Earth ... Everything that matters is pretty spot on.'

Shannon is passionate about Mars and MDRS. She speaks of the hab as if it were a person, a transformative space, a sort of teacher which changes people, and I recognise her pilgrim passion as similar to the way some people talk of mountains and mountaineering – go out and up and meet it with respect and you'll be changed.

'Bill Clancey, a human factors NASA researcher, said to me that he thought of this place as the protagonist of the story.' When you try to tell the story of MDRS and what we're trying to achieve, you know, what do you focus on? Do you focus on the people who changed their whole lives and are now working at SpaceX and NASA? Do you focus on the work that's been done here? Do you focus on the human factors, the disasters, the funny things, the weird ways of coping? Really, the main story is that everybody has come here – to this place to learn something about themselves. I mean, they may say they're here for another reason; they're coming for the adventure – those ones are often those who have the hardest time because it's hard to stay focused on a mission for two weeks when you can't go outside every day and you're limited in terms of your resources, your time to yourself, your privacy, because you have to be part of a team. There's no real freedom once you sign on to be part of a team that has to work together.'

So the first Mars astronauts with current technology would strap themselves in and and fly off for . . . six to eight months?

'Pretty much.'[†]

And then you're there for . . . a year or two?

'The way things are, you'd either stay for one month or have to stay a couple of years. You know, I'm not an

---

[*] William Clancey was Chief Scientist for Human-Centred Computing at NASA Ames's Intelligent Systems Division from 1998 to 2013.

[†] For comparison, Yuri Gagarin, the first human to venture into outer space, spent 1 hour and 48 minutes there. Neil Armstrong's total time in space during his two NASA missions (*Gemini 8* and *Apollo 11*) was 8 days, 14 hours, 12 minutes and 30 seconds. His fellow astronauts aboard *Apollo 11*, Michael

engineer ... but the Mars-500 simulation in Moscow did 500 days – eight months getting there, one month where they could actually go outside their craft, into their *Mars yard*, because they were in a building – and then the rest of the time coming back, and that's when the mission fell apart.'

How did it fall apart?

'People just quit. The first eight months, gung-ho: "On our way, this is a great mission!" They got there, spent their thirty days *on Mars*, and were like, "That was cool." And then they had to wait eight months to get out of there but they felt they'd done the mission, they were just returning; and there was no sense of danger, they knew they weren't in any danger

---

Collins and Edwin 'Buzz' Aldrin Jr's time off-Earth was 11 days, 2 hours, 4 minutes and 43 seconds, and 12 days, 1 hour and 52 minutes respectively. Russian cosmonaut Gennady Padalka is the current holder of the space time world record, having spent 879 days in space over five missions. His compatriot Valeri Polyakov is the holder for the longest single stay in space, with 437 days and 18 hours on board the Mir space station. Six months is around 183 days, eight months 244. The shortest round trip to Mars presently thought possible is 396, although this would require the briefest of Martian stays – like a swimmer tumble-turning at the end of a pool.

* The Mars-500 mission was a psychological isolation experiment conducted between 2007 and 2011 by Russia, the European Space Agency and China, in preparation for an unspecified future manned spaceflight to Mars. The experiment's facility was located at the Russian Academy of Sciences' Institute of Biomedical Problems (IBMP) in Moscow, Russia. Between 2007 and 2011, three different crews of volunteers lived and worked in a mock-up spacecraft at IBMP. The final stage of the experiment, which was intended to simulate a 520-day manned mission, was conducted by an all-male crew consisting of three Russians, a Frenchman, an Italian and a Chinese citizen. The three-part Mars 500 facility sought to simulate an Earth–Mars shuttle spacecraft, an ascent-descent craft, and the Martian surface. The volunteers who participated included professionals with experience in engineering, medicine, biology and human spaceflight. The experiment yielded important data on the physiological, social and psychological effects of long-term close-quarters isolation – mars500. imbp.ru and en.wikipedia.org/wiki/MARS-500.

so they just got bored. And we see that again and again on long-term missions – keeping the crew engaged and focused is the hardest thing. It's really interesting to see here, from my own experience of being on crews, about Wednesday of your second week – because when you arrive it's very intense, you have a period of getting settled, a couple of days because, remember, you're in a crucible here so it's all happening really fast. So the first couple of days you're getting set up, the next few days you're learning: "How do we do this? What are we doing?" You just get in stride and things are starting to work out and it's Wednesday of the second week and you're going to be leaving on Sunday, crews often disengage.'

Back at TGI Friday in the UK, Lucinda had told me about the Mars 160 simulation – eighty days in the desert, eighty days in the Arctic. The standard MDRS crew rotation 'in sim' is fourteen days, so a 160-day operation was a big jump, a real test, but I was told stories of people who'd snapped and gone AWOL in Utah after less than two weeks.

'We obviously prefer people not to break sim but, unfortunately, some crews do. I don't know why they'd want to do that but . . . sometimes they want to go and have an ice cream or a hamburger. We tell them: "Don't break sim. Don't go into the town with your sim-suit on . . . you're not allowed."'

You mean they went to town with their spacesuits on?

'Some did in the beginning. And that was absolutely not okay.'

What did the people of Hanksville think?

'Oh, we've been there a long time, they're pretty used to us now.'

—

I slept alone in the hab, berthed in the Commander's quarters – a small white room with a bunk, a porthole, a desk and a lamp, the sort of berth I imagine submariners get. Shannon lives at MDRS half the year in a mobile home hidden in a nearby series of tumps and barrows – secret custodian of Mars. During the day she'd spoken about her farming background, how she was the first of her family to go to university and now splits her time between highly technical field research here and looking after horses on her ranch. It was strange to look out from the window of my spartan pod, out into deep, still and darkening desert, with the knowledge that 100 yards behind me Shannon was probably tucked up watching satellite TV in the company of her two dogs . . . but waking in the night, sitting up in my dark cell, an oval of stars the only light, I could have been 'floating round my tin can', far above the world.

I dreamt of walking in a spacesuit – the A7L sort worn by Apollo astronauts: heavy life-support system on my back, strangely inelastic knees, giant grey felted gloves, close fishbowl helmet; my face a huge reflective plate. As far as I walked, I kept finding myself approaching the Green River Arby's.* Funny as the image of a suited astronaut sitting in a Hanksville diner had been in TGI Friday, out here I found it disquieting, frightening – a picture doused in a terrible bathos, an admission of failure; panic, guilt and loss.

---

*   Just like Blake in J.G. Ballard's *The Unlimited Dream Company,* Mrs Peel in the Crossness Pumping Station, and the unnamed narrator of Paul Kingsnorth's *Beast,* however far I walked in any direction I ended up back at the start – in my case, the diner at the end of the universe.

Are your sim-suits ex-NASA? I asked Shannon next morning, hoping to try one out, discovering with great sadness that they were all away being dry-cleaned.

'No. They're very nice simulations that we've had made. They simulate the awkwardness. You have a helmet with limited vision, you have air running through it and you have a radio. So, if you do your sim right – and I've done enough of them to know this for sure – you feel like you're on Mars.'

In truth the idea of a spacesuit made me slightly queasy. I imagined it as a constrictive cocoon and it brought back a childhood worry and aversion to hearing my muffled heartbeat nagging in my ears at night like a countdown.

'For me, as someone who's always been a field scientist, I'm very comfortable being remote,' Shannon told me. 'I knew that the first time I came out here. But what I didn't know was that, because I'm a bit of a loner, very orderly and fastidious, I could come into a situation where I was living in a building this size with several people and be very content and happy. And not feel overwhelmed with proximity; you have your own bedroom, for goodness' sake.'

The crew who eventually go to Mars – Shannon's sure it's a case of when not if – will be a new kind of astronaut. Astronauts of the past were heroic risk-takers but Mars requires a different mindset. Distance is the key. Mars is about 100 million miles from Earth; six to eight months. The Moon is 384,400 miles away; forty-eight hours away. 'On the Moon you needed people who'd remain calm in a crisis, calm in the face of any kind of emergency. On Mars you're going to need people who are calm in the face of day to day life. Just like here on Earth, it will be boring and it will be exciting, but they're also going to have a never-ending risk factor.'

Shannon described the risk and worry as a kind of background noise. 'You want people who are a little bit more low-key.'

'When we did the Mars 160, because we selected from a large number of candidates, we did some NASA tests on the final twenty-one. And without understanding all of it, because I'm not a social scientist, you had to be a moderate risk-taker to ace these tests. You couldn't be a supreme risk-taker and go to Mars. You couldn't be totally risk averse and go to Mars. Your position on the risk-taking scale was a huge factor in your suitability to go. I thought that was very interesting.

'But one thing that's never been on any test that I've seen, that I really do think should be included, is the idea that you should be judged by your fellow crew members as to how you treat the equipment. This is my new thing this year. I finally realised that every time we've had a massive loss of equipment, the crew involved had flaws and always a lack of respect for each other. That was always an issue in teams who damaged their kit. Time and again, if a team had trouble respecting each other's views, they had a lack of respect for equipment.'

Antisocial behaviour.

'Exactly. And I do think social scientists could learn a lot here. I'm not saying we make people guinea pigs but there is a lot of anecdotal information that I have which is just going to be lost unless I pass it on . . . For example: a crew of four does not work. Almost every actual crew scenario for going to Mars that I have seen has a crew of four but every time we've had a crew of four here the mission has failed.'

Why is that?

'It's too much work for four people to run a mission. You would be too constricted because you always need to have a buddy – so two people must remain inside and only two people can go on an EVA.'[*]

So crews of five and six?

'It just amazes me that it's always four. It's because of weight and space, basically. We've never scheduled a crew of four here. All of our crews of four ended up that way because people couldn't make it out here. So they'd originally have been five or six. But now, talking to you, I want to put together a crew of four planned from the very beginning! That would be a cool experiment to do, see what happens.' She laughs.

Have you ever done pre-mission training to bond and drill crews beforehand?

'We did some of that for the Mars 160. The first day I found the best possible bonding exercise was to go on a long walk. That's something I now tell crews. Get here, settle, have something to eat and then go on a long walk together. Because walks allow you to break off and talk to other people, especially people you don't yet know, and I think that breaks the awkwardness.

'In fact, another interesting thing – to go back to the fact our crews overlap – the dynamics of that overlap are different every single time. I have never had two crews together in this hab who have acted the same. It's really weird!

---

* Extra-vehicular activity (EVA) is any activity done by an astronaut or cosmonaut outside a spacecraft or hab beyond the Earth's appreciable atmosphere.

'When I started here I think, in retrospect, I didn't care about anything but the science. And I am a pretty hard-nosed scientist but now, given all that I've experienced and observed, I see that we as people are our own biggest challenge.'

Again, it all seemed to come back to the idea of needing to be a bit Zen – an interplanetary aesthete, comfortable in your own skin; at ease with lack –

In space no one can hear you omm . . .

'Repetition everyday' was how Lucinda had described a tour of duty at MDRS. 'You have to get your research done. On my last tour we had a schedule and we were up doing exercises at eight, making breakfast for everybody, we'd clean up, get into our suits, do our EVAs, come back, have lunch – so it was fantastic. If you have someone really organised as Commander you're exhausted by the end of the day. All you want to do is go to sleep, get up and do the same thing.'

Who comes out to Mars, Utah? Would-be Martians mainly. Some are paid to be there: journalists or research students, NASA Academy trainees. They get a lot of MAs and PhDs; field researchers; NASA have sent scientists in the past. It's a test bed for kit and people. And above all it seems it's the atmosphere, exposure and concentration MDRS engenders and demands which sets it apart. Perhaps ironically for a place that's meant to reproduce the Martian world, it's a high-pressure environment. The people who come here, stripped of their comforts, have to sort themselves out and get on with it.

'There's a lot of lack,' Lucinda told me, no telephone or internet, fresh fruit or much recognisable food – hab teams eat processed dehydrated food; the same stuff the astronauts are eating on the ISS . . . 'but lower quality because that stuff is amazing'.

(Another reason people broke sim for burgers perhaps.)

My mind flew back to Kerouac and Snyder and the gulf between their outlooks. Here too people come to test themselves and find themselves wanting or thriving in ways they'd never dreamt.

I asked Shannon how many people had been through the programme:

'I probably should count! We generally have about fourteen crews a year of between six and seven people and then, if you consider the university rover challenge where there are 500 people, and the work parties who come out here . . . by Mars' analogue research standards we impact by far the greatest number of people. We want to be inclusive. People have told me that they'd love to come out here but they don't have a college degree or a PhD and I always tell them that doesn't matter. My best crew engineer was from an oil rig – one of those boats that turn into an oil rig. He could fix anything. He was magic and used to spending long periods of time on his own.'

We return to the topic of what makes a crew work and the nightmarish scenario of sending a team of astronauts to Mars only for them to splinter, clash and the mission – and possibly the people themselves – fall apart; that oft-visited, chillingly effective sci-fi trope of a crew trapped with a monster. You do not want to be in a capsule with somebody who wants to open a hatch and step outside.

'Think about it: what if you do make that mistake? What if you put a crew together that appears on paper the perfect team – and granted, they'll be going through a lot of experiences, tests and training before they go so maybe you'll catch it – but what if you catch it a month before launch or even six months before launch and you replace them with somebody else who appears a better fit, perfect. And then you send them. And it isn't . . . Or it gets better! For example – again going back to the Mars 160 – Anushree, our crew biologist [Anushree Srivastava] was not ready. She had no field experience, added late to the crew; she was flying straight in from India, alone – there were so many reasons for her to fail but she had been a CAPCOM* for us and always very professional, always very cheerful, always very encouraging to the crews and we had lost our crew biologist – the botanist we had lined up was Canadian but the Canadian Government changed as we were going through the selection process and the botanist works for the government in the Museum of Science and suddenly they wouldn't let him take the time off. So he couldn't go.

'I was back-up crew so suddenly I become prime crew and I didn't think I was the asset they needed – my goals were more Earth-based. I could facilitate a lot better from there – I had no ideas for a back-up scientist but it turned out that Anushree had just finished her Masters degree so I emailed her and asked if she'd be interested. So she flew out to F-MARS, this tiny shy girl – but the difference between her when she first arrived and how she is now is amazing. She

---

* Capsule Communicator (CAPCOM). Generally, only the Capsule Communicator communicates directly with the crew of a manned space flight. During much of the US manned space mission, NASA felt it important for all communication with the astronauts in space to pass through a single individual in the Mission Control centre. That role was designated the Capsule Communicator or CAPCOM and was filled by another astronaut, often one of the backup- or support-crew members. NASA believes that an astronaut is most able to understand the situation in the spacecraft and pass information in the clearest way.

became this very eager, confident field scientist. She'd never driven anything before, let alone an ATV, but she became the most amazingly good crew member. It was great. Her Masters was in biotech, in London, in a lab – she'd never been in the field."

Perhaps often the clues are there that such people will bloom in the right conditions – Anushree's ambition to study abroad, say; the fact she got involved as a CAPCOM and then said 'Yes' to the last-minute opportunity you offered her. People flourish given the chance.

'And there was actually a lot of argument against her going because she didn't have the requisite experience and background but she had gone on a Spaceward Bound trip in India with two of the other crew members so I and they already had a relationship with her. She was great as a CAPCOM, then she took it further. It worked out perfectly. And now she's gone back to London to start her PhD. She really bloomed. This place did that. The idea of it and the reality she made of it.'

Like the carpenter who worked on the rigs and boats.

---

* 'My love for space exploration started as a naïve desire to be able to behold the face of Earth from far away years ago. This desire was actually driven by my mere imagination of the cathartic effect this event can leave on you, which I think is inexplicable. Suddenly your sense of self becomes menial or possibly unifies with the unfathomable vastness of the space, vanishing this duality. Hard to say. I felt the similar emotional pull when I saw F-MARS from the sky. I was teary-eyed. I was awed as this single event flashed a series of events in my mind that caused me to witness this. So, what I want to say is being part of such missions significantly contributes towards building an ignited mind and heart along with professional accomplishments and trains you to work with humility and responsibility.' – Anushree Srivastava, Crew Biologist, in an extract from the Mars 160 crew diary – www.mars160.marssociety. org/2017/09/dear-martian-friends.

'Exactly. Great people with wonderful skillsets can come from the most diverse and unusual places. It happens over and over here.'

What's the plan for the future of MDRS?

'Well, at some point we're going to become obsolete. At some point we will go to Mars and we will have commercial space flight and the people coming here now in hopes of getting jobs in those areas will take a different route. I don't think there was ever a plan. If you'd asked me the first day I came here, "How long do you think this place is going to be here?" I couldn't have told you. Could I have told you that it would be growing seventeen years later? No. We have no idea what's ahead.'

———

I spent an early morning walking round the base alone – without a spacesuit but certainly in my own little bubble – looking at the set-up then tromping further out to explore the terrain, heading for a feature named Phobos Peak, printing a line of inch-deep footprints, stopping every so often to look back at MDRS; porcelain cold in the warming day – the ground drying paler by the second, the red world baking orange pink, magnesium sky flaring on the sheen of my skin. Ahead were hoodoos, balanced rocks, massive boulders sat up on wind-sculpted bases. Meteor eggcups. Mortarboard toadstools. Coral horse skull stones. I thought of my father encountering the polar bear pelvis in the white desert of the Arctic whilst I walked over scalloped drumlin dunes and flaking washboard deltas, my boots crusted in frothy bronze mud setting as clouds of hard pumice around my feet.

As Phobos neared, the sun began to pulse, but hot as the day grew the Mars base behind me always looked frosted. Perhaps it was a lifetime of enigmatic science fiction, the otherworldly loneliness of the desert, but I found myself checking and rechecking to see my ship hadn't departed home without me in a cloud of tremolo and theremin squall.

But as I walked I found trash and that grounded me. Plastic bottles, wrappers, polystyrene, foam; yes, I knew this planet. I gathered up as much as I could until I couldn't carry any more. Later I asked Shannon why Mars, Utah was so trashed and she was genuinely sorry and upset.

'Some of the people who come out here are not respectful. It's a research station . . . I get so frustrated. A lot of what you'd see as trash are water bottles from a student rover challenge we hold every year. They're the worst litterers. Of all time. Even though we tell them.'

However, she is fixing it and this last year was different. The competition is run and judged for sixteen hours a day, 'three days straight, brutal days, and there's not a lot of extra time to fix stuff. This last time, IKEA were coming to look at the hab as soon as the competition was done so I made the teams clean up and they could do in half a day what it took me a week to collect. But I don't think there's the respect for this land that there should be, no.'

She trails off and I'm left with the image of her litter-picking Mars.

I asked Shannon about the deuterium. The actual question now I listen back to my tape isn't the most pithy but definitely reflects how confused and heartbroken I felt in the moment, talking to this lady, this wonderful enthusiastic

Mars Mom figure moderating a Martian test bed to what ultimate end nobody's yet sure; whose contribution, insight and knowledge may well be ignored or disregarded when big money fires the starting gun for Mars.

This is hard to ask but almost everywhere on this planet has been spoiled and polluted by human activity. That D.H. Lawrence word: beshitten. We have beshat the Earth . . . and I do struggle with the idea of humanity going to Mars when Earth is in such a state. At some level it feels like a dereliction of duty. Even the crews who come here leave trash. Does that weigh on you?

I think Shannon's answer is extraordinary in its honesty.

'The idea that people really want to be astronauts and go to Mars . . . they really want to do that but they break things here, don't treat this desert or planet with respect? That's becoming a bigger part of our training programme – which is sad.

'My fear, as someone who is an optimist but sees that we have no respect for the planet we live on . . . my visions of Mars stop beyond the first landing scenarios. I'm not sure I want to see even a settlement at this point because I just see that as an opportunity for humans to exploit. So, you know, I want us to go to Mars. I think it's what we do – we like to explore and see things – I hope, like so many people like me, *Star Trek*'s our vision of what can be. And we like that but we know that that's probably not possible . . . I won't watch sci-fi movies with end-of-days kinda scenarios where everything's gone to hell in a hand-basket. I don't want to see that vision of the world. I want to see the good . . . But, yeah, I worry a lot. We're so good at terraforming this planet that we've terraformed it to death. And do I think that Mars is going to save us from the mess we've made of ourselves here? Oh, heck no. Mars wants to kill us.'

Was it weird that I came away thinking of the Manhattan Project? Because that's the analogue which blossomed in my mind.

———

In the hours before I'd flown to Utah, Kate and I had gone to the Getty Center in the Santa Monica Mountains. The complex is reached by a monorail. Nothing shouts 'the future' like a monorail. Inside the largest gallery was an exhibition tracing the development of sacred art and treasures in the Americas from about 1000 BCE to the arrival of Europeans in the early sixteenth century.

The show had over 300 masterpieces, treasures of the Moche, the Olmecs, and the Maya, all the Andean empires before the conquest of the Incas kicked in. The exhibition used the word supernatural a lot but I began reading it as extraterrestrial. The objects were so exquisite, alien and powerful. They seemed to glow in the cool black gallery. I thought of the marvelling Conquistadors, landed in a new world of mesmerising riches. Thesauronauts.

A couple of months later the Santa Monica Mountains around the Getty were on fire. The hills blazed either side of the 405, the flames writhing the angry gold and mottled red of magma. CNN ran live coverage of the infernal pulsing V – much of it from dash-cams – and that was perhaps the strangest thing of all: the fact the pictures showed the 405 highway still open, cars and trucks still rolling, slightly slower maybe, but rolling nonetheless. An apocalyptic firestorm hadn't altered behaviour. The asphalt might be molten, the rippling atmosphere airless and blistering hot, but LA's drivers were still driving come hell.

MDRS, Utah, USA. Photograph: Dan Richards

VI

BOTHIES, SCOTLAND

'Oh, Eeyore, you are wet!' said Piglet, feeling him.
    Eeyore shook himself, and asked somebody to explain
to Piglet what happened when you had been inside a river
for quite a long time.

                                                    – A.A. Milne[1]

B *oggler boggler boggler.*
        Over the moor. *'Boggler boggler boggler'* for a good
twenty minutes. *'Boggler boggler boggler'*, the sound
increasing from a whisper to a murmur to the disgruntled
splutter and growl of the Caledonian sleeper. Had you
been standing on Rannoch's footbridge to watch the train
approach you would have seen it grow from a dot to an
articulated line, seen its caterpillar face form dark-eyed
and yellow-chopped – a green locomotive pulling four
purple coaches curving across the dun bog sea and into
the island platform, drifting underneath you to stop with
a concertina clunk beside the panelled station building,
to settle there and tick. And a few moments later you
would have heard a carriage window drop and seen a hand
emerge, fumble open the door, and two bleary figures step
down trailing rucksacks; peaky-looking figures, red-eyed
and out of shape.

'8.40 a.m.,' the shorter fellow whimpers. 'Do you think the ticket office sell aspirin?'

———

Bugger bugger bugger.

We'd boarded the sleeper at London Euston the night before. Prior to that we'd been planning the trip in the pub, which is to say that we went to a pub and took maps we didn't unpack.

On the train we established that the fitness regimes we'd both planned to undertake had remained hypothetical; neither of us had modified our lifestyle in any meaningful way. Steve had recently walked the couple of miles to work (twice) where he sits at a desk to edit plays. I'd been 'writing and travelling for the book' – but in practice 'writing' meant rewarding myself with tea and Jaffa cakes every 200 words whilst 'travelling for the book' involved damn fine coffee and pie in the Cascades, being marooned at Utah Arby's, and drinking beer in Iceland with the occasional fortnight of sæluhús shenanigans or day at a lighthouse thrown in. Neither of us were fit. Yet we were about to embark on a walk from Rannoch to Braemar; a walk of over 100 miles across hills, moors, mountains, bogs and heath, bothy to bothy* – several of which were over twenty miles apart – in high summer whilst carrying heavy packs. The next week was likely to

———

* bothy | ˈbɒθi | (also bothie)
  noun (plural bothies)
  (in Scotland) a small hut or cottage, especially one for housing farm labourers or for use as a mountain refuge.

be chastening and painful, we agreed. We'd brought it on ourselves, we'd made our beds and now we'd have to carry them to Braemar. In light of this, the important thing was to get a good night's sleep and begin afresh on the morrow. We'd been silly boys but the rot stopped now. We needed to raise our game.

Several half-bottles of buffet car wine later – 'Toy wine!' I announced at one stage, I'm told – things were on the up!

I have vague memories of a cheese board, and running up the ramp in the rain at Preston to cadge cigarettes from the train crew, then possibly an Islay whisky back on board before Steve displayed a remarkable turn of pace around 1 a.m., disappearing down the train and leaving me to pay.

When I eventually crawled into my cabin bunk I found myself beset with such apocalyptic nausea that I feared for my actual life.

Next morning I awoke so hungover that I regretted surviving the night. My eyes seemed to be trying to leave my skull by means of pneumatic drills. The least noise brought pain so exquisite that the train whistle nearly caused me to die. The least touch was agony. My skin crawled. My hair hurt. I was hot, I was cold. Once off the train and over the footbridge I was terribly sick in a ditch.

To make matters worse, Steve seemed to be fine. He ate his breakfast at the Rannoch Hotel with gusto whilst I shivered wan-faced, deafened by the wall-clock.

The hotel is one of three buildings in Rannoch – the others being the station and the old tin school, long closed, now home to the playwright David Greig. In the introduction to his *Selected Plays*, Greig tells a story of how the

Scottish poet W.S. Graham was once lost on the moor in a snowstorm:

> He had struck out of Glencoe hoping for a lift which never came. For some time he wandered lost in the great white blankness of the moor, alone. He was cold. He began to fade. He thought he might die until eventually he was rescued by a shepherd who took him back to his croft and gave him brandy.*

Greig goes on to equate W.S. Graham's experience with the process of writing. For him, the solitude, the emptiness and the whiteness of the snow echo the solitude of his battle with the empty blank page: 'a landscape across which the author moves, stumbling and searching'. Now I too was blank and foundering on Rannoch as if augured or following stage directions – the moor before Ben Alder had become a landscape across which this author was set to move: stumbling, searching and ralphing his guts up.

——

Bog bog bog.

Nine p.m. The sky was teeming, hammering. My hood was like a drum, a loud cowl lashed by hard resolute rain

---

* In the book, David continues: 'That story holds a special place for me partly because the metaphor of the man in the snow is one I once used in *Pyrenees* but also because most of these plays were written in a cottage on Rannoch Moor sitting at a kitchen table and looking out at the very same vast wasted moor across which W.S. Graham was trying to walk that night.' – *Selected Plays 1999–2009*, David Greig, Faber, London, 2010, p.ii.

which had begun falling shortly after we struck out of Rannoch and looked set to continue for ever. The watery light had gone from the day, no match for actual water, and the world was now subfusc – a wonderful word – utterly murky and underexposed. Fog filled the valley. It was dreich dreich dreich and my feet feet feet were wet wet wet. The air was a mizzle of tick-tick, pitter, spit and stipple. The stream at and in my boots was in rowdy spate. The banks were mud and rivulet. Gorse and saturated ferns which smelled of deep musk and humus hissed as we pushed past looking for our path. The stream was a pocked leaden mirror – *even the stream looked uncommonly wet.*

I'd had a lot of opportunity to study the stream since we'd been following it for a good couple of hours from the head of Loch Ossian. Quite why this was necessary, why we were there in the first place, is still the subject of some debate. A mile and a half down the road from Rannoch station we'd swung off on to a gravel access track and begun to climb into the sop. We were in cloud by the time we reached a hydroelectric station, after which we left the track and aimed straight up the hillside over tussocks and boulders into thickening murk and eventually the summit of Carn Dearg. Our plan had been to loop a course over Carn Dearg to Sgor Gaibhre and down to the Ben Alder bothy, using a horseshoe crest of high ground to avoid the slog and slop of a mire which stood in the way of a more direct approach. Also, Steve believed (yes you did, Steve, you know what I'm going to say) that a more direct route up loch-side from Bridge of Ericht would be '*too dull, easy and short*', so he'd scotched it (yes you bloody did! They're your pencil marks on the map).

We ate some wine gums on top of Carn Dearg and Steve introduced me to 'puddocks' aka *Scottish frogs*, shiny little sages with liquid eyes; small gods of heather and haar. The next part of the hike had us walking east across a crest to Sgor Gaibhre but we missed it in the mist, so famously fine, opaque and wetting. We lost our way and ended up skidding down a quaggy cleft, or breabag, losing all our height and good humour in the process. The next hour was spent stumping in circles over an unfolding branching emptiness of brume and bog, compounding our error and aggravating each other, until we reached an area of chest-high ferns, then a pine forest with a timber road we took to the shore of a loch. The wrong loch; Ossian rather than Ericht, we'd gone north rather than east.

———

Blergh blergh blergh.

Tromping, cloudburst, the purl of water. We were now following a burn up from Corrour Shooting Lodge, trying to make right our navigational wrongs. We walked until it was dusk. The ground was sprung bouncy and occasionally tried to claim and keep us, suck our boots off, sink us in sponge. I was tired but no longer wished to die, my hangover had washed away. To celebrate we had another navigational row, best summed up by 'Fine, where do *you* think we are?'

Somewhere on the hillside to our right, we agreed, was a mountain pass which carried a stalker's path which would lead us over to Ben Alder Bothy. But it was hidden by a pall of churning clouds which obscured everything above 100 feet, making it difficult to know exactly where we were . . . and I was frankly buggered if I was going to be a hero and start climbing into Scotch mist in search of a path which might not exist. Steve appeared to feel similarly disinclined so we followed the stream on, on, on until we came across a tent. It was the saddest tent in the world; perhaps the saddest, wettest tent the world has ever known. It was pitched at the side of the stream in what may once have been a meadow but was now very much a swamp. 'Leave me,' the semi-submerged tent seemed to say, 'for God's sake, save yourselves.' I thought of my own tent, snug in my rucksack and my new-found will to live. I shared a look with Steve and, as one, we began to ford the burn and scramble up the far bank, away from the tent of doom.

Everything was sticking, rubbing, chafing, sopping and slopping. If anything I'm underplaying the wet. I had begun to grow gills. Had we been spangin' undersea we couldn't have been any wetter.*

Then we met the path. The beautiful path. I actually cried out in happiness, 'Hello, path!' and for the first time in hours we were definitely on track and knew that we would be sleeping in a bothy with a roof rather than drowning in our boots.

---

* Nan Shepherd's *The Living Mountain* and *The Quarry Wood* carry glossaries of wonderful Scots terms and abound with walking words – my favourite is *spangin'* – v. to walk vigorously.

See also *dingin' on* – raining / snowing hard; *drookit* – soaked, drowned; *drummlie* – physically upset; *thole* – endure; and *tint* – lost.

Bothy bothy bothy.

The stalker's path down Bealach Cumhann ran parallel to the Alder Burn. It was solidly engineered and well maintained. The fact we were on the home stretch lessened the ache in my shoulders and feet. I followed Steve into the V of the valley; an empyrean arrow of broken blues pointing to Loch Ericht and the unsighted cottage where we were set to sleep. There was still a whisper of light in the sky, fading like breath on a windowpane. We were racing the deep dark to the bothy. It was going to be a close run thing. The rain had slackened but there was no moon, it was owl-light only owls could appreciate. The path had dimmed to the palest line, a rope falling into a well. The landscape, already pared back to water, rock and bracken, had lost any sense of depth. We strode on, scuffed along, tripping as we went. Nearly there. So nearly there.

The bothy, when we reached it, was locked. This came as something of a blow. It was now pitch dark and as we stood there, silent, suddenly exhausted having been so up, having raced the night – conscious of the implacable cold of the loch now at our backs and the black mass of Ben Alder overhead . . . knackered now, done, undone by a door, a padlock . . . I felt myself crumpling as I turned to Steve. 'Here we are,' he said, opening a second door further down the cabin. 'Let's get in, eh?'

I swallowed a sob, picked up my sack and followed him inside.

————

Bothies are basic shelters left unlocked for anyone to use – or 'stumble into soaked to the skin' as was the case with us that night. The bothy below Ben Alder is known equally as McCook's Cottage after Joseph McCook, the last permanent resident – a forester and deer watcher for the nearby Ben Alder Estate. McCook lived in the cottage from around 1880 until 1920 when he moved down the loch towards Rannoch.

The building is now divided in two; a dark timber extension acts as a store for the estate and abuts the older stone cottage – slate roof, eared with low chimney stubs, two windows either side of a blue porch muzzle. Inside, a central bunk room is shelved with shallow cots. Either side of this dormitory is a room with a hearth, the largest of which has wide benches built around the walls so parties can sleep beside a fire. When we opened the door of the room with the benches we saw the ingle had embers aglow, and by their light could make out the form of a figure stretched out under blankets, asleep. The room was warm, a sweet fug of lanolin, the steamed ghost of a thousand boots. In that moment it was everything we wanted, to doss down and be done with the day.

When we stirred next morning the sun was high, the sleeping figure was gone and the grate had been swept clean.

——

Today Ben Alder Cottage is overseen by the Mountain Bothy Association (MBA), which was set up by the aptly named Bernard and Betty Heath in 1965 in an effort to save abandoned crofts in the wilder parts of Scotland from ruin. Such buildings had always traditionally been used as shelters and dosses for hillwalkers. In early MBA journals, Bernard uses the wonderful phrase 'rough-stuffing' to describe the act of tramping across the Highlands in hope rather than expectation of sleep undercover; 'rough-stuffians' the cognomen for people mad enough to undertake such ventures. The MBA, like Ferðafélag Íslands in Iceland, helped establish 'bothying' as an organised and sustainable activity by taking the initiative to restore empty buildings and ruins which would otherwise have returned to the earth. The Heaths' nascent MBA pulled together groups already frequenting and patching Highland 'but and bens'* independent of each other – such as the Aberdeen-based Cairngorm Club of mountaineers (est. 1887) who rebuilt Corrour Bothy in the Lairig Ghru as a club hut in 1949.

By becoming a recognised body of bothy custodians, the MBA put themselves in a position to raise funds and negotiate with estates and landowners – landowners who in many cases were only too happy to help. Such was the case with the mid-70s restoration of Bearnais Bothy – a shell of a cottage above Loch an Laoigh in Wester Ross. After an enthusiastic campaign for access and aegis by Betty Heath, a letter of permission arrived 'plus a generous cheque from the Landowner to start the renovations off'.[2]

Writing at the time, Bernard sketched the bothy's situation, as well as expressing his hopes for the future – the note is really a rallying cry and call for volunteers with the vague invocation of a helicopter:

---

* but | bʌt |
noun Scottish – an outer room, especially in a two-roomed cottage.
but and ben
Scottish a two-roomed cottage; a humble home.
ORIGIN – early eighteenth century: from but in the early sense 'outside', specifically 'into the outer part of a house'.

If you can picture Maol Bhuidhe in your mind, you will have some idea what Bearnais is like. It shares with this bothy (its nearest neighbour) the sheer remoteness in an equally wonderful setting of lochs and mountains. Note the nearness of several Munros – Bidean a' Choire Sheasgaich 3102 ft, Luid Mhors 3234 ft and 3190 ft, Sgurr Choinnich 3260 ft, Sgurr a' Chaorachaain 3102 ft and Bidean an Eoin Dearg 3430 ft. Reach for 1" OS map No. 26. Bearnais's ref is approx. 021431 set in a glen bearing its name. Note the hill path approaches. No road to the door here. With special permission heavy materials could be road-hauled to Ben Dronaig Lodge on the neighbouring estate and back-packed on the path to the loch and then overland to site. Near the bothy the old field would take a helicopter if our luck was in with the military!

It's a lovely snapshot and one can quite see why so many were inspired to muck in and help the cause. Bearnais exemplifies the kind of spartan refuge needed to explore the wilder reaches of Scotland. Today the MBA's website lists 'open fire' as the building's sole 'feature' but someone crumping up the snowy glen with dusk approaching would bite your hand off at such a luxurious offer – fire, walls and a roof, lifesavers all. Bothies rarely have beds or water, electricity almost never, but there are often candle stubs and matches, gifts from unknown friends; and this state of affairs chimes absolutely with the MBA's stated object as a charity: 'to maintain simple shelters in remote country for the use and benefit of all who love wild and lonely places'.[3]

In the last fifty years the MBA has overseen the repair of well over a hundred cabins and advanced bothying beyond

the preserve of a hardy clique to open houses for all comers –
weekenders, hikers, mountaineers irrespective of club
affiliation: people perhaps hitherto put off the idea of hiking
too deep into the Highlands by the spectre of 'rough-stuff'.
Where previously there was something of a parasitic, free-
for-all element to bothying, opportunistic use without
renewal, now a charted network of outposts exists. Free,
egalitarian and elegant; Bernard Heath has described it as
like camping without a tent.

In times past, people like Joseph McCook might have
given tea and shelter to travellers passing his cottage – walkers heading up the loch to Dalwhinnie, a distraction from
the red stags he oversaw for the estate, someone to tell him
news of the big smoke; Rannoch, Glencoe, Bridge of Gaur.
Now it was just us, repacking our rucksacks in the sun below
Ben Alder: two men sitting on the grass above the burn
where it laced with the Ericht; two men surrounded by
socks. A day completely different from the day before. So
warm a day that the water looked inviting, the mountain
almost forgiving, the ramble to Dalwhinnie ambitious but
not entirely crackpot, even on shell-shocked pruny feet.

I asked Steve how he felt. Fine, he said.

Likely to be a long day, I suggested, refolding the map.

Shame we're starting at eleven o'clock, he replied, evenly.

What a misery, I thought. I hope he falls in the loch.

———

We were set to join the bothy dots of Ben Alder to
Dalwhinnie, Kingussie to Ruigh Aiteachain, then down the
Geldie Burn to 'the Red House' – a ruin near 'White Bridge'

at the junction of the Geldie and the Dee – Jimi Hendrix by way of David Lynch. Then up the Lairig Ghru to Corrour Bothy* before climbing over Ben Macdui to the Hutchison Memorial Hut, then out to Braemar. Which seems so reasonable put like that but was actually rather ambitious, took very little account of topography, and assumed – *required!* – that Steve and I be fit as decathlete fleas.

The jaunt also necessitated multiple maps since our route wound over the corners and fringes of several orange OS Explorers. Some consideration was given to foregoing a couple of sheets since 'they're nine quid and we only dip on to them for a few miles' (yes you did, Steve . . . or was that me?). Either way, we bought and brought them and they now joined the socks in my pack as we set off northeast up the loch – sun baking, boots damp, shoulders furious.

I'd been in touch with the National Trust for Scotland about staying in the Red House ruin. Head of Natural Heritage, Dominic Driver, had been very encouraging – the trust had plans to return the house to use as a bothy, he said. Perhaps he could meet us en route and explain the works they had in mind.

He copied in a man named David Frew, Operations Manager for the Mar Lodge Estate, on whose ground the Red House stands. 'The Red House has a roof and four

---

* Corrour Bothy is about 43 miles from Corrour station as the crow flies and shares no affiliation. The bothy's name possibly derives from the fact the building sometimes acted as a shelter for the 'currour' or forester's assistant. Like Ben Alder, the bothy was originally home to a deer watcher for the local Mar Lodge estate and was similarly left uninhabited around 1920. – *Mar Lodge Estate Grampian: An Archaeological Survey*, Royal Commission on the Ancient and Historical Monuments of Scotland, Edinburgh, Dixon & Green, 1995.

walls, but that's about it!' he told me. 'Personally I would prefer to camp. Also, I can't officially condone you using Red House to overnight in, because it is currently considered an unsafe building. There are warning signs up to this effect. We know that many people do still use it, and it is for this very reason we are talking to the MBA about them taking it on.'

All of which was fine. We had a tent . . . but then things started to unravel rather. Our trip coincided with the half-term holiday so Dominic was promised to his children, besides which he seemed slightly startled by our 'ambitious itinerary' – I laughed out loud when I received an email with the line *I'm sure that [your] apparently unfeasible route was mainly due to me mispronouncing place names when I spoke to David.*'

Back on Loch Ericht, Steve had donned a bandana which gave him a piratical air. I had on a puckered sunhat pitching somewhere between Acid House and *Test Match Special*. Wrecks en route to ruins in dubious fashions.

———

By mid afternoon we were about midway up the loch, which sounds pretty good going until you recall that Ben Alder Bothy is a fifth to a quarter of the way up to begin with. The water was blue, the path was grassy and now relatively flat. Eventually the single earth hollow worn by walkers' feet became a double track so we could walk side by side and give updates on our failing bodies in measured tones rather than having to shout forwards or back –

'My feet have broken, Steve.'

'Shut up, man, my back stopped working after lunch.'
And –
'I think we're carrying too much weight, Dan.'
'I agree, Steve, feel free to go home.'
And –
'What do you think's beyond those trees there, Steve?'
'Pain, Dan! Pain and death.'
(Etc.)

Beyond the trees we actually found the grounds of Ben Alder Lodge. It was stately and granite and surrounded by pines and signs which told us we'd gone the wrong way, were actually trespassing. Nevertheless we pressed on, tossing a cheery 'Good evening!' in the direction of a man in tennis gear, quite possibly *The Man* in charge. Later, on the lodge road out, we befriended Ben Alder's head gamekeeper, a wonderful fellow with a 4×4.

In Dalwhinnie – let's say we walked all the way – we found our bunkhouse, dropped our bags and retired to the garden for a cold drink. Already in the garden was a novel-reading lady who turned out to be an eminent psychologist (I know!) and who, having politely asked our plans for the week and been regaled with our Scottish travails thus far,* told us about the three types of fun.

Type One Fun – Fun that was actually fun and you enjoyed at the time. 'I'm having fun,' you might say. 'This was fun.' 'We had fun.' 'Fun was had.'

Type Two Fun – Experiences that whilst not fun *at the time* are quite enjoyable later, at a distance, when recounted

---

* By which I mean mine; Steve's from Aberdeen – the very definition of 'Scottish travails'.

to friends or friendly psychologists. For example: 'Steve and I got wankered on the Euston sleeper, so much so that we thought our retinas had detached, got lost in a migraine of dreich and dreck, spectacularly failed to ascertain "east", slid off a mountain, argued a lot, got drenched so much that we're now part newt, found the right path and bothy but couldn't fathom "the door", only survived the supposedly easiest walking day of our trip – a flat tromp on a path along a loch shore: DAY TWO – by hitching a ride with a man who half an hour earlier had probably been told by the local laird to loose the dogs on us for invasion of privacy. THAT':

'Yes, I suppose it is quite funny. *Oh, I can laugh about it now but at the time it was terrible.* Terrible.'

Type Three Fun – Not fun then, not fun now, in fact it horrifies and grimly fascinates everybody in the retelling – raconteur and audience alike. Ernest Shackleton's *Endurance* expedition is a classic case of type three fun. The 'fun' seems to lie in the fact you survived. *Apollo 13* was type three fun.

We thanked the eminent psychologist who, as well as being hugely useful to this narrative, was actually real. She was on a cycling tour of the flatter parts of Scotland. Twenty miles a day, 'so an hour and half after lunch'. Which suited her and her husband just fine. The previous year they'd gone on a cycling tour of southern France but suffered from 'ambitious itinerary' – ridiculous mileages to meet each day. 'We like wine more than bicycles,' she told us and we nodded. These people had the right idea. And all the while Dominic Driver's line recurred – *'I'm sure that [your] apparently unfeasible route was mainly due to me mispronouncing place names . . .'*

———

Next morning we caught the train north from Dalwhinnie. The original plan had been to walk east over mire and mountains to the bothy at Ruigh Aiteachain but this had been vetoed back in London since much of that journey would involve walking off-path over exceptionally marshy marsh, the sort of terrain where people disappear, sunk in unseen sumps. As a map, the area looked like the work of a cartographer with only brown and blue to hand. Tight-packed ginger contours and turquoise watercourses rippled across the page. Op-Art enthusiasts might have acclaimed and framed such an image but no one in the their right mind would wish to walk across it in a straight line from Dalwhinnie east-northeast. 'The last we saw they were limping that way,' eyewitnesses would say, pointing out into a landscape the hue of stewed prunes, undulating endless. 'They were talking about "type three fun" . . . something about a horse in *The NeverEnding Story* . . .'

Plan B, which had been *the plan* until the day before, had been to catch a train up to Kingussie then walk through Drumguish, down the Geldie Burn and reach Ruigh Aiteachain that way.

Today's plan was to ditch Ruigh Aiteachain altogether. The previous night we'd sat up looking at our maps and decided to tear up our ambitious/unfeasible/nonsensical itinerary and begin again from Aviemore down.

The plan now ran: Aviemore, up Cairn Gorm, over and down to Loch Avon, round to the Fords of Avon Refuge (sleep) // a walk over and up to Hutchison Memorial Hut, up up up to Ben Macdui, over and down into the Lairig Ghru with a detour north to see the Pools of Dee before returning south to Corrour Bothy (sleep) // Down Glen Dee with a slight detour to look at the Red House before hiking out to Braemar. Catching a bus to Aberdeen (and sleep).

We were now going to walk in the shape of a Z with Aviemore at the top and Braemar at the bottom, where formerly we'd been set to walk a sort of sickly 5 keeled over.

We caught the train to Aviemore, suddenly fast again, streaming through trees and over roads. I was back in love with trains, the way they speed on an even keel, resolute comets cutting a swathe so landscapes melt and fizz at their passing. We sliced across moors, flashing woods which filled my eyes red, and within an hour we were up at the ski centre on the side of Cairn Gorm from where we could look back over the foaming greens of the Queen's Forest and blue slate of Loch Morlich. It was another fine day.

The ski centre had a funicular railway which ran up towards the summit but for some reason we did not use it. We thought about this decision a lot for the next hour whilst slogging up under the raised tracks, every so often overflown by a purple lozenge of sightseers, winding up its hawsers with a whistle and hum. Why didn't we catch it? we'd ask each other, a question which grew sadder and higher-pitched the hotter and more breathless we became. By the end we were just panting 'Whay?' dry-mouthed.

When we got to the top of Cairn Gorm the wind was whipping at a fair old lick. The summit dome was strewn with ash-pink boulders, grit and moss. It was a glary hard-baked little world – squint and you could quite believe the sharply curving horizon looped under your feet and you were standing on the pole of a tiny moon.

At the summit of the mountain moon was a weather station; a concrete shed banked up with rocks on top of which was a jaunty drum on legs about the size of my Cascades bear canister. Beside the shed and linked by cables was a stubby pylon sporting various instruments and aerials. Whilst I was standing near the shed, the lid of the canister rose to reveal a whirling anemometer and a set of thermometers amongst other meteorological gadgets – it was all very Wallace and Gromit.

Having peered at the weather station set-up awhile, I turned to find a tour guide had snuck up behind me with a party of walkers. He was wearing the sort of fluorescent coat and trousers that mark a fellow out as either tour guide or sewage engineer – 'This weather station exploded,' he shouted over the wind, '*exploded!* 208-mile-an-hour gales blew it up a few new years ago.' That seems very specific, said one of his followers sceptically and the rest nodded.

'Yes, well,' crumpled the Dyno-Guide, 'we added on eight miles an hour. It's designed to withstand 200 and the thought was another eight would do it. *Explode it*, I mean!'

We left him flailing his arms around as the canister shut itself down with a droidal whine.

'Goes to show,' I said to Steve, who'd also been listening in.

'Goes to show what?' he asked.

'I'm not sure,' I admitted. 'Cairn Gorm's windy, something like that.'

'Fine Scottish wind! Awfy strong,' Steve probably said. He said a lot of things like that on the walk, when he was talking to me at all. A proud piratical Scotsman, he took every opportunity to point out when things were *fine and Scottish*, i.e. excellent, and *soft and English*, i.e. me – all attempts to point out I was technically Welsh fell on deaf ears.

Descending over Cairn Gorm's rump towards Coire Raibert, I could see over the battlements of Coire an t-Sneachda and into the bowl where I'd been taught about winter mountaineering safety and survival on a Conville Course several Januarys before. The coire, then an icebox, was now a bare sun-trap – dark in its heat, a half-closed hand cupping twin lochans; lochans totally buried when I'd been down there, digging out snow holes with the adze of my axe. That was January, this was May – amazing to witness first hand how a landscape could be so changed in so few months. Now the idea of snow on this toasted plateau seemed mad, just as the cloudbursts of our first day out of Rannoch felt an eon, a season, a world away. The noise of rain here would be foreign, it would surely sizzle.*

Fireach is the Gaelic word for high barren ground and that's just where we were and just how we felt – exposed on the scorching hillside we'd caught fire-ach(e) – but then our path joined the stream which descends through Coire Raibert and the spray of the cascade and shadow of the fissure led us off the rufous moonland and down to the blues of Loch Avon blazing below; chilly, inviting, delicious, magnetic – the rebirth of the cool.

—

* I was going to write that rain that day on Cairn Gorm would seem 'Martian' but it rained and rained at Mars, Utah the day before I arrived. Funny old planet, Earth.

If Coire an t-Sneachda's lochans were cupped in a single hand, Loch Avon is held in a mountainous pair. Beinn Mheadhoin forms the thumb, flesh and fingers of one side, the lower cliffs of Cairn Gorm the other. The northern flanks of Ben Macdui rise up at the wrist end whilst the River Avon runs from the fingertips.*

When we reached the shore, snow patches could be seen gleaming high on the schist slopes beside Shelter Stone – a flathead mesa-like formation at the loch's end. Even in the thick heat, the snow flashed cold. The loch banks were flared with heather, upholstered with bearberry, blaeberry, crowberry, black mosses and neon lichens splotching shore boulders, cushions of saxifrage, and dwarf trees like those near Hvítárnes; small shifty shrubs skulking round Loch Avon, or Loch A'an as Nan Shepherd had hymned it:

> Loch A'an, Loch A'an, hoo deep ye lie!
> Tell nane yer depth and nane shall I.
> Bricht though yer deepmaist pit may be,
> Ye'll haunt me till the day I dee.
> Bricht, an' bricht, an' bricht as air,
> Ye'll haunt me noo for evermair.[4]

We walked down A'an towards the river's outflow. There were peach beaches where our shadows paddled, further out the loch floor dropped to pits of deepmaist blue, and as we went

---

* Beinn Mheadhoin is the thirteenth highest mountain in the British Isles at 1,182m. Cairn Gorm is the sixth at 1,245m. Ben Macdui at 1,309m is second only to Ben Nevis (1,345m). I later discovered that Loch Avon is a prime example of 'a glacial trough loch' – now isn't that a delightful term? It makes me think of a giant bath / bath for giants.

on the loch shore changed to an almost duney nature, polished rocks rolled round with warm white sand and flowers, all fringed with sharp grasses which scratched at our boots.

In Glen Avon the valley walls rolled out and the flanks to either side softened to resemble giant moles. The floor grew flatter and, joy, the bogs returned so we had slop and dreck anew to jump and skirt, lavender and hyacinth hues resumed their beat and the sound of racing water too, and then – so marvellously early in the day, in the *daylight*, that I was quite taken aback – there was Fords of Avon Refuge. It was small and looked to be barricaded with sandbags but as we got nearer I saw that it was actually surrounded and banked up to its roof with boulders, like the sand-cast of a lugworm or a desert lizard that's buried itself the better to camouflage and chill. When we reached its door the full truth was revealed. It was a storm shelter the size of a potting shed, in fact it was an actual potting shed reinforced in the roof and floor. There was room enough to lay out our sleeping bags and lie full length, so we set ourselves up and then went down to the shore of the river to eat our dinner which consisted, as did every meal on the trip, of salami, cashews, cheese and raisins with either squash or black tea to drink depending on whether we could be bothered to get my Primus stove going.* Tea was generally an end-of-day pleasure. We drank it that night, steaming hot from plastic cups whilst dangling our sore feet in the freezing race of the Avon.

––––

* We ate that all week: protein, healthy fats, fibre, fruit – it kept us going and was occasionally supplemented with treats like chocolate and dried apricots; although Steve took against my apricots early on, saying they tasted 'weird', which they absolutely did not.

That evening the thought recurred of how far was far enough to truly be remote. I was back in the drystone mouth of the bothy looking at the sky, wondering whether to draw my bag up and sleep head out of the doorway, like a snail.

The definition of *outpost* I like best is 'a small military camp or position at some distance from the main army' – which I picture as being the world of roads, mobile reception and people working behind desks. Part two of the same definition suggests, 'a remote part of a country or empire'.[5] Several other definitions substitute *outlying* for *remote part*.[6]

The MBA's website describes Fords of Avon Refuge as 'A small emergency refuge shelter only' and not intended for planned overnight stays. 'No fire or stove.' No windows either but I'd wanted to experience austerity, the barest box in a granite jacket – space enough for ten to huddle and four or five to sleep if caught out in bad weather. That night, however, the sky was golden; clear and warm and still. We could not see the sunset from the refuge but the hilltops around us were capped by pinks skimmed over Cairn Gorm. We sat out with our tea, the glen to ourselves.

'There seem to be some awfy fancy bothies up north these days,' Steve wrote to me a few months before the trip – the halcyon days – 'Perhaps this is a muddily romanticised memory from my teens but the empty little dry-stone bolt-holes I remember seem to have gone.'

Now, he said, there were bothies 'like miniature wooden church halls, complete with guitars, packs of cards, fireplaces and composting toilets' – concessions to the soft English, no doubt – added to which places like Corrour were so 'stowed oot' in summer that the overflow campsites around them resembled 'miniature Glastonburys' – or 'pop festivals' as my grandfather might call them. (He's ninety-three, about the same age as Steve mid-rant.)

One of the Cambridge dictionary's definitions of *outpost* is 'a rare example of something that is disappearing. – *Free jazz has been described as the last outpost of modernism.*'

Reviewing *The Largesse of the Sea Maiden*, a posthumous collection of Denis Johnson's short stories, free-jazz enthusiast Geoff Dyer suggested that Johnson's 'Control [as a writer was] achieved through willing proximity to its loss'.[7] The beauty and fidelity of Johnson's work existed because the author's life bled in and blurred the lines between life lived and imagined. Either way, wrote Dyer, he took the reader to places and states which rang true, had weight, were compelled in their truth.

I think the joys of bothying might be in part due to a similar willingness to forgo the controls of the modern age in order to reconnect with older, deeper truths and needs. The spartan nature of outdoorsing opens us up to the freedom of the unknown. By pulling out the pin that mounts us to a GPS grid we are better able to experience place, space and time. Without our phones we become better connected. Breaking with the digital puts us more intensely in touch with wild country, allows us to negotiate it on the ground and take responsibility for our position. To be present in the moment, to concentrate and orientate yourself, to arrow – *quarrel* in the case of Steve and I – towards a shelter, mindful that you do so on the landscape's terms, conscious of the physical world around you, reminded of your smallness, is a great eye-opener – 'being towards hard-stuffing' to paraphrase that problematic outdoorsman Martin Heidegger.

How much of an anchorite does one have to be to be truly isolated, lost, remote? For many people in 2020 I suggest turning off their phones anywhere unknown – city, countryside, hinterland, metroland – will plunge them into a strange new world of 'off the beaten track'.

———

Next morning we crossed the A'an by means of stepping stones and began to walk south on the Larig An Laoigh Drove Road past the Dubh Lochan and into a beautiful velvety U-shaped valley which funnelled us up to the foot of Coire Etchachan. The path to the Hutchison Memorial Hut and thence Ben Macdui could be seen snaking off to the right across a furzy swell of deep heath flared with juniper.

The Hutchison Memorial Hut bore a plaque:

Dr A.G. Hutchison of Aberdeen, 'Hutch' to his friends and adoring nephews, had been a geologist who, like Roald Dahl, was employed by the Shell Group. After his death in a fall whilst exploring the cliffs of Pembrokeshire, funds were raised to build a bothy in the mountains he so loved.

The cabin was empty. Inside, the window was covered in condensation but there was a stove, a sense of insulation and a padded bench-cum-sleeping-shelf, all of which gave the impression it could be kindled cosy. A new storm porch and solid roof told of recent MBA works and there were candles and dry-bagged matches on the sill. It felt a good place, cared for. We left in good spirits to climb a couple of hundred metres more to Loch Etchachan, which lies around the 900-metre mark, 409 below the summit of Ben Macdui.

Geographically and emotionally, as things turned out, it would be all downhill from there.

———

We ate lunch in a solid ruin near Ben Macdui's summit. The building, named Sappers' Bothy, was built to house cartographers and soldiers undertaking the mapping of the Cairngorms as part of the Trigonometrical Survey of Scotland, which ran through the first half of the eighteenth century. Now the building is roofless but the thick walls are remarkably intact – the fireplace is over a metre deep, the stone lintel an absolute beast – and provides an excellent dugout to avoid the scudding wind. Lunch had, we went over to look at the summit, which was crowded and clouded. Summit seen, we began to descend into the Lairig Ghru down a precipitous . . . I mean, 'path' is and isn't the right word inasmuch as we followed the path of a stream named Allt Clach nan Taillear straight down the mountain, hopping back and forth across its channel like goats or reckless pillocks depending on your stance. Reviewing our near-deaths in the *Guardian*, Geoff Dyer might have noted that 'Control(ed descent) was achieved through willing proximity to loss (of life).'

On the way down – and there was a lot of down to do, 700 metres or so – I thought of how serene Loch Etchachan had been that morning. A still sky mirror, as if the true summit of Coire Etchachan had been cut through with a cheese-wire and toppled to reveal the mountain's insides glass.

Finally down on Lairig Ghru path having flown the stream's flume and spilled over the bracken, catapulted through the gorse, pitched into the shin-deep mulch – become acquainted with all the watery ha-has and hillside rebarbatives at nature's disposal – we took off our rucksacks and tidied ourselves up a bit. Would we go up to the Pools of Dee? We would, but we'd leave the bags hidden here. That done we set off in the general direction of Aviemore, following the Dee to source, hobbling slightly. It had been the hottest day so far, albeit rather overcast, but now the air was growing sultry and the atmosphere felt charged.

———

Thunder smashed around the hills like bricks inside a mixer. In the past hour the sky had dropped from frost to putty to jaundice, the life sucked out of the day. Night fell in ten minutes, the sky became a metallic bruise, then the rain began to fall – softly softly to begin with then harder harder, thrashing, belting – drops the size of your hands and face. By now the sky was indigo, at least that's how it seemed. You couldn't raise your face to it, the water was falling and rising all around – sky down, ground up – already the rain was down my back, my trousers were saturated, my boots were full. We were walking as fast as we could down Glen Dee, properly yomping now, sweating, breathing hard, our packs were heavy, soaking; this was not mank, it was not subtle or misty, no, this was a stair-rod deluge. This was biblical.

And the thunder was phenomenal, ear-splitting, tremendous; the crack of it, like trees being uprooted and thrown about; a rending tearing sound – every few seconds a cannonade of rubble smashed into the valley's skip. And the lightning was amazing, the pyrotechnic heavens arcing, shredding the cobalt sky, crazing my retinas, the world turned white and deafening, blue, magnesium white and deafening, blue . . .

The Pools of Dee had been slightly underwhelming, although we agreed it was 'a good thing to have done'. When we got to Corrour Bothy we discovered it full and overflowing with *weekenders*.* A discussion was had about whether to camp or press on to the Red House. I was unwilling to unpack the tent. We were there for bothies. We agreed to carry on. It was just over seven miles to the Red House and we had gone just under halfway before Ragnarok began.

So we walked an hour or two in the storm, along the river, swishing ferns, past Scots pine saplings doffing crazily, through mire and streams, straight through – for what was

---

* Steve's term, 'weekenders' – muttered in the manner of a man with a grudge.

the point of avoiding them now? – and at some stage the thunder and lightning lessened but the rain kept coming and the night grew darker. Blue, blue. I was soused to the point where I really didn't care. I had water trickling into my eyes so everything looked muzzy, blurred; blue. The world had run together in a new-jeans wash.

The Red House, so sought, now appeared hollow-faced, set back from the track over grass; we ran, got in, the noise changed, we slumped down, we stopped. It was indeed a ruin but a ruin with a reasonable roof. The floor was compacted dirt and grit. Turning on a torch we saw that there was nowhere we could comfortably sleep. We undressed and hung up our clothes, made hooks of random nails in joists – I strung a makeshift line up of belts and string. We found a towel at the bottom of a bag and dried our hair a bit. I unpacked the tent and built it inside the house, turning it sideways to get it through the doorway, dashed outside, pegged it down, and dashed back in for tea. We drank the tea. The corrugated iron roof made the gutted house a drum, the high hat hiss and clack of it, white noise with thunder noises-off, 'the angels moving the furniture about' as my great-gran used to say. Through the window openings the world poured and crackled. After tea we made for the tent, crawled in, burrowed down into our feather bags, then I fell straight asleep.

———

Next morning, damp but undefeated, we walked out towards Braemar. At Linn of Dee we met the road and a man with a Land Rover in the trailhead car park who was awaiting a group of walkers due down the Lairig Ghru 'at some point'. He was happy to give us a lift into town. A lovely man. He'd been at Corrour Bothy the night before as well and walked out in the storm as we had; perhaps he'd been just before or after us on the path. He lived in Aviemore and ran an outward bound adventure group, taking children and teenagers into the Cairngorms 'to show them a bit of nature, a bit of wildlife', he grinned, such as the previous evening. 'A banger!' he said with pleasure. 'A stunner.'

The Cairngorms are a unique mountain range in the sense that they take the form of one great plateau, a different experience from climbing in the Swiss Alps, say, where one might climb up a series of valleys to a defined linear line of peaks then over, down and out. Nan Shepherd wrote that one walks *into* the Cairngorms rather than up and along, echoing John Muir's suggestion that where exploration of the natural world's concerned 'Going out is really going in.'

In Iceland I'd worked on the fabric of bothies. Here, we'd worked to get amongst them and join their dots and in so doing we'd come to appreciate the pleasure of seeing one's haven appear out of the landscape. And here's a circular thought: the presence of the bothies draws people into the wilds, the romance of them perhaps, that dream of 'camping without a tent', the promise of a roof as safety net from hard-stuffing. Yet, instead of being an easy option and softening the corners of mountain hiking, the bothies inspire further questing out, on and into the landscape, providing a solid base to light out into the Cairngorms, or moorlands or Highlands to the west beyond the Great Glen. The joy of approaching a dry bunkhouse after a day's hard walking saw both Steve and me welcoming the buildings into our lives like old friends, talking to them, thanking them for existing. Without them we'd never have waggled our strange route from Rannoch to Braemar, met the people we met, nor had the chance to spend a couple of evenings alone in the still pink/trouncing blue. The approach transformed our reading and appreciation of the cabins at day's end: the simplest sheds became castles, knights in shining armour.

Of all the outposts I'd met so far in the book, the bothies of Ferðafélag Íslands and the MBA seemed the most open-hearted, the best able to transport people a distance from the main army. Our Scottish campaign had also revealed the other side of the sæluhús coin: the animating aspect of human agency, praxis – can a bothy be said to exist unless footsore walkers stop awhile under its roof? To my mind the meaning, indeed the very name of these hybrid cell/shed/hostels, is dependent on their patronage – unfrequented they lie dormant as tools without a craftsman to clean and deploy them; working shelters akin to working dogs – designed and honed to serve, they grow rusty waiting.

As of 2020, the MBA oversees 105 bothies and two emergency shelters. I wish them all the best for the next fifty years and hope they do work with the National Trust for Scotland to refit the Red House for public use. As it was, Steve and I had had a taste of the rough-stuff but as we left the Cairngorms we agreed the trip had been all the better for that; a mix of type one and type two fun, certainly, but no type three. We'd

---

* And we were never cold, did I mention that? I was never once cold all trip – a bit chilly that first night maybe, that first night walking down Bealach Cumhann in the dark, but after that the days were hot and the nights mellow gold. In retrospect the walk was topped and tailed by a warm bath and an electric shower.

had real fun and could recall our endeavours with pleasure – indeed we did, in a pub, shortly after being dropped in Braemar.

So we ended as we'd begun, with beer and maps, only this time they were all out and open on the table – spattered holey relics, tattered weather-beaten plans – the better to relive our Highland escapades.

Steve King approaching Hutchison Memorial Hut, Cairngorm Mountains, Scotland. Photograph: Dan Richards

VII

PHARE DE CORDOUAN, FRANCE

I do not know much about gods; but I think that the river
Is a strong brown god – sullen, untamed and intractable,
Patient to some degree

– T.S. Eliot*

In late October I went to Bordeaux for a weekend with my good friend Nick.

We rode shiny trams to closed museums, explored cavernous concrete U-Boat pens and took a tour in a dodgem-like 2CV. I saw in a birthday at a spit-and-sawdust bistro amidst a happy wreckage of oysters and white wine whilst Nick, having declined to play Carpenter to my Walrus – declaring my mollusc pals 'off-putting' – supped his plonk mistrustfully and suffered my bivalve jamboree with thin-lipped odium.

I have always loved the sea. The first few years of my life were spent overlooking the blues of the Bristol Channel and Mediterranean Sea from Penclawdd and the island of Spetses. The salt was good for my infant eczema. The air was

---

* According to a note by Eliot under the title, 'The Dry Salvages – presumably *les trois sauvages* – is a small group of rocks, with a beacon, off the north east coast of Cape Ann, Massachusetts. *Salvages* is pronounced to rhyme with *assuages*.' – 'The Dry Salvages', *Four Quartets*, T.S. Eliot, Faber, London, 2001, p.21.

good for my lungs. As a toddler I used to bob driftwood boats in rock pools on family holidays in Cawsand, Cornwall; the first clank of the Torpoint chain ferry marking the moment of 'nearly there' – the tidal Tamar the holiday rubicon beyond which our family relaxed.

Seas and rivers held sway in my early reading too. The estuary of *Borka*, the goose without feathers, the misadventures of *Towser and the Water Rats* and Mr Gumpy in his punt. The 'messing about in boats' espoused by Ratty in *The Wind in the Willows;* games of Pooh sticks on the River Avon, epic sandcastle competitions on the beach.

My grandfather, Bob, had worked on the Travelling Post Office (TPO) trains between Bristol and Plymouth for most of his life. Although he'd retired by the time I was born, he used to tell me stories of his days on the railways. After the run down to Devon, he and his crew would often go for a swim at the YMCA or the Plymouth Hoe lido below Smeaton's Tower, an impressive red and white striped lighthouse which resembled the beacon in a favourite book, *Tim to the Lighthouse*.[1] Bob was an inexhaustible source of tall stories – about the tower, about his exploits as a motorcycle messenger during the Second World War, his subsequent army experiences in Egypt, India, a year at sea, then latterly his life on the Great Western TPO. He seemed to have lived

---

* Smeaton's Tower is the upper portion of John Smeaton's original Eddystone Lighthouse of 1759, which originally stood on Eddystone Rocks, a little over twenty-two kilometres to the south of Plymouth. In 1877, when erosion of the ledge on which it was built forced the construction of a replacement beacon, Smeaton's Tower (the third on the site) was dismantled and rebuilt on the Hoe.

a *Boys' Own* dream.* And he was a great swimmer, something I am not, but sometimes I forget and jump in, enthused by the fun other people are having.

I recently took a dive into the Croatian Adriatic, over-whelmed by its brilliant blue. I sank. When I resurfaced, gasping, I had a foot full of sea urchin.

'Why did you do that if you can't really swim?' I was asked.

'To check,' I explained, digging needle barbs out of my heel with a penknife. 'To see if I'd improved . . .' by which I think I meant 'become proficient' because, to me, the sea is synonymous with proficiency and skills I don't have. Sailors able to sail, swimmers able to swim, all those knots, itchy roll-neck jumpers . . . perhaps this added to the mystique of lighthouses over the years – secluded seamarks manned by unseen mariner-types protecting shipping in the foulest of weathers. *Tim to the Lighthouse* was very clear about the perils of being a lighthouse keeper, the solitude, the continual need to polish the bright glass of the light, the constant threat of being coshed and trussed up by wreckers. They might resemble helter-skelters but light-houses were a serious business.

---

* A favourite tale he particularly enjoyed telling was about the time his train smashed through a set of oak crossing gates on the Wellington Bank in Somerset and 'blew them to matchwood, nothing left. We were going like the clappers, a hundred miles an hour down over the bank, then BANG! The steam locomotive, not a scratch.' See also – the time he drove his motorbike from Clifton Downs to Temple Meads station, through the centre of Bristol in under three minutes, at an average speed of eighty miles an hour, during blackout; the time he loosed a box of mice into the Post Office typing pool; the time his army unit accidentally blew the windows out of Lincoln Cathedral; the time a tin of molasses spilled over the conveyors at Bristol Sorting Office . . .

When I later learned that many of the towers were automated it didn't diminish my fascination. Instead the sentinels assumed a haunted quality, a lonely spectral aspect beautifully realised in the work of Eric Ravilious, whose watercolour and pencil works of Beachy Head lighthouse and the Belle Tout lantern room – at once subdued and dazzling – I've had pinned beside my desk for years.

I've always carried a torch for such outposts.

The last manned lighthouse on the British Isles, North Foreland in Kent, was computerised in 1998, ending a tradition of keepers dating back 400 years. Casting about for a manned tower to visit, I discovered that, save for a pair in Holland, almost all of Europe's lighthouses are now empty. Those few that remain occupied are closed to the public, save one: Phare de Cordouan.

———

On the last day, pre-dawn, we padded through cool deserted streets to Gare de Bordeaux Saint-Jean. At 7 a.m. when our train pulled away the daylight was only just beginning to muster muzzy pink.

The journey was quiet; we soon left the city and began to shadow the Garonne river, running northwest to the coast, passing strung-out vineyards, forests, villages, a dew damp world, blue pine and terracotta.

Our first contact with the Garonne had been rather more hectic. On the afternoon of our arrival in the city we were booked on a boat tour but misjudged the time and had to run for it, Bordeaux streaming around us as we hared along.

Beyond the opera house we tore hard-right and met the river, a vast chocolate monster. But there, there was a boat and here, here was a Wonka-like figure with great moustaches, a flowing mustard scarf, bright green trousers and tweedy blazer. As we arrowed his way, he held his arms aloft, beaming, eyes wide. Slow yourself, he gestured, slow yourself, slow, catch your breath; the very best gestures for my thumping run-out heart.

Bruno Beurrier. *'Phew!'* he said, clasping his chest in solidarity. *'Have you humour?'*

I have! I panted, puffed but game. I ha-ave. Just give me a moment.

(Humour pronounced so wonderfully, 'Oo-Mah', that I couldn't help but smile.)

'Your boat is there. Your captain is here!' Bruno announced with a flourish, pointing to a handsome craft moored below us and introducing me to an open-faced mop-headed fellow in a roll-neck jumper. We all shook hands.

They had not left. We were not late! All was well. We would go to the ball on the river . . . now where was Nick? Oh gosh, his camera kit, poor man . . . he was with me at the opera house, but now . . . feet caught in a tram line? Fallen in the river? I hoped he hadn't suffered. Oh, no, here he puffed now. Did he have a limp before?

Installed on the boat, Bruno took up his post as guide – a Janus role he played as both delighted host and needling Grand Inquisitor. He asked as many questions as he answered and expected cultured responses. Why, he wondered aloud, fixing me with a saddened eye, were we all so ignorant about Bordeaux, the most wonderful of cities. It was small comfort that he toyed and lambasted everyone on the boat similarly in a variety of languages, I felt that I'd personally disappointed the man.

Why, for example, was I unaware that Bordeaux's name flows from the French *au bord de l'eau*, 'along the waters', and *why* (Dan) did I know next to nothing about Eleanor of Aquitaine, the reason Bordeaux is so synonymous with wine in the English-speaking world?

Sorry, Bruno, we all thought, shamefaced, shifting in our seats.

Forgiving us with a winning smirk and twirl of his scarf he launched into Eleanor of Aquitaine's meteoric life and times: Queen Consort of both France and England and Duchess of Aquitaine in her own right, she was Bordeaux. The people loved her and the fact her second marriage made the city an English territory in all but name was absolutely fine with them. It was this, her second marriage to Henry Plantagenet, which opened up the region's wine to the English market. So much was exported to Britain that red wine en masse is known as Claret in the UK to this day, *Dan*.

Thank you, Bruno.

All the time we were tootling '*all aboard de l'eau*', past the vivacious doughnut whirl of La Cité du Vin – a museum dedicated to the wines and viticultures of the world. Designed by architects Anouk Legendre and Nicolas Desmazières to resemble wine swirling in a glass; ribboned gold and buxom. Older blocks of a Bauhaus nature jostle with silos and new dockside towers whilst thump in the middle growls the massive concrete bulk of a German U-Boat base, a brutal cave which, having survived the Second World War intact, has now been repurposed as an exhibition space and venue. In contrast to the submarine pens' solid implacability, the fishermen's sheds perched up on bandy footings which pock the riverbank beyond Pont d'Aquitaine were brilliantly eccentric.

The Garonne is not a dirty river, announced Bruno at one point, daring us to defy him. In fact the people of Bordeaux do not consider the Garonne a river at all! We call it *'the sea'*, he concluded triumphantly, pointing to the rise and fall of the massive tidal range which milled and darkened the banks either side. Later that night I watched the dark waters run north from the city's eighteenth-century heart, surging under Napoleon's Bridge towards the Atlantic, flexing molassed and muscular. Undeniable. Vital. Deific.

—

Le Verdon sur Mer was the end of the line. Our train was an incongruous silver bug in the red rail yard. We were two of three people to disembark. The air smelled of pine sap, salt and tar. It was only just after nine o'clock but the day was mugging up. We crossed the tracks, walked through the town towards distant cranes and along a pristine beach to a marina where we found coffee, the Cordouan ferry kiosk and our boat, *La Bohème*. Also at the marina was Jean-Marie Calbet, one of the foremost lighthouse experts in France and President of the Association pour la Sauvegarde des Phares de Cordouan. He greeted me with a firm handshake and explained, to my delight, that he was there to accompany and inform. Ahead of my visit I'd spoken to Magali Pautis from SMIDDEST – Joint Association for the Sustainable Development of the Gironde Estuary – for advice about visiting Cordouan. At the time I'd sensed I was talking to someone of phenomenal organisation but I'd no idea she'd be so helpful and pull out all the stops to provide me a tour by a world leading expert. This rather flew in the face of my general modus operandi – 'Normally I'd flag down a boat, turn up unannounced, and knock at the lighthouse hoping someone was in,' I told Nick, only half joking. Jean-Marie was an enthusiastic barrel of a man in white polo shirt, shorts and crocs. He would be delighted to guide us right to the top, he said, to the lantern room normally locked 'because of poisonous mercury fumes'.

Delight all round. How exciting! This was more like it – a most welcome frisson of danger. Nick! Did you hear that, Nick? Mercury! *I know!* Oh, don't be like that . . .

I later made a video of Jean-Marie inside the Fresnel belvedere, demonstrating the mechanisms of the light and rotary shutter floating on their quicksilver bath. 'The lamp is fixed. The only moving thing is the screen,' he explained, spinning the tricorn octagonal shade. 'Turning, it gives the impression that the lamp is flashing. You cannot see the mercury but when there is a tempest the top of the light-house moves and we have mercury on the floor. I was here for a storm of about 180kph, it was quite a good one. [He smiled, we laughed nervously.] So, of course, it moves but you can't appreciate it.'

I'd be too busy rocking in the foetal position, I thought, and noticed Nick was looking rather green – but that might have just been the vitrine's emerald glass. Myself, I was cast scarlet by a red wall which painted sea and sky as a world-ending fire. I was having a brilliant time.

To reach that highest hothouse paned red, white and green – tricoloured more Italian than French though it stands at the mouth of one of the largest estuaries in France – we'd climbed seven storeys, some sixty-five metres, 301 interior steps. We'd spiralled round warm stone walls like freckled parchment on stairs which began counter-clockwise then reversed, 'to stop the keepers getting dizzy'.*

Cordouan had grown from the moment *La Bohème* rounded Pointe de Grave and slipped into the swim of the mercurial Gironde, the Garonne's massive fishtail endgame. At first I saw it as a far-off peg, a nubbin, but every time I turned to look again, *every time I blinked*, the lighthouse grew – subliminally at first, then in startling instalments, until the moment we landed on the sandbank foreshore when I looked back at the boat then up at the tower to discover it grown exponentially, having apparently torn towards me whilst my back was turned – a pale king hanging over all.

We entered Cordouan's fort-quoit base through a stepped tunnel, meeting and shaking hands with the keepers beside the several-inches-thick front door. Then we were into architect Louis de Foix' ornate interior. The base dates from 1611. The atmosphere is church-like, the echoes rich and sonorous, corkscrewing stairs like a belfry. First floor, an apartment for the French king, of course. Second floor, a chapel to the Virgin Mary and the architect, it seemed. Ho ho. She has a statue and altar, he a handsome bust below a rapturous inscription which he likely dictated, beneath a coffered dome ceiling akin to the Pantheon in Rome. The stained glass was exquisite, although Jean-Marie suggested it was 'hanging around' at the glaziers' at a time of renovation and

---

* So Jean-Marie Calbet told us then and so I repeat here now in absolute good faith.

slotted into the chapel with minimal tweaks. None of the saints or scenes depicted relate to Cordouan or the sea, he told us, before adding as an upbeat afterthought, 'Of course, they all look very nice!'

Onwards. Up to two more floors of intricate tiling and interlocking limestone – our steps and conversation turned the helter-skelter whirl of stairs into a whispering gallery – it was actually quite moving just how beautiful the space sounded and looked bathed in oblique afternoon sun.

In 1786 it was decided to add twenty metres to the original base. Everything above the chapel was rebuilt by architect Joseph Teulère and the masonry attests to his artistry and skill. The strength and functionality of the space around me were clearly assembled with the most deft craft and pride, each block honed and fitted with such precision that the lime mortar joints were almost invisible. Here a keystone shaped like a half-moon radiated fine lines, manifest beauty and stability. The ivory colour of the tower's interior – the rounded cantilevered stairs – suggested that we might be climbing to the top of an organic carapace, a helical shell.

Equally, we could have been ascending a castle turret or cathedral spire – as, in a way, we were – but reminders of the beacon's function were everywhere in its high hollow form. Here was intricately coiled rope below a winch. This was the lamp room where fuels were raised for the lamp which burnt, at various stages in the signal's life, wood, whale oil, coal, kerosene and petrol.

Sixth floor, the watch room, a circular bunk vault of dark wood where the keepers took turns to sleep and tend to the lantern lit above them.

Top floor, a short flight of metal stairs – a strange aberration, new sounds – then a sudden inundation: the lantern room, a crystal world of prisms, glass. The sound expanded, the view exploded, the sea, the sea; the Atlantic spread red, green and blue to the ends of the curving Earth.

Cordouan is unique – the only operational offshore lighthouse in the world both manned and open to visitors; the first to be listed as a historic monument; the first French beacon to employ parabolic reflectors and the test bed for Fresnel's rotating system of concentric lenses.* The lantern room, whilst generally closed to the public, can be viewed very well from the external balcony which runs around the lighthouse top. On the day I visited a brisk wind was whisking, so a buffeting turn about the outer circle was thrilling. I hugely recommend it.

Jean-Marie and his team are doing the most wonderful job of preserving and safeguarding the fabric of Cordouan. When I visited, some of the tower's lower flanks were caged in scaffolding as part of an ongoing effort to restore and replace carved limestone features blasted and smashed by the sea. It is a constant battle, one the sea will always win, Jean-Marie told us with a cheerful shrug, 'but we carry on'. And it's not only the ocean which wishes to carry Cordouan away – 'One day a keeper arrived by boat, this was many years ago, to find two people already here, trying to crowbar the statuary. He asked them what they thought they were doing and they were shocked that anyone would care. They

---

* Augustin-Jean Fresnel (1788–1827), French physicist and civil engineer who correctly postulated that light has a wave-like motion transverse to the direction of propagation, contrary to the longitudinal direction suggested by Christiaan Huygens and Thomas Young.

thought the lighthouse was too old to be working, they thought it was . . . *redundant*? Is that the word?'

Around the base were lodgings for the workmen and the keepers, curved and fitted together like everything at Cordouan with cabinet-maker's care. One apartment, allotted to the lighthouse inspectors who used to sail around checking the fitness and upkeep of the beacons in their care, had been kept as it was built in the late nineteenth century. Panelled walls, a marble fireplace, a snug cot-style of bed, and a most intricate double door arrangement – two stout doors hinged parallel so they closed together, a sound-proof box to shut out the roar of tempests.

A large-scale map in Cordouan's entrance hall depicted the different coloured quadrants of its light as a kind of navigational pie chart. When sailors were positioned so they saw Cordouan's light as green, they were on the right path to enter and exit the Gironde, deep waters, clear channels, safe passage. When they saw red, they were not. The map also showed the area's other lighthouses and beacons and I suddenly saw Cordouan in context, one of a number of towers and transmitters controlling the seaspace here – collecting, instructing and handing ships on, each to the next, in weather fair or foul, high tides and low. Some signals were radio, some were of light, some called you forward – specifically asked you to arrow and home – whilst others were guides in a broader sense. Cordouan stood out like a traffic policeman, pivoting to beckon, slow, start, pause, stop – ordering and steadying the estuary flow. Working its debouchment beat for over 400 years.

As we sailed away at the end of the day, I kept my eyes on Cordouan – a solitary chessman, apparently aloof on its amber sandbank but actually a figure in a much bigger scheme. The lighthouses I'd always imagined as single stars had been revealed by Jean-Marie to be a close-knit constellation. Rather than intransigent monoliths booming 'HALT' and 'DOOM', Cordouan and its brothers keep the sea lanes moving.

I'd known remarkably little about lighthouses before today, it turned out, but that was part of the reason why Phare de Cordouan had been such a pleasure to visit and explore. The beacon had raised questions of what constituted 'the edge'. The word 'hidden' is antithetical to lighthouses, they're there to be seen and regarded. As so often in this book, I saw I had to better define my terms; Cordouan had revealed a world of ships and shipping which whirls away unseen and likely unsuspected by those of us ashore – a system beyond our purview.

How far is the horizon? How far out must one sail before slipping beyond the scope of those on land? A ridiculously short distance. As little as three miles.

Cordouan – King of Lighthouses – reigns 4.3 miles offshore.

The fanal frontier? It depends where you stand.

---

* For an observer of average height (5ft 7in) standing on the ground, the horizon is at a distance of 2.9 miles. The same person standing on a hill or tower of 100 metres (330ft) in height can see the horizon twenty-two miles away. Were they to climb to the top of Mount Everest (a mountain of 8,848 metres) the horizon would be 209 miles' distant.

Phare de Cordouan, France. Photograph: Nick Herrmann

VIII

FONDATION JAN MICHALSKI POUR L'ÉCRITURE ET LA LITTÉRATURE, SWITZERLAND – NOVEMBER/ DECEMBER 2017

> A writer is a person for whom writing is more difficult
> than it is for other people.
>
> – Thomas Mann[1]

I am in Switzerland to write. I'm here for six weeks. So far I have transcribed a lot of Mars conversations and written up my recent trip to Cordouan.

Every hour, like clockwork, a train passes below. Two green carriages appear through a gap in the woods and amble a wide arc down to Montricher station, pause a moment then carry on to L'Isle, passing back a half hour later. It's very comforting, as much a part of the landscape as the farms and barns, trees and cows – the tram-train's whistle as familiar as the klang clonk of their bells.

In the morning, when the Alps beyond Lake Geneva glow, I sit with coffee by my window and read. In the afternoon I write – sometimes in the cabin but more often in the library where the feeling of being amongst other people spurs me; makes me feel 'at work' rather than just 'scribbling'. Lunch is communal and important for that because some days it'll be my only conversation. In the afternoon I'm back in the library or I might go for a walk a little way into the woods to think – it snowed this morning, which frosted the pines and lacquered the leaves and spun the paths sugar so they snapped beneath my feet. I think on the walks and I think in the shower – the percussion of the water on my head opens me out, gets ideas and associations bouncing. I drink a lot of tea. In the evening I might drink a bit of whisky. I go on until the words on the page become thin or unconvincing. A sudden surfeit of similes or adverbs sends me upstairs to either shower or sleep.

My cabin is a treehouse named Fuhrimann suspended from a canopy of openwork concrete which covers the whole foundation. The canopy itself is supported on tens of columns which give the impression of a strange forest. The large library and auditorium sit at the centre of the campus. Four administration boxes and the refectory float close by. Seven fellow writers' pods hang around the edge of the complex – six on the south side, one on the east – each different, the result of a global competition which asked architects to design something compact in concrete, wood, metal and glass – a living space with a kitchenette, bathroom, bedroom, and a space for writing.†

---

* 'Switzerland, land of Toblerone and Dignitas. At the moment I deserve none of the former and will be wheeled into the latter by my publishers if this manuscript doesn't take off soon.' – Author's diary entry, early November 2017.
† The competition stipulated that all the entry designs must hang suspended from the canopy by steel ties and hawsers; hawsers being famously key to the writing process, up there with pens.

Fuhrimann was designed by the Zurich architectural practice of AFGH and I reckon the CNC routers of Switzerland must have been running hot for days when the blueprints were delivered because the cabin is a palace of prefab ply.

Everything is plywood. The stairs are a climbing wall of alternating treads. Ply walls jut ply shelves. The desk on the top deck is a boxy mutation of a ply balustrade. Hinged ply blinds whir up and down the cabin face. Fuhrimann is a wonder of origami. Front door portholes, mat and lampshades aside, there isn't a curve in the place. The cabin is a machine for writing, Bauhaus severity all the way – straight lines for clean minds.

At night, lights off, all the shutters open, the landscape around is so deeply dark that the headlights of far distant cars burst over the cabin in waves. Lausanne, sixteen miles to the southeast, is a swirling galaxy. The moon is a limewash flood.

——

Publishers Vera and Jan Michalski moved to Montricher in 1983 and soon after had the idea of creating a literary gathering place, 'a haven for lovers of the written word', in the peaceful surroundings they enjoyed at the foot of the Jura Mountains. A site was acquired on the edge of the village but following Jan's premature death in 2002, Vera decided to create a foundation in his name to celebrate and foster literature, writing and writers. Established in 2004, the foundation welcomed its first resident writers in 2017.

——

To get to Montricher one first takes a fast train to the town
of Morges then changes for the Bière–Apples–Morges railway, a narrow-gauge tinpot local conveyance which climbs
into the hills north through vineyards, cutting under castles
and through stippled woods, arriving at Apples where one
changes again for the even smaller two-car tram whose clack
and whistle were to frame my writing days. North again,
sloping up a field of pylons, a stop for a farm, a handsome
barn, and there in the distance, to the right of Montricher
at the point where fields cede to forest, is the grey palisade
of Fondation Jan Michalski (FJM). The lightest of light rail
slows to stop by a station house a mile below the village it
serves, you get off and walk on roadside verges, past horses,
more farms, the twin of the filling station I met in
Marblemount, linhays, another farm – all of which brought
back walks I had made up to Alpine huts when last in
Switzerland. Those outliers had their heads in the clouds
whilst FJM is built on pasture, but the sense of having
made a journey and crossing an uncommon threshold is
comparable and the longer I'm at the foundation, the more
I think of the Goldilocks principle;* the sense that some

---

*   Circumstellar habitable zone (CHZ): in astronomy and astrobiology, the
CHZ is the range of orbits around a star within which a planetary surface
can support liquid water given sufficient atmospheric pressure. The bounds
of the CHZ are based on the Earth's position in the solar system and the
amount of radiant energy it receives from the Sun. Due to the importance
of liquid water to Earth's biosphere, the nature of the CHZ and the objects
within it may be instrumental in determining the scope and distribution of
Earth-like extraterrestrial life and intelligence. The habitable zone is also
called the Goldilocks zone, a metaphor of the children's fairy tale of
'Goldilocks and the Three Bears', in which a little girl chooses from sets of
three items, ignoring the ones that are too extreme (large or small, hot or
cold, etc.), and settling on the one in the middle, which is 'just right'.

destinations need to exist in the right geographic location to excite a visitor's imagination and fulfil their function – to exist in a bubble far enough away from distraction yet close enough to civilisation to be practical.* FJM is a bubble squared in the sense that each resident writer is assigned their own Goldilocks cabin, a box designed to be 'just right' for writing.

Judging from Fuhrimann, the architects think massive amounts of storage and vertiginous stairs essential to the writing process when, in truth, having crash-tested the cabin for several weeks and 'the writing process' more generally for two decades, I can tell you that the real essentials are a chair and a table of good height, a pencil, some paper, a door that locks and a comfortable bed. The view beyond the table, chair and bed are extraordinary here and the winter light is wonderful but when it comes to writing the important thing is getting it done, the act itself, so whilst it's a great thing to have views and light – views to stare into distractedly whilst thinking of the right word, light to find your chair and table – I'm only able to truly appreciate such things when I'm not writing. And if that suggests that I write with my eyes closed, that's not so far from the truth. When I write I'm blinkered, everything else becomes peripheral, atmospheric. I might have music playing but I won't be listening to it; I'm aware of it playing,

---

* Or to exist so far beyond civilisation that the mission is possible in the sense of MDRS in Utah, Ny-Ålesund at the top of the world, the Halley VI Research Station on the Brunt Ice Shelf at the bottom. From the Mauna Kea observatory on Hawaii to Skellig Michael and Eel Pie Island – any child's den or treehouse – all crucibles which carry the fervid far-flung fire of worlds apart.

the sounds, but they become diffuse. Yet, I applied and travelled out here to take up this position, I left my perfectly serviceable desk at home to sit here in Montricher. Why? To see what happened. To see how I worked elsewhere, meet fellow authors and revisit Switzerland; to see if everything I've just said was true. To see if a ply-glass tree-house was a key factor missing from my writing process. Added to which, I'd visited a number of other writing desks and chairs in other boxes in the months before travelling to Montricher – Roald Dahl's was one, Roger Deakin's another; a man who collected and built a positive armada of writing vessels in his lifetime.[†]

———

*   In recognition of Fuhrimann and AFGH's functionalist Bauhaus aesthetic I've been listening to CAN, Bowie, Cate Le Bon, Radiohead, Talking Heads, New Order, and St Vincent . . . and Steely Dan, because they're great.

†   Roger Deakin was a celebrated writer, wild swimmer and environmentalist who lived at Walnut Tree Farm in Mellis, Suffolk. The farm and land around it featured prominently in Roger's writing. His books often began there, sprung out from the farmhouse moat and meadows he bought in 1969 from a local farmer who had been keeping pigs in the semi-derelict house. Roger stripped the Elizabethan-era structure down to the original skeleton of oak, ash and chestnut timbers, gradually shoring up and rebuilding the homestead, sleeping in a bivouac inside the huge central fireplace until he created himself a bedroom. More information about Roger's remarkable house can be found in the book *Notes from Walnut Tree Farm* – a diary/compilation assembled from the notebooks Roger kept the last six years of his life, and *The House* – a documentary recording he made in 2004 for BBC Radio 4.

ROGER DEAKIN'S SHEPHERD'S HUT,
MELLIS, SUFFOLK

19 March 2017 – I have spent this morning writing illegible immediate notes in a grey notebook I brought back from my trip to see Simon Starling in Copenhagen. Having seen Roald Dahl's reanimated hut in aspic, I've come here to write in Roger Deakin's hut in hawthorns.

I have a copy of *Waterlog* here on the little desk, next to the bed, in the wood-lined cosy of the hut, rich in bird, fire and farm-song – whistling, singing, purring, pop and crackle and the whirr of unseen saws and a chipper making a meal of trees unseen. *Waterlog* begins with Roger talking of water, immersion and sadness – 'I was living by myself, feeling sad at the end of a long love . . .' – I too am sad, a ridiculous aching sadness which I can't shift from my chest. It sits. I sit. I write.*

A magpie flies up to a dead elm.

The wind frisks the trees.

Bees buzz.

Trains pass – fizz becoming rumble which builds to a peak as they flash past then trails off, rails singing . . .

I sit and I know that I shouldn't be sad. I should be writing about this hut all elbows, bashing away like Kermit on his typewriter – because I'm here in this privileged secret space, so iconic and charged in the minds of a million

---

* I was rather heartbroken at the start of this book and whilst I was already set to go travelling to remote parts, it gave the premise a bit of a kick and perhaps I travelled further and faster away than I might otherwise. I got out of London, I travelled and wrote myself better. Two years later I'm hardly sad at all.

readers; I'm here within sight of the famous moat around which the birds sing see-saw songs and chip like coal chisels, spinning lines of music in through the window here to say, 'Come on, old man, get on with it, you silly lovelorn pillock.' And they're right, of course, quite right.

There are three hooks on the back of the hut door on which are hung my wax jacket and scarf. The door is green, paint peeling in places, the floor is a patchwork of faded threadbare rugs. To the right of the door is a little cast iron wood-burner, the Summerford #10, which I notice is running a bit low so I open the top and drop in a few more of the sawn ash chunks and banister bits which fill the wood basket here at my feet, and then I close the lid and the thing gets roaring again, and I bank it up and hope that any bugs got out of the wood.

The copper flue runs up the right-hand corner of the hut, disappearing through the roof. The burner corner is clad in metal sheet but the rest of the walls are planked – old planking mellow and creosote-dark, maybe a hundred years old, with scratched initials and graffiti. Most of the windows are recent – the old ones were rotten – so the hut is fairly wind and watertight and cosy with the burner. In fact it's so rapidly filled the hut with soupy heat that I need to stand up and open a window.

I've coffee here in a Charles and Diana mug which matches the faded gilt on the mirror frame – and round we go to the panelled double bed which takes up over half the room; the multi-paned end window, spotted with ladybirds awoken by the warmth, a wicker chair, then the other long wall with its two square windows. The ceiling inside is pitched whilst the roof itself is corrugate-curved.

The basket of wood, a broom and a corner cupboard.

The floor is dusted with insulation shredded by either birds or mice in the roof.

The burner stands on thick terracotta tiles, surrounded by a few green coins – dug from the fields around perhaps – a kindling axe, a couple of pokers, a small shovel and a pair of gardening gloves.

The glass in the windows is wavy and flecked with bubbles. The view rippling as you move your head.

The caravan's outside is flaking maroon. The front is flaking worst – the rear/door end is backed into the hedge, sheltered, facing the house and moat.

The roof overhangs the door to make a small skew-whiff porch.

The cast iron wheels are slightly bigger at the back than the front.

I warm more coffee in a pan on the top of the burner.

Another train.

Overcast now.

A pheasant kooks.

The fire flutters.

A shotgun woofs somewhere behind me. And again.

The fire growls.

I went round to look in the railway wagon, another place I know Roger wrote. I climbed in, up the step of a milk crate, to find a big bumblebee pottering, looking at itself in propped mirrors before leaving slowly, flying like a dumpy man walking deep in thought, hands behind his back.

More rain, misting in from the west, showering diagonally, passing across the field. Hissing. And now the wind rises, shaking everything slightly, moving through the trees and hedges and over the moat, hatching its surface; and now the rain swells to come down harder, sheeting and swishing about in waves on the roof, pulling down the sky.

Last night I slept in the bed here, warm beneath quilts on the horsehair mattress. At 2 a.m. it began to rain. 'An amazing thunderstorm last night as I lay listening . . .' A radio set between stations; familiar patterns dance across the tin; the rain plays train songs; my carriage sways; the cabin of a ship far out at sea.

I drift off.

The gun woofs again.

The birds are lying low.

I can hear the hut gutter running into the brimful bucket beside the back door.

I open the door and walk out in the rain and the rain is rather warm and that takes me aback.

The ditches are dark-sided, recently dredged.

A digger stands over by the house.

I return to the shed and shut the door, peel and eat an orange, put the peel and more wood on the fire and sit down to write. This.

———

Now, in Montricher, eight months later, I read these notes and reflect how Roger's writing shed so matched Thoreau's description of his house at Walden pond – 'a frame, so slightly clad; a sort of crystallization; not so much within doors as behind a door' – finding himself neighbour to the birds having caged himself near them.[2] A wooden hut in a wood, a few mil of glass, a piece of tin, the width of a plank away from the outside world. Robert Macfarlane once noted that Walnut Tree Farm was a settlement in three senses: a habitation, an agreement with the land, and a slow subsidence into intimacy with a chosen place. Looking round, I see the sandwich ends of Fuhrimann's ply, each layer a slice of woodgrain laid at right-angles to its neighbour to curb any natural tendency to weft and warp. Environment controlled. The laminate glass of the doors and windows* keep sound as well as weather out – I can't but compare my glossy box with Roger's shepherd's hut.

A few nights ago there was a snowstorm and the windows flexed, their reflections warping. Every so often the gentlest tremor ran through the treehouse and that was almost more worrying than the rocking sway I know would have afflicted the shepherd's hut were the same storm to have hit Mellis. I know why Fuhrimann is overbuilt, of course, I'm not suggesting AFGH should have made it out of balsa, but in making their treehouse so terrifically solid and secure they took away the occupant's ability to do anything other than write. Where is the need for running repairs? Where is my eccentric little fire to stoke? *That would be a fire-risk, Dan. Besides, the treehouse has underfloor heating.* Where are the birds? *You could open the balcony doors, Dan, although I would not advise you to do so since it is night-time and snowing.* Yes, I know it's snowing but I want to hear the birds all the time, HAL. Where are the leaks for me to plug whilst racking my brain for another word for 'hawser'?†

There's nothing for it now but to write and I hate

---

* Which can be opened but it's snowing so they're closed.
† Hilariously, there was a leak after the snowstorm abated and the ice and drift on the cabin front began to melt. I put a bowl underneath it, as one would, and next day a handyman with a thermal imager arrived to fix the issue.

writing ... *I'm sorry, Dan. Would you like me to make you some warm milk?* Yes please.

I think Roger Deakin similarly cherished distractions, the world beyond his window, delighted in daydreaming. But no! We must be disciplined like Roald Dahl, pull the curtains, sharpen our pencils and crack on.

———

The rain makes roundels in the moat and the ditches.

The birds are back up and the fire is rumbling.

The peel has dried out and is burning and filling the hut with a good smell.

I feed in more wood then, suddenly restless, I put my jacket on and walk over to the house, over the sliced clean clods and digger tracks, the turned earth of the dredged moat.

A moorhen starts, aghast, and runs towards the far ditch, a startled tucked-up strut – all legs, white arse and affront.

Titus, who now owns the farm, makes me tea. We talk about Alfa Romeos and he shows me pictures of the last time the moat was dredged, twenty-odd years ago – the banks pulled up smooth as silk as they are now – as well as photographs of people walking on the frozen moat's surface and two old Citroen DS estates, parked up near the railway wagon, squat like frogs on the lawn. They still sit somewhere, grown through by brambles and ailing elms, forms lost in the thorny mass. Titus tells me the farm is whelmed with 'finds' – trucks and farm tools; a tarp-wrapped tractor-driven bandsaw, harrows and ploughs – skewed sheds full of doors and sash windows Roger used to rescue from London skips.

Things keep turning up.

The wrought iron Victorian grave surrounds, tiles and old glass bottles, the cider turned to vinegar buried beneath a greenhouse.

'I took everything out,' Titus told me, 'the house was too full of Roger so I took a great load of stuff outside to store, those two trunks there, that table: I cleared a space, let the place air; de-Roged it a bit . . . then I moved it all back in, put it back, mostly in the same places as before . . . that piano's still got to go . . .'

Five p.m.

Suddenly the light's drained out the day and the ditch and pool beside the hut are pocked-white with the downpour and now the wind rises and sheets of rain begin to lash the side of the van and the fire gutters and roars and the bright mouth of its low vent shivers.

I think of Titus with his tea in the beamed kitchen, the parquet-patterned brick floor, the dog snoring on the sofa, the Aga warm at his back.

Titus and Jasmin live in what was Roger's house but it's their house now, they're moving the story on. Walnut Tree Farm is not a reliquary, it's a worked and working smallholding. Roger wasn't the beginning and end of the story here, he was part of something bigger, a custodian, a link in a chain, an inspiration but an inspiration forwards, *to action on*: towards something else, be that writing, rambling, wild swimming, a deeper knowledge of habitat or the protection of hedgerows – his story doesn't solely live in Walnut Tree Farm, it's run out into the world, moved on, become innumerable other things . . .

—

There are occasional tours at FJM when the writers are pointed out, like the penguins in Regent's Park. 'Here are our tame writers,' someone whispers in French and the craning sightseers, as one, go 'Oooh!'

Last week a man knocked at my door – I heard his feet boom on the diamond plate of the metal stairs up.* It was after dark. He waited a moment at the top – peering in – then knocked. I immediately opened the door. He was taken aback. He gabbled a bit. Oh! I was a different writer! He was expecting the lovely American lady. Kristen, I thought, yes, she warned me about this: visitors. 'She was so welcoming,' my visitor explained, looking hopefully past me, into the blond interior. It was dark and snowing outside but it was also 9 p.m. on a Sunday night. I couldn't invite him in, I explained, because I was writing. Sorry about that. (I wasn't sorry.) The man's crest visibly fell. The American had invited him in, he mumbled. 'I bet she didn't,' I thought.† 'Did you bother her at 9 p.m. on a Sunday as well?' We said goodnight and he clanged back down the steps – no longer trying to be quiet. I'd gently suggested perhaps he shouldn't knock at anyone else's door. People were probably working. By which I meant 'You'll probably scare somebody silly or they'll call the police.'

After he'd gone I pictured the foundation viewed from the road below, as I'd seen it walking up from the station or coming back from the village shop; it didn't look overly inviting. On nights when it was snowing hard, dark

---

* The steel stairs up to Fuhrimann's front door were notable for being one of the cabin's few non-ply parks.

† I checked, she didn't. 'Bollocks,' she said.

mountain looming behind, it glowered. Yet this man had thought it a good idea to wander round the concrete box park forest in a snowstorm tripping the security lights, booming on the steel stairs, peering in through windows and knocking on doors. He hadn't come to use the library. He wasn't lost or an urbex adventurer, he was just nosy – *spying on the writers in the writer zoo*. I'd told him to go away in a gentle manner but had he been duffed up by one of my fellows I wouldn't have been surprised. Nancy in Décosterd might punch him in the solar plexus so he doubled like a pocket ruler. The silent French poet everyone is secretly afraid of might kick his knees off.

But otherness attracts scrutiny. As much as the complex has been built in a remote part of the world to lessen distraction and focus concentration, it becomes the story, a curio – 'What's he building in there?' as Tom Waits once asked. 'What's he building in there? We have a right to know.'

The FJM's otherness may seem aloof from without, but writing is a solitary business; and, to the foundation's great credit, had I arrived and never once left my cabin, kept myself entirely to myself, I think that would have been fine. Nobody checks up on me other than to pass on information* – I could quite easily have been anonymous and invisible here but I'm not like that, I'm not very good on my own; so, from the start, I work in the library and drink coffee with the librarians and went walking with Kristen for the few weeks our

---

* Guillaume Dollmann, the brilliantly droll Head of the Residency Program, popped by every so often to tell me such things as that the thermal imaging handyman would be coming back next day to have another crack at fixing my leaky roof and that tomorrow was laundry day – but the intranet handled most of that.

stays overlapped. She was writing a book about growing up on a boat her parents sailed around America, an itinerant childhood of abnegation – and she also wrote about dancing and high-altitude ballooning so there was much to discuss. And then, shortly after she'd flown back to San Francisco (and I'd moved into her cabin), Nancy arrived from Oxford to work on her manuscript about glaciers and the world's northernmost museum at Upernavik, Greenland,[3] which is great since we can compare notes on ice and mountains. Brilliant Mikołaj is still here: a Polish poet of great kindness and punctuality who I always see through the high library windows, already at his desk, as I make my way over. And Perrine from France, a resident who crossed the tracks and fell in love with Alex, also French, Head of Library Operations.* The foundation is home to a most diverse mix of people: Alexandra, Administrative Assistant and Cultural Mediator, originally from Sicily, with a passion for Japan and Taiji taoism in which she hopes to become a master; Shadi, also of the library, who originally met Alex when the pair worked together in Israel, and sets great store by Palestinian tobacco – a young, interested and interesting group who probably speak ten languages between them and could not have been kinder to me. I've learnt all about their lives and passions at lunch, a time when staff and residents come together to eat and talk. Sometimes Vera Michalski pops in

---

* They married in early 2018 and we all received an email from Perrine with pictures of the service:

> Miko was our witness
> It was raining
> We are HAPPY!
> And we kiss you very hard!

to see Guillaume, Head of the Residency Program, or just generally say 'Hello'. She must be very proud of her team who so animate the site and fill the library, galleries and auditorium with life; exhibitions, installations, concerts, talks, and festivals. The light at the heart of the forest.

———

Each departing resident is asked to leave something from their time – a document or object for future residents to see and read. I noticed that a lot of the items on display in the refectory pigeonholes were a pretty poor visual show. Files of paper don't razzle-dazzle. A pine cone with a haiku is a bit of a cop-out. So I built a scale model of Fuhrimann a few inches high from my FJM welcome pack. I took it very seriously, bought some glue, borrowed a Stanley knife and ruler from the library; it took several days. It was frankly amazing. When I finally presented it at lunch in my last week, Guillaume and Shadi were so impressed that they took it outside to compare with the real thing.

'You didn't do any writing this week, did you?' said Guillaume.

I admitted I hadn't done much.

'It's far better than the pine cone,' Shadi assured me.

Kristen's parting gift was a translation of the Morse code cut into the cladding of Décosterd, Nancy's cabin:

IN ADDITION TO SIMPLICITY
NUDITY

H D THOREAU

WALDEN
OR LIFE
IN THE WOODS *

Fuhrimann, FJM, Switzerland. Photograph: Tonatiuh Ambrosetti

---

* Eight months later, reading a proof of Nancy's book *The Library of Ice*, I discovered that she too had been drawn to translate Décosterd's Morse morsel: 'It takes me a few weeks to realise that the irregular perforations on my cabin wall are Morse code. I decide to translate my home. I stand outside in the snow and jot down the sequence of dots and dashes. I look up a history of Morse in the library and get a crib sheet for the code ... The letter-by-letter decoding of Morse is much more laborious than the work I've been doing on Greenlandic songs ... Gradually I impose order on the stream of letters, spelling out a quotation in French. I realise it's a translation of a work originally in English, although were it to be translated back again, it would only faintly echo the original.'

Which indeed proved to be the case since, going one better than Kristen and me, Nancy discovered the gnomic fragment's source: 'The very simplicity and nakedness of man's life in the primitive ages imply this advantage, at least, that they left him still but a sojourner in nature. When he was refreshed with food and sleep, he contemplated his journey again.' – *Walden; or, Life in the Woods*, Henry David Thoreau, Penguin Illustrated Classics, London, 1938, p.36.

IX

投入堂 NAGEIRE-DŌ,
三仏寺 SANBUTSU-JI,
三徳山 MOUNT MITOKU,
日本 JAPAN

門前の小僧習わぬ経を読む – An apprentice near a
temple will recite the scriptures untaught.

– Japanese proverb

The night after my arrival in Japan, a dragon with a
mouth of fireworks spat flames over my shirt, setting it
alight. The man holding the serpent's severed head nodded,
apparently satisfied, and strode on to slay further dragons and
rescue a maiden whilst I, on fire, began to flap myself out.

The dragons were part of a Shinto theatrical dance called
Kagura (神楽) – a rollicking highly stylised means of enter-
taining the Gods* – a mix of epic legends and origin myths.
The Gods, mostly female, love a dance and yarn, which is
lucky because the plays take place in the shrines where the
deities dwell.

The dark outside the shrine was black as jet; lights on
the road lens-flared and threw the horned silhouette of the
building back into the cold forest behind.

---

* Kagura 神楽, かぐら translates directly as 'God-entertainment'.

Lamps shone through the fret-screen windows – inside the shrine was warm. As people began to gather for the performance, the shoes on the front steps mounted.

Backstage, behind black and gold curtains, the young players were dressing and making up. Each process was complex and involved. I saw a warrior being helped to robe in several layers of embroidered silk. A red dragon head rested on the floor beside its concertina body. An actor turned and looked at me, face half white. The air was full of talc and incense.

A traditional band knelt on the floor stage-right, dressed in kimonos before drums, pipes, gongs and cymbals. The audience had filled up the shrine space and children sat wide-eyed as the first play began. It was the story of the meeting of the warrior Benkei and a young nobleman named Yoshitsune, who battle on Gojo Bridge. Fearsome Benkei, all severity and power, stamping and dancing whilst flashing his sword to all quarters, wore a furious mask of rage. The audience were suitably impressed, there were gasps; the children squealed. Then Yoshitsune arrived and the pair squared off. The fight that followed was mesmeric – the choreography fantastic. It recalled the acrobatic courtship of grebes – symmetrical and gravity defying. The two whirled around as the music thrummed.* A great spectacle. All the more amazing for the fact the swords were clearly very real and sharp. The second play was a classic – a hero saved a maiden from dragons – three dragons! They were evil beasts with long snaking bodies

---

* Such dances take a minimum of three years to learn with practice twice a week, a performer later told me.

which coiled about the stage. At the end, when the hero cut their heads off, the dragons and I combusted and everyone cheered

> And for the next minute I slapped my shirt,
> Smuts flew, and round me, mistier,
> Farther and farther, all the Gods
> Of Shimane Prefecture and Japan
> Laughed.*

———

I travelled to Japan to see Nageire-dō (投入堂), an ancient temple of the Sanbutsu-ji complex on Mount Mitoku – a most bewildering building, perched on stilts up a sheer cliff face, far-flung in every sense – its name translates as *tossed* or *thrown-in* hall.

In 706, the story goes – the sort of story a Kagura company could tell uniquely well – the Japanese mystic En no Gyōja (円の行者) threw three lotus petals into the air and instructed them to fly to places sacred to Gods and Buddha, pledging to establish temples wherever they landed.

The petals flew away to Mount Yoshino in Nara Prefecture, beyond Osaka; Mount Ishizuchi on Shikoku Island; and Mount Mitoku in Tottori Prefecture, the most northerly of

---

* With apologies to Edward Thomas. Later, I was allowed to try the dragon head on and can report that visibility was minimal and the thing weighed a ton, which satisfied me that my immolation hadn't been targeted. It wasn't until several days later that I remembered that it had been the Hero rather than the Dragon that had thrust the head towards me as it issued death, so the jury's out.

the three. Each of the mountains became a revered spiritual centre but I was drawn to visit Nageire-dō in particular because it looked such an exposed and theatrical structure – as marvellous, precipitous and implausible as a Ukiyo-e woodblock print by Hiroshige.*

Believed to have been completed in 849, the temple's construction still baffles historians and archeologists. A very early example of kake-zukuri, or 'hanging-style', Nageire-dō's slender scaffold architecture has its origins in China – a means of creating a level platform on sloping ground without having to cut into the mountain or hillside around. Writing about this uniquely organic approach, architectural scholar Kevin Nute notes that because the length of each timber column supporting these structures was 'individually cut to fit the particular profile of the land [they] would literally be unable to stand in any other location'.[1] Nute points to this extreme site-specificity as the reason kake-zukuri buildings evoke such a powerful sense of harmony with their setting, often seeming to merge with the landscapes around them as intrinsic organic structures rather than as built objects . . . and now might be a good time to mention that Nageire-dō resembles a crab. The moment I saw an image of the temple, I thought so. A spindly crab backing itself up into a tidal cave, porch mouth open in concentration, roof brows knitted, pencil legs pushing down on the foreshore, seaweed and algae greening the rocks around. Hesitant arthropod, patient, ancient – custodian of the cliff. Unique creature of personality and agency. I can

---

* Hiroshige (1797–1858) was a master of Ukiyo-e, as, later, was his protégé, Hiroshige II (1826–69).

absolutely understand how Nageire-dō keys into Shinto's essential animism and why it is seen by many to stand as both manifestation and celebration of the care and respect followers pay to Japan's powerful environment. Beyond any crustacean attributions, a huge part of the temple's mystique lies in the fact it still exists 1,300 years after it was apparently thrown into place. Its survival would be remarkable enough somewhere stable but to have remained standing so long on islands so regularly beset by earthquakes and typhoons is incredible. The sacred kami spirits must truly care for it.

———

Since ancient times, the Japanese have celebrated and addressed the divine energy or life-force of the natural world as kami (神) – a word which roughly corresponds to 'deity' in English. Kami are myriad and reside in nature. There are kami of the mountains, the forest, and the sea. Kami are all around, in every thing and every person. At one point in my trip to Sanbutsu-ji I was shown a diagram of NATURE, a circle full of constituents, geographic features, flora and fauna – the elemental and the individual: mountains *and* rocks, blossoms, forests *and* trees, the sea *and* rivers *and* water, and human beings* – under each was written (kami).

---

* Individuals who have made a great contribution to the state or society may also be enshrined and revered as kami and this idea interlaces with ancestor worship, Shinto's other central strand, to illustrate the permeable sense of time at the religion's heart, as explained in *Soul of Japan: An Introduction to Shinto and Ise Jingu* – 'Shinto has shaped the past as an integral part of Japan's cultural heritage. It will continue to shape the future through the deep influence it exerts on Japanese thought. Yet, as a fundamental aspect of daily life in Japan, the focus of Shinto is omnipresent. For honouring the kami, and receiving their blessings,

It was touching in its thoroughness. *Everything is kami*, said the diagram, polite but firm.

Such interconnectedness is particularly important at Sanbutsu-ji since the steeps of Mount Mitoku are home, unusually, to both Shinto shrines and Buddhist temples. Sanbutsu-ji's lotus petal-loosing father, En no Gyōja, is considered the founder of Shugendō, a syncretic religion which incorporated aspects of other, older doctrines such as Old Shinto, Japanese folk animism and shamanism, Taoism, and esoteric Buddhism. Shinto and Buddhism evolved symbiotically for centuries, splicing and parting as tree roots knot, until the establishment of the Empire of Japan in 1868 when Emperor Meiji sought to reorganise and enshrine Shinto as the official religion whilst banishing Buddhism from national life, framing it as a foreign Chinese ideology. However, the reformative zeal soon waned and only a couple of decades later the two faiths had grown back together.

The idea of such upheaval seemed strange at Sanbutsu-ji, so rich green and enclosed, where even the relatively recent temple buildings are several hundred years old. Today the forest path which climbs up to Nageire-dō passes by – and in one case *under*[†] – six Buddhist temples and a Shinto shrine. Undertaking the route, it was easy to feel that I was

there is no time but now.' — *Soul of Japan: An Introduction to Shinto and Ise Jingu*, Public Affairs Headquarters for Shikinen-Sengu, Tokyo, 2013, p.12.

[*] The term Shinbutsu-konkō (神仏混淆) – literally, 'the jumbling up of kami and buddhas' – describes the amalgamation of Buddhism and kami worship which existed in Japan prior to the Meiji period.

[†] A strong earthquake in October 2016 cracked the rock beneath Monju-do Temple. The temple's stilts remained sound but an alternative route for walkers and pilgrims had to be made.

passing through an eternal landscape, that nothing but the seasons had changed for an eon; that the architecture was as primary as the forest around it; the halls of Monju-do and Jizo-do kin to the towering stands of sugi (杉) – Japanese red-cedar, some nearly a thousand years old.

———

To begin with, several hundred weathered steps lead up the hillside from the road. Then, in a lower temple beside a pond of Koi, the first purification rituals took place. I passed beneath a sacred torii gate (鳥居)* to a temizuya (手水舎) font where I cleansed my hands and mouth – dipping a special bamboo ladle into water to wash first my left hand, then my right, before wetting my mouth and finally tipping the dipper up so water ran down the handle. Such rituals punctuated my time in Japan. Several times every day they served notice that now, to cross *this* threshold was to cross a frontier from the general into the particular, the prosaic into the sacred; to encounter ancient realms in which new rules applied. At the mighty shrines of Izumo and small halls en route to Nageire-dō, I felt I was walking a thin line through time, that here was a porous world of rifts, repetition and rhyme, that my path was wound and rewound over terrain not purely physical. The stone staircase into the sky-scraping cedars from Sanbutsu-ji's first temple was one

---

* A torii is a traditional Japanese gate most commonly found at the entrance of or within a Shinto shrine, where it symbolically marks the transition from the mundane to the hallowed. However, the association between Japanese Buddhism and the torii is old and profound and it is unknown whether torii existed in Japan before Buddhism or arrived with it.

such instant where the air seemed to blur and new frequencies flow. The vanishing point of the staircase drew me upwards, the rhythm of my feet met and joined with the tread of my fellows'. The forest seemed to join us in the ascent, gathering either side to channel and coax us up to the emerald apex where, a few minutes later, I met my mountain guide, Yoneda Ryojun, second son of Sanbutsu-ji's Head Priest, most recent of many generations who have studied and practised on Mount Mitoku, once home to 300 warrior monks.*

Another ritual and a higher temple, Hon-do Hall; this time the act was composed of bowing and clapping – a bow at the main door, two claps and a final deeper bow. Then we passed on and I was presented with a white sash, a wagesa stole. Everybody who climbs to Nageire-dō wears a sash as both blessing and permission to be on the mountain. 'The mountain will cleanse our six modes of perception,' Yoneda told me – the eyes, ears, nose, tongue, body, and mind – to climb one must live in the moment and look forwards, keeping a close watch on the path ahead for hazards. 'This is Zen,' he nods. 'The path we undertake today is also The Way of the Ascetics, a form of training intended to purify the senses, and by putting our lives on

---

* I later discovered that Sanbutsu-ji and its primeval forest inspired the world of *Princess Mononoke* and that made perfect sense, for if ever there was an supernatural stage and crucible for battles between shape-shifting forest Gods and humans, Mount Mitoku is it. *Princess Mononoke* (もののけ姫 Spirit/ Monster Princess) is a 1997 Japanese animated film set in Japan's late Muromachi period (approx. 1336 to 1573) – an epic historical fantasy which follows the young Emishi prince Ashitaka's involvement in a struggle between the Gods and monsters of an ancient forest and the humans who consume its natural resources and harm its environment.

the line attempting to reach Nageire-dō we will sharpen and hone them all.'

This statement formed part of Yoneda's cheerful pre-walk pep-talk. Snakes were also mentioned briefly. Also peregrine falcons. But the main thing was to keep one's wits about one and hands free to grab and grip the branches, rocks, ropes, chains and halls which would form the rungs of our next couple of hours' climb. Now, what was our footwear like? Like a fourth official inspecting a footballer pitch-side, Yoneda ran an eye over our boots. He himself, I noticed, was wearing geta (下駄), a traditional Japanese form of footwear like a flip-flop clog. Traditional straw-rope sandals named waraji (草鞋) are offered to any walker whose shoes fail to pass muster. All cleared, sashed and blessed, we made our way down to another torii, beyond which a small red bridge named Yadoiribashi crossed a mountain stream. Everything after the gate was sacred, a province of Gods, making that little wooden gate one of the most holy portals in all Japan.

Yoneda reckoned that he scales the path 100 to 150 times a year. Sometimes he'll go three, four, five times in a week. Sanbutsu-ji's climbing season runs from 1 April until the first snow of winter, generally early December. An average of sixty people might hike up the mountain on a weekday but the numbers of walkers and mountain aesthetes may shoot to 200 on a weekend, and triple to

---

* He thinks he probably first climbed it when he was six or seven years old and, by happy coincidence, we had a seven-year-old along with us today, chamois son of a National Park Ranger, and a constant source of encouragement and delight. All the sure-footed sons shone on Mount Mitoku that day.

600 during the Golden Week* public holiday of late April/
early May.

'Six hundred people a day,' Yoneda repeated thoughtfully,
rolling the number over.

'How many fall off the mountain?' I asked him with a
grin.

'Very few,' he smiled back. 'Most people can hang on.'

———

We climbed through rhododendrons, bamboo, grasses,
ferns. In some places the paths were dusty, in others soft as
the bark of cedars – springy, dusky, the earth a foxy ginger –
the colours in the hollow runnels russet, rich rust and
copper. The trees grew around and over the path. Sometimes
we had to climb around or within them, picking a line
through their vascular lattice. On some steep sections we
ascended ladders of roots and later pulled ourselves up chains
over rocks polished by devoted bodies scaling, sliding,
scrambling to heaven.

About a third of the way, Yoneda decided that a hearty
mantra was in order to get us into a true pilgrim trance. He
taught and took up the chant – a repetitive relation of the
'Everywhere we go' call and response rounds I'd long ago
endured in Scouts – before stopping to instruct the group
to sing from the diaphragm. I did my best to sound vigorous

* Golden Week (ゴールデンウィーク) is an annual public holiday in Japan
which runs from 29 April to early May. The week contains a number of
important dates and festivals – such as the Emperor's Birthday, Greenery Day
and Children's Day – and many Japanese take the opportunity to travel around
their archipelago to visit family as well as cultural, historic or sacred sites.

and enthusiastic but in truth I rather wished he'd pack it in. Chanting is a tiring business when one is hacking up a height and rather than blissing me out to a state of mindful now-ness, I found it pissing me off to a state of vengeful hoarseness. But Yoneda appeared to have lungs of steel, so on we ascended, singing away, arms and faces shining, air shimmering, until I remembered that even the hardest task-master guide generally likes to answer questions about their mountain. 'Yoneda,' I panted, as soon as Monju-do Hall became visible ahead, 'can you tell me something of the architecture here?' Indeed he could, and did! Respite. But the little boy climbing with us saw straight through my ploy and met my eyes with a knowing grin; he spoke no English, he knew my game.*

———

Monju-do dates from the Azuchi-Momoyama period in the sixteenth century and, like several other halls on the climb, is built on a cliff using kake-zukuri, but unlike the spindly pegs of high Nageire-dō, Monju-do and Jizo-do beyond are supported on the sort of wooden trestle frames Denis Johnson hymned in *Train Dreams* – a boxy timber scaffold on top of which the temple sits, a natty hip-and-gable roof

---

* Scribbled down phonetically, the mantra ran:

> *Sange!* / Sange!
> *Locum Sho-jo.* / Locum Sho-jo . . .

We started well but ran out of steam. Several people clapped me on the back for my architectural ruse and took it on themselves in different forms, so the real team-building chant became, 'Yoneda, I wonder if you could tell me . . .' followed by a question about a tree, snake, rock or view.

of cypress bark shading an unguarded walkway, from which one can see a full panorama of mountain forest, an explosion of broccoli pom-poms bobbling to every horizon. To the east Mount Daisen – Mini Fuji – to the north, unsighted today but *absolutely there*, Yoneda assured me, the spectacular islands of Oki.

Having padded around the veranda, a narrow platform a metre wide, observed the drop and noted that this would be an excellent spot for forest bathing, a precipitous diving board above the sylvan world, we put our shoes back on – shoes off for temples – and carried on up to the slightly older Jizo-do Hall* which, my guide announced with great pride, was built back to front.

'At this temple one prays behind the God, Dan. Very unusual.'

I quite liked this being the home of 'the God, Dan' – it would be a splendid spot to live – a small library, a simple bed, a kettle . . . to be a bodhisattva amidst birds and trees, to pass the time with the legendary eighty-seven-year-old man who collects chestnuts on the mountain every day.

'He is the man who goes to rescue anybody who falls off the path,' Yoneda informed me. 'He will rescue them and carry them down on his back if a helicopter is unable to help. He regularly carries fourteen kilos of the chestnuts so is in wonderful shape.'

---

* Jizo-do Hall is reckoned to date from the late fifteenth / early sixteenth century, the end of Japan's Muromachi period, although, like all the temples on Mount Mitoku, it was founded several centuries earlier. The sumi ink writings of a Buddhist priest were recently unearthed, which tell of the temple being repeatedly burnt down and rebuilt in the medieval ebb and flow of wars fought around Mount Mitoku.

Yes, that sounded good. I'd talk to him and live here, although there would be the small matter of walking parties crawling under my feet – this being the temple hall under which the recent earthquake cracked the rocks. Now the path runs below the building, through a trestle maze; that might be slightly clonky and irksome ... as might the constant booming of that massive bell.

'Can you tell me about that massive bell?' I asked my friend Yoneda.

It turned out that the massive bell dated back 850 years and, like so much on Mount Mitoku, no one is quite sure how it got there. Another of my walking companions suggested it could have been made in situ, cast in two halves, nobody knows. The monster brass bell currently hanging – *'resounding'* – in the eaves of Shoro-do Hall was recast from the original bonshō (梵鐘) in 1680.* Pilgrims announce themselves to the Gods by ringing the bell before undertaking the final stage of their journey to Nageire-dō.

I rang the bell, having clambered up to sit beneath a suspended beam which, having set myself, I swung into a boss on the mighty bell. The boom which followed rippled the air and grew for several seconds, inflating from the initial thud, the moment the beam hit the great clocca. As the reverberations rang around my head, everything apparently in motion, fizzing – I reflected that whilst I'd called on many mountains, I'd never before rung the bell.

---

* Both current bell and bell-striking hall / kanetsuki-dō (鐘突堂) date from the late seventeenth century / early Edo period.

I'm told that the priests of Sanbutsu-ji proudly refer to Nageire-dō as 'Japan's most dangerous National Treasure' but I think they're selling it short. The path up is certainly slightly precarious – there was a stone ridge to be negotiated after the Shoro-do fukihanachi (吹放ち),* named either Horse or Cow-back depending who you ask, which was very much like dancing along the delicate nobbles of a spine – but beyond that there's little to fear and the trail resumes a spring footing. I quite see how *'Japan's most dangerous National Treasure'* has a definite pizzaz that *'One of Japan's more lofty but perfectly secure National Treasures reached by a testing path with brief interludes of knackering acclivity'* does not. I'm sure Japan has more dangerous treasures,† but my real point is that to call Nageire-dō dangerous is really to misrepresent it. Nageire-dō is actually one of the ancient world's great wonders – one of the modern world's great survivors – the Oz of shrines – the greatest wonder of a mountain of wonders – the final revelation after several hours of encounters. *Nageire-dō is astonishing.*

Imagine: you've climbed through gnarled and knotted forests, scaled chains and ladders, crawled a dusty maze under temple trestle struts, shimmied over several rock formations which seemed set to send you skidding, rung the most colossal doorbell, and now – having passed tiny path-side temple boxes of sutras, some dating back to the thirteenth century – you reach a cave before which sits one of the final halls before Nageire-dō. But before you can glimpse that, you stand beside

---

* A fukihanachi is a type of timber-framed bell-striking hall without solid walls.
† The Hello Kitty Theme Park sounds terrifying!

the exquisite Kannon-do Hall, and are told that, for centuries, it has been understood that to pass through the darkness of the cave behind the temple and emerge into the light the other side is to be reborn. So you stoop to be ushered through the tunnel they call 'the womb' and emerge on to another part of the mountain where there is another small temple, the last, the gatekeeper – beautifully crafted and panelled as all the others, feathered roof a vermiculation of cedar fronds, four-square on six uneven legs, each a different height, the secret-handshake of all the nimble temples soft-shoeing on Mount Mitoku – and here you learn that this holy kiosk was the receptacle for the hair of all the monks of antiquity who passed this way. They'd reach this point and shave their heads, a last offering before, cropped and cleansed, they walked the final few steps, aware that they were on the cusp, about to enter a realm reified by a temple En no Gyōja himself threw into place by means of magic. A few steps on to where a great wall of mountain, a hip-like lug, allows the path to continue around and then . . .

There it was.

Mount Mitoku fell away green.

The cliff was a sheer wash of bare rock, marbled by water, blotched sage. Wiry saplings hung from fissures. Grass and moss fringed in tumps low down, ferns too, but the severity of the face had seen off all but the most acrobatic life.

Halfway up, the rock was gashed back in a great mouth, an ashen tongue ran down from this and on that tongue stood Nageire-dō, impossible beast. It stood poised, as if just woken – just as I'd seen it in pictures, only now, up close, its presence was electric. It was so charismatic it held your eye. I felt lucky to have caught it, despite the fact it's apparently been stood in the same spot for 1,300 years . . . I remembered a story a friend once told me about Francis Bacon opening and closing his studio door, opening it a crack to peer inside, closing it quickly, opening it again. 'What are you doing, Francis?' my friend asked.

'I'm trying to creep up on the painting,' he said. 'I'm trying to truly see, catch it off guard.'

Nageire-dō felt like that.

Less a building than a moment.

I felt suddenly, incredibly happy. Recharged. Alive.

And of course time flew – as time always flies when one is part of an excellent crowd or falling in love. I had maybe fifteen minutes there with it, time when I tried to take in its form, fix it as Hiroshige might have, properly behold it.

Impossible scene.

Slender legs and ochre roof. Lopsided but totally sound. It looked absolutely 'thrown up' in the sense I couldn't see it any other way. I decided I didn't care how it was done. Who wants to know how they disappear the elephant? I'd never been more delighted by a story.

Nageire-dō is made of stories. That's where its magic lives. And people are made of stories too.* That's how we make sense of the world. All the worlds. And I knew leaving Nageire-dō that I was fuller of story than when I arrived; fuller than when I first set foot on Mount Mitoku, than when that dragon had set me on fire, than when I first set foot in Japan or began this book, driven on by the story of a great white bear. Story spurs us on, helps us stay in the moment and consider the past. It makes us better, human; better humans.

---

* Stories and kami.

日本 JAPAN

投入堂 Nageire-dō, Japan, Dan Richards

I'll leave Japan with a poem by Gary Snyder – one of several poets and storytellers who drew me to Japan in the first place drew me over from Desolation Peak to carry a story on.

Saying Farewell at the Monastery after Hearing the Old Master Lecture on 'Return to the Source'

> At the last turn in the path
>   'goodbye–'
>   –bending, bowing,
>   (moss and a bit of
>   wild
>   bird-)
> down.
>
>   Daitoku-ji Monastery[2]

X

SVALBARD, NORWAY

Isfjord Radio, Svalbard. Photograph: Alex Edwards

When I started painting the pelvis bones I was most interested in the holes in the bones – what I saw through them – particularly the blue from holding them up in the sun against the sky as one is apt to do when one seems to have more sky than earth in one's world . . . they were most beautiful against the Blue – that Blue that will always be there as it is now after all man's destruction is finished.

– Georgia O'Keeffe[1]

Svalbard. Land of polar bears.

Like my father thirty-six years before, I first flew to Norway, then further north. After several hours of night we overturned the Tromsø sunset. A feather of horizon slowly focused to a shard, blue falling red then flaring fire so Svalbard dawned as knapped ice islands and mountains shadowed pink; the sea, a dark mirror ceding to floe. I thought of shrouded furniture in shuttered rooms, cotton sheets rippling down to cover the floor.

The cold on the walk from the plane to the terminal at Longyearbyen was bitter. Inside I met my first polar bear. A stuffed creature, frozen in a posture of livid umbrage. My friends and I collected our bags and found a bus to take us into town – Alex Edwards, who runs sustainable safari camps in East Africa. A tall man with a beard, more likely to smile than frown, he'd told me several stories in Tromsø airport about such things as trying to remain calm whilst flying a small plane solo through a tropical storm, trying to remain calm when a lioness walks into your tent, trying to remain calm when the sail snaps off your sailboard and you begin drifting rapidly out to sea, and trying to remain calm when a hippopotamus bites your kayak in half. The latter story was clarified by another member of the party, Horatio Clare – travel writer, ornithologist and explorer – who was sitting in the kayak at the time.*

The others were Alex's son Ralph, a seraphic, surf-haired teenager of great affability – and Dominic Taylor, a friend

---

* Horatio: 'It was on the Kafue river. Alex had asked us to position the thing downriver of the hippopotamus so he could fit us all into the shot. He didn't expect the shot that he got, however, which was of a hippo apparently trying to climb into the kayak while biting it in half.'

from Alex's university days who occasionally came along 'on mad trips like this'. I had yet to find my fit, having only met Horatio before, but everyone seemed friendly and similarly sleepy as the bus began to crunch its way up Adventfjorden, past the cronky coal port's silhouette – dark ice to our left, dark crags to our right – towards the town which lay a few kilometres east from the airport.

We were staying in a simple clapboard hostel of the sort traditionally used by miners. The bus pulled up, we piled off, found our room and collapsed into bed just as the first sun began to overspill and fill the valley the other side of the heavy felt curtains.

Early breakfast was a buffet and seemed to happen only moments after I'd gone to sleep. Horatio and I both looked rather haggard but jam, charcuterie and coffee soon jiggered us up. The new day, this new world, blazed hard. I now saw that we were up a side-valley from the main fjord drag, a gigantic Belfast sink chipped along the side with chevron rock-forms and gantries – towers of an extensive cableway which once ferried coal hoppers out to the port. As we assembled by the front door, layered up and bulbous – long-johned and jumpered, muffled and hatted, breath steaming – it struck me that I was finally here, in long-dreamt Svalbard, childhood Arctic phantasmagoria. There was a road sign warning of ice bears – a white bear in a red triangle. Our barn-like boarding house was one of maybe fifty brightly painted wood and concrete buildings which line the several circuits of frost-lacquered roads that lead back down to the frozen bay. In the distance I could hear a klaxon sounding, heavy plant engines and dogs barking. A snowmobile passed. The sky shone blue. Everything pointed to the fact that we were on the cusp of a great adventure.

Longyearbyen* was named after John Munro Longyear, a lumber and coal magnate from Michigan, USA. In 1901, Longyear took a holiday to Hotellneset – now the site of Svalbard airport and dock but then home to a small hotel and post office. There the American happened to meet some coal prospectors who told him about Svalbard's rich reserves. In the years that followed Longyear established 'Longyear City' as a major coal-mining centre. By 1916 the town had two mines and was home to 500 workers. In every picture I've seen of him, Longyear sports the sort of stern Edwardian beard and moustache which accentuate a glare. His is the face of a man who once had such a nice time on holiday that he returned the following year to knock the place down and build a coal port.

—

Alex had organised the trip as an experiment to see what sort of bespoke expeditions were available in the Arctic; to see, in his words, 'how the Norwegians do it'. He was keen to expand his safari company's range and to this end had organised the tour to test the water – or ice, perhaps. Horatio was there to write a travel piece for a newspaper and I'd managed to tag along having failed to gain permission to go to Ny-Ålesund to revisit either Tim's shed or the glaciers of Oscar II Land.

In the early stages of writing this book I was filled with hope that I would reach Ny-Ålesund. As those of you who've

---

* Motto – 'Unique, secure, and creative'.

followed me through earlier chapters will know, I usually get to the places I set my heart on. I fly, hitch, walk, sail, call up Utah raptor experts I've not seen since university . . . apparently impossible journeys take slightly longer than very difficult ones but I usually get my outpost. Oscar II Land was a bridge too far.*

Ny-Ålesund itself is difficult but not unattainable. Cruise ships occasionally stop there in summer to let people disembark, stretch their legs, post a card from the world's most northerly post office and visit the world's most northerly museum and shop. The problem was getting permission to walk out and explore the landscape beyond the town, which is a highly protected area of global scientific interest. It's not possible to fly into Ny-Ålesund without permission. Just like Newhalem below the Skagit dams, Ny-Ålesund is a company town, a closed community of research scientists. Nick Cox, the man in charge of the UK Arctic Research Station at 78° 55' N. – a man of unwavering politeness and patience who I emailed a lot in the several years of this book's gestation – was very helpful and identified Tim's shed as being a cabin named Jensebu but summed the situation up in an email of November 2017:

Dear Dan,

The international station primarily conducts environmental research. As I think I mentioned in

---

* I didn't get to Big Creek Baldy lookout either, you'll recall, because the forests around it were on fire – another case of wintery emails – but that episode turned out very well: I changed tack to Desolation Peak, met Jim and that bear – hopefully Ny-Ålesund's proxy would prove a similar success.

earlier correspondence, securing permission for non-scientific projects can be difficult. The ten nations operating stations in Ny-Ålesund protect as best they can the natural environment. Every footfall must have scientific merit.

[. . .]

I have just returned from a Svalbard science conference in Oslo where we were shown photographs and data concerning Kongsvegan, Kronebreen and Uvésbreen. In the past Kongsvegan provided the only safe route to Jensebu hut. Warming is causing dramatic changes to the topography. The snout of Kronebreen which is on the brink of surging has retreated 400 metres in the past year. It has exposed the snout of the Kongsvegan to the sea which has eroded the snout to a narrow strip which is crevassed and to be treated with great caution. Another year might see that strip disappear. The other route via Skara and Uvésbreen might be possible. There are crevasses high on Uvésbreen.

I am sorry access to Jensebu hut is not straightforward.

Could I describe my plan in detail on a Natural Environment Research Council (NERC) station application form, he asked, offering to circulate and discuss it with his approval team and key international partners. I couldn't. My odyssey was non-scientific in the extreme. The idea of filling in the form made me wince; the part where I explained that my trip was inspired by my father's purloining of polar bear bones in 1982 would doubtless raise a few eyebrows at NERC Towers. 'Oh great!' they'd surely think. 'Let's absolutely have the pillock progeny of the Kongsfjorden pelvis-napper back to break his neck down a few of our crevasses . . .'

If the problem had just been the presence of bears, I could probably have found a couple of guides with guns and we could have gone exploring – indeed I did sound a few out, including Annette Scheepstra and Ronald Visser, a well-known guiding pair who explained that, were I somehow to convince the BAS* and NERC that I was actually David Attenborough, and be allowed to buy a devastatingly expensive ticket to fly over from Longyearbyen, I'd still need to negotiate the shed keys from Kings Bay, the arm of the Norwegian Ministry of Trade and Industry who operate Ny-Ålesund and own Jensebu.

Ronald stayed there once in winter, Annette told me. He found it very small.

Some evenings I'd call up Ny-Ålesund on Google Earth and slowly scan along, panning east, until I got to the junction of Kronebreen and Kongsvegen where Jensebu apparently still stood, beyond my zoom capabilities but there, down there, somewhere. The fact the glaciers were in such poor condition and declining so fast, the brutal costs of getting there and hiring two guides, the time and

---

* The UK Arctic Research Station in Ny-Ålesund, Svalbard, is funded by the Natural Environment Research Council in Swindon and, rather confusingly, *hosted* by the British Antarctic Survey (BAS) in Cambridge, England – www.bas.ac.uk

organisation involved, together with the moral questions of whether I should be going to such a vulnerable ecosystem I would surely damage further – such a trivial project in the face of that. After a while I accepted that Jensebu would remain beyond me, as it always had, a place my father once visited before I was born. Now, more than ever, I marvelled that he'd been and perhaps it's befitting that this book end with the realisation that some places are beyond us, *outwith* as the Scots say, not because they're physically unreachable but because they're so delicate you should not go.

The worst thing I could do to celebrate Jensebu and Oscar II Land would be to fly or sail there, burning money I really didn't have on jet fuel and diesel to explore a melting world, thereby damaging it further. It would be utterly callous. My father had been there at a tipping point. In the winter of 1982 there was ice a metre thick in Kongsfjorden, in the winter of 2017 there was none. Nick Cox reports that Kronebreen retreated 400 metres in 2016, that's over a metre a day, over 4.5 centimetres an hour. That's terrifying. Why would you go? First do no harm.

When I originally began to think about this book, wondering where I might go, a friend suggested that one of the places be imaginary: a terra incognita dream, a speculative mirage. At the time I thought it was a lovely idea but wasn't sure whether it would fit. It turns out it was at the heart of the book from the beginning – Jensebu, my Xanadu, Godot's shed – Hotel California.

I have one photograph of it and a sketch map where it's marked 'HUT' at the point where the Brøgger peninsula dives under the grind of Uvésbreen and Kongsvegen, a black square surrounded by the dots and dashes of the journeys the three groups on my father's expeditions made – ant tracks across a carbon world. The sketch is a distant relation to the sort of maps J.R.R. Tolkien drew of Middle-earth whilst writing *The Lord of the Rings*, to help author and readers alike make sense of his epic quest.

'Maps are worrying me,' Tolkien wrote to his editor, Rayner Unwin, in April 1953, three months before publication. 'One at least (which would then have to be rather large) is absolutely essential. I think three are needed: 1. Of the Shire; 2. Of Gondor; and 3. A general small-scale map of the whole field of action. They exist, of course; though not in any form fit for reproduction – for of course in such a story one cannot make a map for the narrative, but must first make a map and make the narrative agree.'[2]

My map and narrative would remain at odds unless I changed my focus and picked up the story elsewhere. Jensebu was fine where it was, where it had always been, a place of imagination. Antoine de Saint-Exupéry wrote that deserts are beautiful because somewhere they hide a well, and one doesn't need to visit the several deserts where he crash-landed to appreciate the universal truth of those words.

I determined to get to Svalbard as sustainably as possible and hire a local guide to explore less endangered areas. I would try to stay in a shed akin to Jensebu and perhaps, if I were lucky, wave hello to distant cousins of my father's bear. The fact Horatio and Alex offered me a spot on their expedition was a godsend; the luck that our interests and agendas coincided, unexampled.

In the months before we travelled north I wrote to Philip Pullman, whose *His Dark Materials* trilogy paints Svalbard as a fantastic world of armoured bears, dæmons, balloonists, witches and sinister scientists.

'Oh, you're going to Svalbard!? Home of the armoured bears,' people would say – lots of people. Several even asked if it was a real place, 'beyond the books' – suggesting Pullman might have upped Tolkien in making his map and narrative agree to the extent that the magical world he thought up is better known than the Norwegian reality.

But when I heard back from Philip through our mutual friend Katy, my hopes of an Arctic pow-wow took something of a dent. 'I'm afraid he says with regret that he can't help,' Katy emailed. 'It turns out he's never been to Svalbard! He did all of his research at the Bodleian Library.'

Svalbard, just like Middle-earth – a world fashioned in Oxford. I found that strangely comforting.

Somewhere in the heat haze shimmering over Kongsfjorden a solitary bear approaches Jensebu, crosses into the shadow of Mount Grensefjellet, stops, raises its head and sniffs the air. It looks enquiring at the little shed up in the rocks. Sunlight reflecting from its armour plays across the wooden boards. A moment's pause. Then the great bear stretches and turns away northeast, crump tread fading until the only sounds are the breeze and the tick of ancient glacial ice.

———

* The day after I finished writing this chapter, E.H. Shepard's original map of Winnie-the-Pooh's Hundred Acre Wood sold at auction for £430,000 – a new world record for a book illustration.

Sotheby's described the 1926 sketch as 'possibly the most famous map in children's literature'.

Erlend Øian was our guide. A fiendishly young, brilliantly knowledgeable and enthusiastic Norwegian with shaggy hair and glacially blue eyes. He collected us in a minibus and we drove out of town to his company's base – a building originally built to store dynamite for a Norwegian coal company and later pressed into service as an aircraft hangar. There were maps of Svalbard on several walls along with large photographs of Arctic explorers – men with gruff Edwardian beards, women mainly there for scale; look how tall these long-skied heroes were! And what excellent pointy hats! Erlend drew our attention to one particular map and began to sketch the week to come. Today we'd travel west out to Barentsburg for lunch, then round Grønfjorden to Kapp Linné and Isfjord Radio where we'd eat dinner and stay the night. Tomorrow we'd explore the west coast before heading back inland for lunch at a glacier face . . . Several days were reeled off like that: a meal, a 100-kilometre drive with a break for more food along the way, each night a different place to stay. The way he moved his hand across the map it looked like we'd be scooting a massive figure 8 with the final night at Pyramiden, a Russian mining ghost town at 78° 39' N., the furthest point north on our trip and the closest to Ny-Ålesund.

In a room next door to the main map hangar we all got changed into thermal boiler-suits and boots in preparation for the snowmobiles. Big black boiler-suits, balaclavas, face masks, gauntlet gloves, layer after layer until we resembled well-upholstered Hells Angels – hell having frozen over; a

---

* A friend who read an early draft of this chapter remarked to me that 'Northern Scandinavians in the Middle Ages believed Hell to be a very *cold*

chapter of accidents waiting to happen. We lumbered out with our bags to meet our machines which were lined up on Adventfjorden's frozen shore. Hedge-trimmer transformers. To get their measure we pootled about on the ice a bit. A thumb trigger accelerator on the right handlebar, a break on the left. Horatio and I took one bike, Alex and Ralph another. Dominic had a bike to himself but was assigned a sled to pull of fuel and food, as did Erlend whose snowmobile was notably more beasty than ours – bull-chested and mantis-emerald. Once our bags were lashed to the sleds, their tow-bars double checked, and everybody happy, Erlend led us off.

Horatio drove, I sat behind. We crawled up through Longyearbyen, crossed the main road and pitched into the flume of a frozen river bed. We followed that back past the hostel and up the chipped enamel valley to a halfpipe channel which wound up in a series of loops before debouching us on to the Longyear glacier top. We accelerated then and zoomed. Ice crystals began to form inside my goggles and my exposed nose burnt numb but none of it mattered in the

---

place', and this note led me to research *Niflheim;* 'Abode of Mist' or *World of the Darkness* according to the OED – one of Norse mythology's Nine Worlds which seems to have overlapped with notions of *Niflhel* or *Hel* – as well as descriptions of Hell in Buddhism, particularly Tibetan Buddhism, where there exist an equal number of hot and cold Hells. The Qur'an describes the gate of Hell as being overseen by Maalik (aka Zabaaniyah), leader of the angels who guard the underworld. Whilst Hell is usually described as a furnace, there is one pit named Zamhareer which in Islamic tradition is unbearably cold, with unbearable blizzards, ice, and snow.

* There are no roads connecting settlements on Svalbard. Roads run within the few towns but rarely beyond – town to docks, mine to airport – there has to be good reason for infrastructure here and generally the drivers are coal-based.

minutes and hours that followed, time in which we zipped across a series of vast white panoramas, a world of diamond dust flaring to the tops of the mountains which swooshed around us, luxuriously quiffed and toga'd steeps. The land-scape was astounding. I cared not a jot that my eyes were streaming and my beard regularly froze to my mask; when-ever my feet went to sleep I'd wiggle life back into my toes – besides, every time we halted I roasted in the sun so the windchill was mostly a boon.

I enjoyed that first day of bike-life immensely, although, as the days went on, the thrill began to thin. Alex in particular became tired of the judder and his role as Ralph's windbreak, oscillating between 'Bloody thing's like riding a motorcycle with a flat tyre' and 'Kick me again, Ralph, and you're walking' as opening statements whenever we'd scrunch to a stop for either coffee or sweet blackcurrant cordial drunk steaming from carved birch cups named kuksas.

My irks were minimal. The main frustration was that I wasn't allowed to drive. I found Horatio's driving very conservative but since I didn't have a licence I was the passenger so I rode and I rode, slowly. 'You drive like a old man,' I would tell him every time we stopped for Ribena. 'Shut up,' he'd retort and that would be that. But on day three, when we were far far out, truly plumb in the middle of nowhere, Erlend suggested that Ralph and I could 'have a go' – a prospect which rather pleased Alex since by that point he'd decided that several lionesses walking into his tent were preferable to driving further with *an insensible arse*, or 'Ralph' as we still called him. 'Excellent. Let's see how you like it!' he grinned at his son, who ignored the murder in his father's eyes and gleefully hopped up front.

Horatio was less keen about my 'having a go'. Perhaps it was the fact I'd pointed out several times that the dashboard speed dial went up to 150kph and 'it wouldn't go up that high if it wasn't designed to go that fast'. 'You're a menace,' he'd say, and we would continue to beetle along at 50kph but now, at last, it was my turn – after all, Ralph was allowed and he was basically a child. With utmost reluctance, Horatio relented, shuffling back to pillion himself like a martyr, and let me take the reins. By this point the others had raced ahead so I sought to immediately make up the distance with a run in the high 80s. 'This is better!' I shouted over my shoulder, 'see how smooth this – BUGGER! Ha. Wow. Sorry. Ha! You okay?' but I wasn't sure if Horatio could hear me over the wind, the engine or his hysterical screaming.

Erlend had demonstrated 'tactical leaning' to us all at the very beginning, how to shift ourselves about the bike and counterbalance its weight. That had been very useful and necessary when negotiating the slaloms out of Longyearbyen. However, for the most part we were able to open up and arrow across the snow-flats as young Luke Skywalker sped across Tatooine, with only the occasional switch-back pass or snaking descent down a glacier muzzle requiring more than a swivel of the hips.

In broad Grøndalen we made good speed and passed a herd of stumpy reindeer snuffling for lichens and grass beneath the snow. Once out of the valley, we climbed north

---

* Or, more Svalbardian, the Battle of Hoth in *The Empire Strikes Back*, which was filmed on the Hardangerjøkulen glacier near Finse in northeast Norway.

towards some derelict mine workings which looked more crash-landed the closer we got. Broken, half-buried, dangling hawsers, all open iron mouths and blind windows; the buildings seemed to reel in their ruination. Below us, dimpled Grønfjorden dazzled, so brilliant we had to shade our eyes. Across the water, further mountains formed a rumpled blue meringue, their folds trailing on to the frosted fjord. Turning north I saw the cloudless sky smudged black: Barentsburg.

——

'Porridge with meat' may not sound appealing but it's actually very nice. Perhaps the uniquely breakfast associations of 'porridge' and worrying non-specificity of 'meat' let the union down, I don't know, but as I say, it was perfectly fine. The Russian salad was similarly *fine*, although by that stage I'd come to the conclusion that everything was either named ironically – 'salad' – or with such potent honesty the mind shut down.

'It's porridge with meat.'

'Sounds good!'

The highlight was the borscht. The borscht was wonderful but borscht is always either wonderful or terrible – there seems no middle ground with borscht. This was the first time I'd had Ukrainian borscht and I can report that it was superb. It had more in common with the hot clear Polish sort than the creamy cold purple type and I could feel it fortifying my soul on our post-lunch walk around the town. Both Barentsburg and Pyramiden are mining outposts. But whilst Pyramiden was abandoned in 1998, Barentsburg still excavates unprofitable coal in order to keep the Russian flag flying – 'It's political,' Erlend told us with a shrug, which was actually quite unusual to hear, a strange jabby word in that shrouded scape because Svalbard seemed a world away from politics, at least those of the twenty-first century; because, yes, there was Lenin: the second most northerly bust, red granite head on a pedestal. And there were faded murals of chiselled miners inspiring Cyrillic dictums – 'Strong hands create heat and light!' Timeless yet close at hand – hibernating rather than forever asleep. Beyond Lenin was the governor's house, Palladian and arsenic green. Down the hill towards the harbour was a Russian orthodox church, dark timbered spigot, one of very few buildings to survive when the *Tirpitz* shelled the town to pieces in 1943. And beyond all these, the Russian Embassy, with its high fence and cameras; the most anonymous building of the lot.

Later on the trip we met Sergey Chernikov, a Muscovite who works as operational manager and specialist field guide for the Arcticugol Trust* – Arctic Coal, the company who run Barentsburg and oversee Pyramiden. 'We are not political people here,' he told Horatio, 'but we come for political reasons. Many of the Ukrainians fled from the war but life up here is not political. Russian tourists come to Pyramiden to see polar bears. Some remember Soviet life but the young are not interested. It is British people and Westerners who are interested.'

How would I describe the people I met in Svalbard? Strange as it may sound I'd call them young and diverse. On our trip we met Poles, Ugandans, Brits, Americans,

---

* Арктикуголь – Arctic Coal.

Vietnamese, Ukrainians and Russians, most working in either guiding or hospitality – hoteliers, restaurateurs, dog-sledders, guides – most under thirty, seeking new starts at the top of the world. Svalbard must feel like a blank canvas to many incomers – a prospect made more attractive by the fact that, uniquely, Svalbard is a visa-free zone so anybody may live and work there on an indefinite basis regardless of country of citizenship, provided they can support them-selves – not always an easy task since the cost of living is high.[4] A place of prospectors, then, Arctic émigrés; people set to have a go, independent thinkers and refugees. Longyearbyen is a frontier town and each day new faces arrive, some planning to stay a weekend, some intending to stay full stop; to test their mettle in the winter when the sun is absent from late October until the beginning of March and the truly dark season from mid November to February when it's pitch black twenty-four hours a day and temperatures can drop to –30° C. Add to this the need for a snowmobile, dogs or skis to get anywhere out of town and the fact one can't do so without 'bear protection' in the form of a rifle or heavy revolver and it's easy to see the old west in the high north. Longyearbyen's gold rush is tourism.

Barentsburg felt very different. Where Longyearbyen was flux, Barentsburg was statuesque. Where Longyearbyen was Huf Haus-ish with wood eaves in sweet-wrapper tints, the blocks of Barentsburg were slightly bottom of the box; the away-kits of sports teams facing relegation – maroons, sharp greens, beige vanilla fudge, mustards at the back of the fridge. Khrushchyovka – generic concrete pre-fabs with the occasional curved corner to assuage the Arctic wind. The mine workers' living quarters had a Tetris fascia reminiscent

of naval aquaflage. There were boxy black garages nearer the
fjord. The mine workings, conveyor-ways, steam vents and
cranes were corrugations painted blood and custard.

Barentsburg is building its tourism industry but it's a
way behind its neighbours. The former company town now
has a hotel for visitors, a restaurant and a bar, but it's still
very raw and this sets it apart. As we left, tracking back
towards the mountains under gantries and flues, I reflected
that the past couple of hours had been some of the most
uncanny I'd ever known, but why? I couldn't pin it down.
Was it the relative lack of people or the silence which made
it so eerie – the sense that everyone was either underground
or no longer there at all? Only later did it strike me that
perhaps the strangest thing was that, whilst I'd seen some
workers – distant figures in overalls – I saw no coal. No
coal at all. The heart and purpose of the town remained
hidden under snow.

———

That night we suppered and slept at Isfjord Radio – once a
vital link between Svalbard and the Norwegian mainland,
now a hotel. The journey there was remarkable in terms of
the country we covered, the long run down and round
Grønfjorden which featured several steep climbs over pillow
drifts, cutting up in zags, taking run-ups to better attack the
scoop and whip of it. We cut over a long stretch of ice at the
fjord's end, conscious of the darkness of the water below but
Erlend instilled great calm. Like the climbing guides I'd met
in the Alps, he led the way, cheerfully beckoning us on
having showed there was nothing to worry about. I liked

him a lot. He took his job seriously, thought about things before giving an opinion when we asked him questions about distances, terrain, names and meanings – that peak like a scallop shell over there, Erlend – and bears, of course, and weather. During our walk around Barentsburg he'd lit a pipe and begun to smoke it, as Horatio might roll a cigarette. From then on whenever we stopped awhile, for kuksa coffee, say, or so Alex could fly his video drone round a glacier, they'd smoke. About day four I noticed that Erlend had a sooty mark on the pocket of his jacket where the pipe had burnt a hole.

'Has anyone seen it?' Alex would shout, every so often. 'Can anyone hear it?' ... Nothing heightens an Arctic silence like the inaudible purr of an invisible drone. 'Bloody thing's gone! Can anybody ... damn ...' – but the glacier was massive and silent. The only sounds as we strained to listen, other than the automated voice telling Alex that his drone was dangerously low on power, were the cooling click of the snowmobiles, and Horatio and Erlend puffing their tobacco. We looked to the sky but the sky was empty. Then a tiny mosquito whine was discerned, swelling in a half minute to a solid chop above our heads then softly down into Ralph's raised hands. It had a homing function, apparently. 'Bloody thing,' muttered Alex, packing it away. Horatio and Erlend puffed on.

Before Kapp Linné we trundled over a lake, up and down great waving slopes overflown by pinnacles which looked to contain some excellent routes – 'sadly bad rocks', Erlend told me later, explaining that the mountains were a mix of grit, shale, and sandstone; the sort of loose 'rotten' rock that climbers call choss.

All the while we'd been traversing those white sweeps or nosing along shady chutes, Erlend had been keeping watch – an eye on us, were we falling behind? A weather-eye on the world around, were we alone? His rifle was stowed in a case on his bike so he had it in easy reach should anything occur. But nothing occurred, the crystal lake was still, the summits silent, nothing moved. Only us, spiders in a giant bath, making for the coast and the distant dish and thistle of the radio station, long shadowed on the cape below.

———

Save sled dogs, reindeer and people, the only other creature I saw in those first few days was an Arctic fox. People crowded the window to see the creature, passing binoculars, dinner forgotten. I saw it over their shoulders, an amethyst flash out beyond the tethers and station antennae. 'Ninety-nine per cent of Svalbard foxes are white,' Erlend told us, delighted.* What luck! Such a rare creature accounting 100 per cent of my day's wildlife – vivid life out on the glare ice. I can picture it now, flinty blue, violet where it met the sun.†

---

* This is true, 99 per cent of Svalbard foxes are white *when Svalbard is white,* but all Arctic foxes moult and become brown in the summer. Also, a tiny fraction remain brown all year round and these are also, confusingly, referred to as blue – thanks to Dr Nick Crumpton of the Royal Society for this note.

† If Svalbard's fauna had been hard to spot, the flora was almost entirely hidden. We'd passed by a few bare twigs pushing up through the snow. There was a bit of scurvy grass and moss in Longyearbyen but nothing in the way of bushes, nothing above knee height. 'Yes, Spitsbergen isn't big on trees,' Erlend told us at one point. 'If ever you're lost in a forest here, just sit up.'

Later in the twilight that passed for night, I stood outside with Erlend as he smoked. He'd been walking people back and forth to the dormitories, a frozen hundred metres from the main hotel, and still had his rifle on his shoulder. 'Bears,' he'd said simply, when we'd arrived. 'When we're outside I walk with you. If I'm not there, you wait.'

Are there many bears out here? I asked him. He nodded. 'There can be, and bears are hungry and unpredictable.'

Three months after our stay, a bear broke into the station garage and ransacked a store room, ate some chocolate and a jar of jam, smashed a lot of wine, then squeezed through a small window and escaped back on to the cape. The next day it repeated the raid before disappearing down the rusty coast for good.

Bears on Svalbard generally eat seals, which they hunt on landfast sea ice or out on the floating pack. However, warming seas and a lack of ice-floe are taking their toll. They're hungry. And whilst they'll also eat reindeer, birds, eggs, whale and walrus carcasses if they get them, they aren't well adapted to hunting on land and, historically, such things have only ever supplemented seals. In recent years the bears' lack of access to seals has made them bolder scavengers, so whilst their new taste for jam and chocolate is tolerated – garage doors and windows can be replaced – everybody knows that things are unlikely to get any better for the bears and the jam sits at the thin end of a wedge which ends at people.

The next morning, stopped for a drink and drone misadventure an hour out of Isfjord, Erlend told us of bears who swim out to sea ice that isn't there. This is happening more and more, he said. Polar bears are used to leaving land and swimming out to ice they cannot see. Generations have made that journey beyond the horizon but in times past it was never a leap of faith. They can't see it but they've swum to ice they couldn't see before; a deep urgent drive compels them, but the ice is often no longer there. So they swim and swim, further out in search of ice and they drown. 'It's awful,' he concluded, to silence.

Last year a mother bear and two cubs were seen swimming out from the south coast of Svalbard. Several weeks later the bear was seen on Bear Island with a single cub. That's over 400 kilometres.*

How tired they must have been, those two. Beyond imagination. But what then, swim back? Swim back having eaten less, been so thrown out of kilter, so physically stressed – the idea of that becoming the norm, year on year, because the will to swim out from land to the ice with the seals is hard-wired into them, as swallows and storks migrate, so deep in the bears is the urge to find that ice . . .

—

* I can find no record of this swim but during our trip to Svalbard the story was repeated and acknowledged by several guides – some even suggested that the bears swam to Jan Mayen, 1,000 kilometres south of Svalbard, rather than Bear Island/Bjørnøya, which seems impossible. So the bears become modern myths and ghosts, and people conflate stories of survival or endow them with superpowers to endure. Epic sea swims are not unprecedented – journeys of over 400 miles/650 kilometres have been documented – but bears pushed to such feats more often drown than survive. As the fast-ice melt accelerates and sea ice coverage diminishes, bears swim ever further to find floe. Erlend told us that bears now have six to seven weeks less of hunting every season. – 'Longest Polar Bear Swim Recorded — 426 Miles Straight. Study predicts more long-distance swims due to shrinking sea ice', *National Geographic News*, Anne Casselman, 2011.

Huge frozen deltas, shining flats, several-mile-wide estuaries refrigerated and milled to a fine finish so we ran through clouds of powder at impossible knots beneath the glare of Lewis Chessmen alps.

Ice-cave interiors electric blue, eons of ice veined and rippled and us standing in its cortex, luminous vortex, back-lit and boggling. The old coal mine, little more than a wooden shed so blasted it was furry and the entrails of a steam engine which once hauled trucks blinking from inside a mountain, out along a pier, now gone.

The frozen Barents Sea, solid to the skyline – conceivably solid all the way to the pole. We rode out from Svalbard's coast about a mile, stopping now and then so Erlend could check the depth of the ice with a hatchet, hacking down a foot or two in a cloud of swarf, giving a thumbs up and waving us on once satisfied.

Beneath us the solid sea subtly undulated, the faintest memory of waves. We circled neon green icebergs locked in epoxy – so much of the ice resembled glue – superglue verglas, clear ice hacked white as PVA, the thick pearl-escent resin of the sea ice, the pressure-ridge ice which burst in petrified eruptions comparable to expanding foam.

Other ices were more glassy: tumbled sea glass, Bristol blue glaciers cut with lazurite and soap. 'The bluer the ice, the higher the pressure in the glacier,' Erlend explained, adding that a metre of snow could become compressed to a svelte smidge of ice over millennia. Later he put a chunk of glacier in a pot on the wood stove of a cabin and bade us listen to the pop of age-old air. The pressure in the ice was clearly immense; occasionally the block spat a bubble which made the room resound. I made some tea from the melted water and it was damn fine tea.

And so the week went on. Finding ice features on glacial moraine: frozen humps like breaching whales bursting from the permafrost. Opening cabins, defusing 'bear measures' – Heath Robinson barbs and barricades – sleeping on floors, sleeping on elderly sofas, waking to find the windows not only covered with condensation but the condensation frosted to pearly rime. The moment when, having stopped for lunch atop Spitsbergen's largest icecap, after Erlend had probed with his crevasse-finding stick to make safe and check we could all dismount, we as one turned to discover that the lunch, the fuel, almost all the supplies, were missing from the back of Dominic's snowmobile. 'Oh shit,' he said – the most sincere 'oh shit' Svalbard has ever heard – and back we went and found the sled, forlorn but intact, a few miles behind and then, out of sheer bloody-mindedness, I think, Erlend re-hitched it and returned us all to the same spot as before for lunch *there* because there was good. And we had lunch – Norwegian army rations, enlivened by hot water, mixed with wooden spoons – and discovered that meals on icecaps taste better than meals anywhere else to the power of ten. Each mealtime I'd think of Billy Pilgrim in *Slaughterhouse 5*, dipping a finger in malt syrup on pain of death with the result that every cell in his body shook him with ravenous gratitude and applause.[5]

The only thing that really irked me as the trip progressed was the snowmobiles' noise, their fizzing whine. Such miffs were focused and increased every time we met another group like ourselves. We could hear them a mile off, even through our helmets and thick balaclavas, high-pitched and insistent, wasps at our picnic, bombinations the lot of them. And they probably thought the same of us, of course. The problem was 'people like us'.

We were careening past Svea* up the frozen Van Mijen-fjorden, over bumps and ruts beneath the snow and solidified rilles above. There was a lot of judder; I thought again of Alex's description of snowmobiles being like punctured motorbikes. I'd once been in a car that experienced a blow-out. We'd been on a motorway travelling fairly fast. For a few seconds, as the burst tyre span and whomp-whomp-whomped – but louder than that, loud as thunder – we might have been in a Chinook. The snow near Svea was all hard-shoulder roar, but in a sense I was still on a motorway – either side of us the trident impressions of runners and caterpillar tracks coursed out: ten, twenty, thirty wide. Sometimes we drove on valley floors grooved as vinyl, buzz-sawed by legion riders – if they were all also two to a bike, the mind reeled as to how many people there were skirling round the archipelago at any given moment. Up and down between Longyearbyen and Pyramiden, that was the main highway. Over towards Barentsburg and Svea it was quieter but if one looked at any pristine wilderness close enough you'd find it chopped up somewhere, score-marks left in the wake of people belting elsewhere. And we'd pass them and wave, as bus drivers wave when their buses pass – I always

---

* Svea – full name *Sveagruva*, meaning 'Swedish mine' – was a mining settle-ment at the head of Van Mijenfjorden, closed by the Norwegian government in 2017. The third largest settlement on Spitsbergen after Longyearbyen and Barentsburg, Svea had no permanent inhabitants – workers would commute from Longyearbyen. Today it's a ghost town but moves are afoot to try and emulate Pyramiden's success as a tourist attraction.

liked that as a child, the bus drivers raising a hand as they passed, but that's Bristol, it isn't the Arctic . . . and we passed so many people, people like us, whizzing by, foil-faced, flash-helmeted, faceless, and whilst I mostly raised a hand or nodded 'hello' – even on the regular occasions when chapters overtook us; *zip, zip, zip, zip, zip* . . . five, six, eight, ten at a time – it wasn't normal, it was more a resigned acknowledgement that they were here too. 'Here we are,' my wave said. 'Here we all are . . . too many. But it's nobody's fault; it's everybody's fault. Here we are.' And all the time I had the image of those poor bastard bears swimming out to ice that didn't exist. The spectre pursuing me over the snow. I couldn't shift the sadness however fast I drove, however loudly Horatio screamed.

I'd travelled to the end of the world to discover that there are too many of us travelling to the end of the world – I mean, who saw that coming?

Completely nonsensically I wanted it all for myself and I wanted it left alone. Give ice-land back to the ice-bears. I wanted us gone, starting with everyone else on a snowmobile; *those guys* – I was a frigid dog in the manger; fractious fox in an icebox. And those poor bears kept swimming before my eyes, disappearing over the horizon.

———

We knifed off Nordenskiöldbreen's enormous glacial maw crazed turquoise, shattered windscreen fathoms thick.

Down we tacked, helter-skelter, tactical leaning all the way, on to the shaven Artex fjord, flat and scratched a thousand times by people who'd ridden down like ourselves or motored over from Pyramiden, on the far shore, to see the sapphire face up close. The snow and ice were raked in doughnuts, scuffed in crazy patterns; Nazca Lines of scoot. We circled too, to look more deeply into the blue supreme. I'd never seen anything like it – a vault of a sort of insect iridescence, the metallic cyan of dragonflies, the holographic carapace of beetles blown a hundred feet tall. We hovered as gannets over a sardine shoal, silent and awestruck. Then slowly, unwillingly, we turned and aimed ourselves towards Pyramiden and on the way it dawned that this was why Erlend guided; the ecstatic reaction of people who'd never seen a glacier being shown one of the finest glaciers on Earth – reactions of gibbering googly-eyed wonder in our cohort's case. He was using his knowledge and experience to get us to the right place on respectful terms with the landscape – observing and preserving the tape on the gallery floor, as Stefán likened his job at FÍ – and Svalbard's tourism industry is certified sustainable, the Governor's Office have published a masterplan[6] to future-proof and grow Longyearbyen as a destination and staging post for Arctic adventure. This will not happen if there is no Arctic left to explore, all parties agree. The visitor numbers involved are much lower than Iceland – Longyearbyen airport isn't a stopover to anywhere other than Ny-Ålesund – which brings me to another point: Ny-Ålesund – a settlement essentially closed to all but climate scientists, surrounded by a protected zone. The rest of Svalbard is not like that, although some areas are safeguarded to the point of 'out of bounds', but, in general, people visit Longyearbyen, Barentsburg and Pyramiden, shuttling over the country in between or sailing round the coast and up the fjords in summer. This has been the case for the last hundred years, except now clean tourism has replaced dirty coal and, short-stay visitors aside, the permanent workforce is two-thirds that of the 1980s.

In summer, jet aircraft land daily at Longyearbyen but in the dark season flights are massively reduced as the archipelago holes up for winter. Before 1900 there was large-scale industrial whaling. Now there is far less whaling. In 2018 the wildlife is revered and protected as never before, there are *rolls* of tape on the gallery floor . . . so, looking coolly at the situation, things in Svalbard seem pretty good. Yes, there are some crazy inconsistencies – Longyearbyen doesn't recycle its rubbish, it's either incinerated or shipped to Sweden – but things are pretty good. UNESCO states of Svalbard that '[T]he natural biological diversity and the ongoing ecological processes are largely intact. Major technical encroachments are mostly concentrated in the few settlements, and Svalbard can be regarded as the largest and least disturbed wilderness area in Norway.'[7]

So why think and write myself into knots over Svalbard's situation? Because it was so magnificent. So spectacular. So unlike anywhere I'd ever been. Truly unspoilt and elementally pure to the extent that the immediate need to protect it hit me like a lightning bolt. I felt it deeply, a sense of revelation which bypassed my brain, all the usual checks and balances, and arced straight into paternal instincts, the need to conserve and protect; the 'overview effect' psychologists have identified in returned astronauts; a cognitive shift towards custodianship following an experience of awe.

'In the mountains you are small compared to the surrounding view so you more easily and more intensely feel that you are a part of something greater,' wrote Arne Naess,[8] and there in that crucible of frozen fjords, I felt myself part of something great beyond words.

Ahead, Erlend raised a hand in the air, the sign for our peloton to slow and stop. He'd skewed off right, I noticed, into an area away from the beaten track. When we arrived he was off his bike and standing, pointing at the feathery deck. Prints. Massive prints. A deep heel, a rounded palm, five toes – the three in the middle tipped with inch-long claws. Bigger than my face, bigger than my head, 'Big as a bin lid!' I said to Horatio. 'Big as orchestra cymbals?' he suggested, kindly – 'Better,' I agreed. 'More splendid than bins.'

I placed my wool glove next to the print. The glove was large, oversized on me, but would have fitted comfortably within the snow paw. It would have swallowed my bare hand five times over – as would the bear, of course. 'A young female,' stated Erlend. 'Maybe three years old.'

'Are males much bigger?'

'Much bigger, yes.'

'I see,' we all said in unison.

———

Pyramiden appeared as a long black line, a charcoal wharf, a Meccano crane. The pyramidal mountain after which the town is named loomed behind – the sudden summit streaked with snow, the umber under of the lower flanks poking through, as if it had been gone over with a sepia crayon – a massive brass rubbing of a mountain.

We passed the coal port with its several buildings, unadorned blocks of washed-out red. Grey depots, single-storeyed and flat-roofed. A wharf, a silo, a conveyor, a pylon, a fence. It was actually a jolt to see buildings again. I took note of each. A wooden chapel. A set of swings. Here was a pipeline up on stilts. There was a Constructivist monument shard.* A humpbacked bridge! How fun. A group of snowmobilers ahead were making a hash of it, stalling, revving an awful din. Back they slid, took a run-up, one, two, three – bashful Evel Knievels. We followed, keen to do Erlend proud. No problem. We stopped one after the other in front of Hotel Tulpan – the most northerly hotel on Planet Earth. Pink-bricked, curve-cornered, the Tulpan was a twenty-four-room palace on concrete legs beneath which three semi-tame foxes were seen to gambol – two white, one blue. 'I thought you said they were rare,' I teased Erlend. 'They are,' he shot back. 'I am shocked. I've never seen a fox so tame.'

The first floor of the hotel featured a restaurant bar decked out in garish Overlook Kubrick, red and orange with a parquet floor, a few pentagrams and eagles thrown about, the bar overseen by a barman who seemed to have been taught customer service by Mark E. Smith.

'You smoke these. Russian cigarettes,' he told the fellow next to me as I waited for a beer.

'Um, but they're not the cigarettes I asked for,' he queried, 'you have the cigarettes I want just over . . .'

'Russian cigarettes,' repeated the implacable barman, already focused elsewhere, 'the best.'

Erlend was on the third floor in a 'European' room. Everyone else was on the second floor where the rooms had

---

* A red stela akin to Vladimir Tatlin's *Monument to the Third International* (1920) but a higher spire splinter built without curves. The final ton of coal extracted from Pyramiden's mine sits at its base in a hopper.

been preserved 'old-style Soviet'. The European rooms had showers. My room had a shower tray with a complementary can of deodorant but no shower head or shower plumbing. 'Ha!' announced Horatio in finest Bond-villain Berkoff. 'You wish for shower? Maybe you try American hotel.'

Old-style Soviets clearly liked their own space where twin rooms were concerned. The two single beds were as far apart as the architecture allowed, hugging opposite walls. The rest of the room contained a mismatched desk and tiny chair, a cast iron radiator without controls which threatened to boil us in our sleep,* and a square window bolted shut. Between the corridor and the bedroom was an anteroom lined with massive coffer cupboards as if, as well as being haphephobic, old-style Soviets habitually packed a change of spacesuit.

It was marvellous, gloriously eccentric.

After dinner, Erlend and I stayed up to drink another beer and I took the opportunity to quiz him about his life in Longyearbyen. Did he guide on snowmobiles all year round? No no! In summer he guides in sea-kayaks on Adventfjorden or crews whale-watching tourist boats – occasionally having to bop a walrus with an oar if it gets too close to the dinghy.

'Are you sure this is real, Erlend?'

---

* The heating radiator is a Russian invention, of course – thought up by Prussian-born Franz San Galli, a businessman living in St Petersburg, in 1855. The Russian for radiator is радиатор. The Russian for, 'Excuse me, my radiator is dangerously hot, can you help?' is 'Извините, мой радиатор опасно горячий, вы можете помочь?' . . . 'No, seriously, I think this radiator wishes me dead': 'Нет, серьезно, я думаю, что этот радиатор хочет, чтобы я умер.'

'Oh yes! Absolutely. They get quite truculent around the boats.'*

And then there was the story about the group of Hasidic Jews he'd taken out camping in the early dark season.

'I don't think they'd ever been out of New York before. It was a disaster,' he confided. 'Completely mad. I was trying to watch for bears but several refused to change out of their wet clothes when they slept.'

So they got cold?

'They got very cold. One kept screaming he was going to die, that he had hypothermia; how he hated yurts.'

Did he have hypothermia?

'No,' sighed Erlend, 'but nobody slept. They hated it. Complete disaster.'

So you're saying our group are a dream, Erlend?

'Oh yes! Absolutely, Dan.'

———

Next morning Sergey Chernikov met us on the hotel steps. Erlend had asked him to give us a tour – everyone knowing everyone else. Sergey had on a red quilted jacket over which ran a strap to a rifle which he wore on his front – a solid bolt-action carbine with a fine birch stock. He also had a sidearm in an orange holster, possibly a flare gun to frighten bears, and a large bunch of keys which rattled as he walked. We all shook hands and Horatio got out his pad and pencil. He had on his charming professional face, I noticed, a

---

* Erlend was constantly dropping in words like 'truculent' – his English was outstanding and impeccable.

pleasant open demeanour at odds with my slightly leaden head. To rub it in, he began speaking Russian. And Sergey, smiling, clearly understood. What a terrible git. He began to good-humouredly enquire whether Sergey's employers, Arcticugol Trust, were *all right* – were they oligarchical, incompetent or cynical? Good questions. The questions of a cosmopolitan cultured man. In contrast, I reflected, the previous evening I had pressed Erlend to clarify how one best bops a walrus on the nose with an oar.

It took only a moment to step beyond the hotel's ambit and pass into Pyramiden's silent centre. It truly was a ghost town. We were the only people on the streets.

The buildings were laid out around a central park of monuments and grass. As we walked up this centre aisle, Sergey showed us a large dormitory, formerly home to miners' families. Empty now, the windows streaked, although kittiwakes return each summer to nest on the sills.

Pausing in the process of unlocking an ornate door, Sergey drew our attention to the boxes on the outside of the building opposite. Rather than the air conditioning units we might assume, they were small fridge boxes 'for milk and such'. People didn't need refrigerators, he went on, turning back to the door, because everyone's food was free and served here, in the canteen. Beyond the door was a shadowy foyer and a double staircase which led up to the food hall, above which was a mosaic mural of mountains and fjords, surging clouds and a cosmic Byzantine sun. The canteen floor was further parquet. Either side of the serving station were ornate wooden pillars topped with pineapple-like florets. Gold sun streaked through high windows, illuminating flock wallpaper and delicate pendant lights. Out back the giant soup vats and ovens in the tiled kitchens looked as though they'd been abandoned weeks rather than decades ago. But the petals of flaking paint, fallen in drifts from the walls and ceilings told of the true time passed since the day in 1998 when Pyramiden was abandoned. The atmosphere prickled. The kitchens felt charged. A service lift stalled between floors. A stopped clock, flex pulled out at twelve minutes past five. Round steamers with their fly-trap tops sprung open. A series of overhead extraction hoods yawning square, fine rust creeping on their balalaika bodies. The wallpapers here were mid-peel, the plaster underneath beginning to develop varicose veins, the floor dusted with strange pollen – a bright crush of plaster, mould and pigment. Empty offices, chairs and desks at odd angles as though the person working had just pushed them aside, upped and left. Run away. Alex and Ralph padded past, we all padded, it felt wrong to stomp about, the place was as much memorial as museum.

'Wonderful, isn't it?' Alex whispered. 'Incredibly moving.'

And he was right. Abandoned, the building marinated in memory, human traces, story. The fact it was left alone was key. Its dilapidation lent it a sadness and dignity, a unique character; the abandonment felt personal. Unique. Larkin's words again:

> It stays as it was left,
> Shaped to the comfort of the last to go
> As if to win them back.[9]

I returned to the main hall to find Horatio and Sergey discussing socialism. Pyramiden was one of the places where it worked, Sergey said, describing the outpost as 'a snow-dome; somewhere where the USSR could show off how things could be'. Wages were as much as seven times higher than on the mainland, living standards were extraordinarily good and so there was much competition to be posted to Svalbard. Everything was subsidised. When the Soviet Union dissolved in 1991, things carried on for a few years but without the USSR's support coal mining at Pyramiden was unsustainable.

We passed on to the school where Sergey, proud as a parent, showed us classrooms he'd salvaged from dereliction, with exercise books, paintings, murals, and a project on Little Red Riding Hood all crisp and fresh as the children left them. 'My friends on the mainland go from school to university to work,' he said. 'Where is the passion? My passion is restoring this place. I want to show how people lived here.'

He loves the history, he tells us, he feels it important to document and preserve how people lived here, his people. The Russian success of Pyramiden, the far flung utopia of it, this community which existed, endured and succeeded beyond any cultural caricature or stereotype. '*This was extraordinary*', Sergey's sensitive curation declares. '*This was not for nothing. It was not all propaganda. The people here achieved great things.*'

He told us the story of the town's central crest – a polar bear before a red banner above a blue globe emblazoned 79°* – a grand version of the Arcticugol Trust's insignia several metres tall.

---

*   Which it isn't – it's at 78° 39' N. – the proud Russians clearly rounded up in celebration of Pyramiden's great works and perhaps to kick a bit of snow in the more northerly face of Ny-Ålesund.

'They got a famous Russian artist up from Moscow to paint it,' Sergey told us with a broad smile. 'And the man arrived and said, "I've never seen a polar bear, what do they look like?" And, because it was the wrong time of year for bears and there were none around, they said, "Okay, just paint a really big white dog without a tail." And so, if you look closely, that's what it resembles. Although I think he did quite well.'

At the head of the town was the Palace of Culture and here again we met Lenin, red on a pedestal, his expression slightly softer than that of his Barentsburg twin. The palace contained a grand concert hall, cinema and gymnasium – parquet flooring off the scale! And again we found rooms apparently left untouched, although some – the room with the piano set up for a Soviet singalong, hammer and sickle flag draped over the keys – felt like they *might perhaps* have been staged. But for every curated room like that there were ten which gave me chills, a birch bench in a room of books, slowly bleaching, behind which the windows looked out on to silver ice flats, mountains and sky.

And so we toured the swimming pool named after Yuri Gagarin. The olympic-size pool, drained; dark chamber cut with sun – lane ropes hanging loose, the public gallery empty. The silence was such that we held our breath. It was impossible not to imagine the great room peopled, the sounds of swimmers splashing, turning, talking, the gallery full. As with the kitchens, the pool felt electric, the silence expectant – the patient building dormant, paused.

Back out in the sunshine we thanked Sergey. Apparently our half-hour tour had taken two. Time had flown. I'd only seen inside four buildings. We'd hardly begun to scratch the surface of Pyramiden's history.

Pyramiden's crest, Svalbard. Photograph: Dan Richards

Somewhere around us a twenty-bed hospital mouldered together with the remnants of a radio station, a brick factory, fire station, the jail, greenhouses, power station. We'd not touched on the coal mine workings at all and my eyes were drawn to the mining lifts which ran up and into the mountain's face. Two covered cableways scaling the scree behind a handsome administration building and further out, near the port, the Mechanical Institute with its huge compass emblem – aspic treasures unexplored, slowly acceding back to foxes, reindeer, birds and bears. I don't think Sergey mourns the decay, he's fighting a beautiful battle fully aware the war is lost. The arctic climate slows the decline but Pyramiden's atrophy is a huge part of its beauty. The tide has turned and humanity's grip is loosening, year on year.

A final handshake, a brief farewell and we were back out on the fjord, streaking back towards Nordenskiöldbreen, back towards the bear prints, possibly even some bears.

Pyramiden's mechanical workshops below the mountain summit. Photograph: Dan Richards

EPILOGUE

The female bear was dozing, two cubs by her side. Erlend had stopped his snowmobile and was stood up on the running boards, scanning through binoculars. He pointed and passed me down the glasses.

I found her turned away in the shade of an iceberg, her back like a furry pear.

A periscope ear flicked and swivelled, the only sign she was awake, alert. I realised I was doing mental calculations as to how fast she could get over here – twist on to her feet and cover the 300 metres of ice between us – forty seconds perhaps. A fully grown bear can cover a short distance at 30 to 40kph. But everything was still. Calm. As so often on the trip, people were whispering. Through the silent tunnel of the glasses the cubs began to wrestle. Joshing, nipping playfully. Wonderful to see. I couldn't hear them, the wind was blowing away from us, towards them. They would have heard us coming from miles across the fjord, the mother knew exactly where we were, that circling ear – her attitude of sleep was just that; she was acting, she was not relaxed, she was lying down, senses cocked. Polar bears can smell a seal twenty miles away. For us it was a thrill to see some bears at a safe distance. For them it would have been like trying to ignore another person in the same phone-box.

The bears weren't actually white at all, they were creamy, peachy, straw – particularly round their necks; slightly blue on the muzzle with black lips and noses. Their pads were slate. They lay as my cat at home sprawls in his basket by the Aga, except they were lying on a frozen fjord in the Arctic a few hundred metres from three Englishmen, two Welshman and a Norwegian . . . and about forty Russians with snowmobiles standing fifty metres to our right.

We'd been late getting over to the other side of the fjord after our tour of Pyramiden, added to which we'd stopped en route to watch a ringed seal basking on the ice beside its hole. Like the bears, the seal had seen and heard us coming. It stared at us blearily from a posture best described as 'trying to carry on a conversation whilst lying on your back and reaching under the sofa'. After a few seconds, it seemed to blink and, with great gravitas, disappeared. We beetled over to the hole and looked down. The seal wasn't there, obviously, but it was an extraordinary portal, scooped and rounded with slush. The water below was darkest green. I didn't fancy it. The impressions of the sharp flippers on the ice where the creature had lain revealed the tools with which it kept its egress open. A seal has several holes on the go at

---

* 'What time of the day did you see them?' asked my zoologist friend Dr Nick Crumpton when I got back to London. Late morning, I told him. 'Ah, well, polar bear hair is actually transparent and not white at all – it's hollow and merely scatters light, making them appear white – their skin is actually black. It's pretty neat optics. But when the light is softer, around sunset, they can look pinkish. Of course, they might have been blood-stained too . . .'

any time, Erlend told us, and being only semi-aquatic they need to haul out regularly to rest, to get warm and dry, to moult, and to give birth to their pups in spring. But polar bears are perfectly capable of lying silently beside a seal hole for a week, and whilst the bears can operate at any time of the day or night, their activity generally follows that of their main prey and seals are larks, so polar bears are most active in the morning – the early bear catching the seal.

Good luck with that, I thought, good luck trying to do beary things when you're surrounded by pungent people with strident cameras and snowmobiles. Each spring the bears must steel themselves for Pyramiden's paparazzi circus.* And the camera, as John Berger pointed out, violates an animal's normal invisibility and deprives the animal of its own ability to observe:

A recent, very well-produced book of animal photographs (*La Fête Sauvage* by Frederic Rossif) announces in its preface: 'Each of these pictures lasted in real time less than three hundredths of a second, they are far beyond the capacity of the human eye. What we see here is something never before seen, because it is totally invisible.' In the accompanying ideology, animals are always the observed. The fact that they can observe us has lost all significance.[1]

---

* At least nobody's out here hunting them any more, you might say, but the presence of tourists inevitably means that every year bears are shot 'in self-defence' – a term that rather suggests that it's the bears who act inappropriately when most often the opposite is true; most often the ill-prepared housebreakers shoot the ursine owner. Erlend was firm: 'When bears get shot, it's rarely their fault.'

The cubs had gone back to sleep, tired from their tussle. We all stood quietly, conscious of our luck, the great fortune to see *Ursus maritimus* in the wild; because it was wild, deeply so – Svalbard and the bears. We were the interlopers and had been ever since we stepped off the plane a week before – had been ever since we started whaling there in the seventeenth century; will ever be, perhaps, and thank goodness for that.

Erlend leant forward to restart his engine and turn the snowmobile away. We followed, leaving the polar bears be.

———

What to think about all this? What to say?

In the moment, as we were driving away, my feelings were many and mixed. Here we were and here also were a great many others. Too many – and not just snowmobiles but *people*: too many people because the bears had been bothered, and people should not bother the bears. But I had seen them and been amazed and moved by the experience. I felt hugely conflicted. In the immediate aftermath of the trip all I wanted to do was suggest to other people that they not do likewise. Don't go to Svalbard. Don't get on a snowmobile. Don't buzz off in search of ice bears. Don't bother the bears . . . like I'd done.

I tried to make sense of the experience in a letter to my Swedish friend, Gonz.

I struggled to explain it, dancing around the idea that perhaps more landscapes need to be conserved as Ny-Ålesund is protected by being placed off limits. Fewer snowmobiles, more BBC nature programmes – I tied myself up in knots

of well-meaning, aware all the while that I sounded sancti-
monious . . . so I was delighted when Gonz wrote back to
say that he'd been interested in what I had to say and understood my perspective because he'd had similar ideas himself,
many times, and occasionally still caught himself having
'selfish and condescending thoughts for others' – something
I took on the chin.

'I have to say I don't agree with you,' his letter continued.
'All places should be explored because we as humans are
explorers – nomads – and it's as pure a feeling to explore as
it is to breathe or eat. But I do agree more must be done to
make sure explorers and explorations are matched in more
logical ways. If you can't reach a summit by training and
preparing, you shouldn't be allowed to do it.'

He made the analogy with climbers wearing oxygen to
summit Everest. Should oxygen be banned to reduce the
numbers? Of course not. But the current situation is environmental ruination – there, as at so many other exploration
Meccas.[2]

Gonz told me he often discusses such things with a
friend who's an eighth-generation mountain guide in
Zermatt. Over many years they've come to the conclusion
that the PADI certification system used by divers is a
model which could be mirrored in the world of exploration – a set of standard tests every would-be explorer and
guide would undergo so both knew what they were dealing with.

Such a system would go some way to ensure that everyone
would know rescue basics and guides 'would no longer have
to guess a client's level of skiing, climbing, etc., or most
importantly, take a client for purely monetary reasons'.

Which is all very well, but the wellbeing and safety of people hadn't been foremost in my mind as I rode away from Pyramiden. Human beings aren't endangered, in fact we've never had it so good; and the world gets smaller as more people lift themselves out of poverty and have disposable income for travel . . . and nobody has the right to deny people the opportunity to see the world. But the Earth is a delicate, finely balanced planet and a sustainable approach is vital.

So if the question is really *how* not *if* we travel, a realisation and acceptance of our place in the scheme of things – that everything is connected; that we are an intrinsic part of nature rather than elective visitors – seems to me essential.

In this the plight of polar bears is an excellent example. Their diminishing habitat and evolving behaviours to cope with that lack – the fact their pack ice hunting grounds are melting away – has not been caused by a surfeit of snowmobilers on the fjords of Pyramiden. We live in the Anthropocene. The Earth is warming and people all over the globe are responsible but the effects, at least until recently, were observed and felt by only a few, a fraction of the whole. This is now changing. Things are accelerating, escalating. We need to slow down. Take stock. Rein ourselves in, take responsibility.

And if the question is really *how* not *if* we travel, because humankind are a questing lot, I suggest we begin by physically slowing down and changing the focus of our travels from ground covered to quality of experience and connection. Rather than globetrotting, globerambling or even globestanding and -sitting should be the goal. What's the point of racing through a longed-for landscape if the means of travel renders it a blur? I suggest a return to animal speed and heightened awareness might be the way to go.

———

A few days after my return from Pyramiden, I took a trip with Astrid Dillner, a young Swede who teaches dog sledding on the outskirts of Longyearbyen.

At a boxpark of square kennels built on stilts, each home to an Alaskan husky, we harnessed our team:

Nelson & Emile leading the way
Radar & Luna in the middle
Cox & Mika at the back.

Muscular, handsome, patient dogs. Warm white fur against the cut snow's blue.

The sleds were wood, bound together with cord to create the necessary flexible frame. The driver stood at the stern, one foot resting on the rake of a brake, the other on one of the running skids. The passenger sat in front, swaddled in rugs, along with the bags and supplies.

We ran up into the mountains in smooth snow channels. Sun glare. Shadow chill. The only sounds were harness jingle, the pants and padding of the team, the shush of the runners and occasional call of encouragement from Astrid behind. Otherwise it was silent. Just us, darting clean through the landscape.

It felt ancient, balanced, peaceful. Wonderful.

On the return leg I had a go at driving the dogs but really it was effortless because they knew the way. My only real challenge was to stop them going too fast, something I tempered with a touch on the brake – at which point Luna would turn her head and shoot me a glare of 'Spoilsport!'

Too fast? you might be thinking. Too fast after a snow-mobile safari? Well, yes, because it's all relative, isn't it? The skidoos were zippy but I was lower in the sled so the world appeared to pass at a similar speed but, crucially, it wasn't and so I was able to take in the landscape and feel immersed in a way that the cat-bikes hadn't allowed. Added to which: a dog team know how to get you home in blizzards, they know bad ice and how to avoid it, and they know if there is danger in the immediate area. Machines cannot do any of these things.

———

So much of this book has been about the search for spaces which afford clarity, be it Kerouac's dream of peace in the high Cascades, the brutalist ply of the Swiss writer zoo or the far-flung temples of Japan. Spaces apart, places to think 'some distance away from the main army'.

The urge for going to the ends of the Earth that so many of us share in one form or another – the dream of going further in the case of a few – has a mirror in the teams of people who prepare the way, creating and caring for the stations en route, the rungs of the ladder as I think of it now. So Stefán and Atli shore up the sæluhús and Dr Rupert oversees the MDRS, and the Cordouan keepers keep watch over the Gironde's shipping, and Erlend leads parties out into the Arctic and keeps them entertained and safe.

And all the time the question of why we go circulates and percolates about.

I think it has to do with wonder and faith, a need to explore and discover and light out into the unknown, *to see*.

Nick Cave recently wrote that he thinks humanity needs to draw itself back to a state of wonder. His way has always been to write himself there, to reach such a state and place through work, repetition, a process – Cave famously used to work office hours to write new songs.

People build sheds, word-splashing cabins set apart from the everyday. Dahl and Deakin, Thomas and Starling – the latter's *Shedboatshed* an amazing hymn to the transportive power and possibilities of the humble hut.

But maybe the thing all these examples have in common, the thread that joins all my outposts together, is that they allow people to engage with the world inside and out in various ways. In this sense, all outposts are lighthouses – sites of illumination.

Sometimes they afford an immediate sense of revelation, sometimes their secrets must be worked for and earned. But in writing this book, I've learnt that an outpost doesn't have to be somewhere you go to get something specific – a place to juice, a plot to mine; an outpost can simply be somewhere to go to be, to find something new of yourself – something magical and unexpected which might change your life; as my father felt changed by Svalbard, and the strange stories and artefacts he brought home inspired and fired me.

So, yes, I agree with Gonz. The need to travel and explore for ourselves is deep within the human animal. But one can go and leave no trace, go and do no harm. Travel slowly. Take it all in. Remember our place and duties of care.

And if you go to Svalbard, maybe take dogs – give my regards to Erlend, Astrid and Luna. Lay off the snowmobiles if you can and leave the bears alone.

Polar bear print and wool glove on frozen Billefjorden, Svalbard, 2018. Photograph: Dan Richards

ACKNOWLEDGEMENTS

To my family – Annie, Tim, Joe, Bob and Moz. All my love.

Outpost was written with a lot of people's help and I have tried to name and thank as many of you as possible below. Looking back over all the adventures, I'm struck by how generous people have been, the amazing friends I've made along the way, and how so often the unexpected tangents and apparent setbacks gave rise to the greatest wonders and meetings.

To begin with Iceland, I'd like to thank Chris Gribble and his team at the National Centre for Writing in Norwich; Dr Katrin Anna Lund of the University of Iceland; Anna Selby, dear friend and poet; and the Íslanders: Kristín Viðarsdóttir, Sjön and Haraldur Jónssen, who put me on the right track, drew me maps, and were so gracious and kind in their hospitality.

Stefán Jökull Jakobsson, Atli Páls and Hekla the dog, thank you for letting me work with you, showing me sælu-hús and opening my eyes to the realm of the huldufólk. Thanks also to all at Ferðafélag Íslands, Halldór Óli Gunnarsson for allowing me to reproduce elements of *Draugasögur úr Hvítárnesskál*, and Hannah Walker and Dr Oscar Aldred – my love to you both.

ACKNOWLEDGEMENTS

I'm hugely grateful to Simon Starling for taking the time to see me, furnish me with scrumptious Danish lunches and generally gad about Copenhagen. The trip to the zoo was an excellent highlight. Thanks to you and your team – Maja McLaughlin, Marta Merovic and Kath Roper-Caldbeck. I am also thankful to Rachel White, Collections Manager and Archivist at the Roald Dahl Museum & Story Centre, Great Missenden, for allowing me access to Roald's archives and letting me explore the writing hut.

America happened rather on the hoof and I was supremely lucky to have Colin Cady with me for the first half – terrific friend and writer, long-suffering hiking, climbing and driving partner. Thank you, Colin. *'Exit, pursued by a bear.'*

There's a moment in every book where I believe things will be all right; that I'm inside a project which will surely come good. In the last book it was the mad descent and wonderful meetings at La Sage post-Dent Blanche benighting; this book it happened when I met Jim Henterly on the summit approach of Desolation Peak – a great blessing. Thanks, Jim, all power to your Pulaski.

I'm much obliged to John Suiter, author of *Poets on the Peaks: Gary Snyder, Philip Whalen & Jack Kerouac in the North Cascades*, for allowing me to quote from his splendid book. I also wish to salute the good folk of Marblemount, the staff and rangers of the Wilderness Information Center (7280 Ranger Station Rd), and Peggy the square-dancing Samaritan, wherever she may be.

Dr Shannon M. Rupert, Dr Lucinda Offer, and Michael Stoltz of the Mars Society were incredibly generous with their time. The fact I was granted unique access to MDRS made the Utah chapter possible – thank you for taking a punt on an odd proposition. Good luck in Martian land-scapes home and abroad.

Kate Morein and her family made me feel incredibly welcome in LA and Long Beach. I was a little bit bedraggled after my Cascades trip, awaiting my call from Mars and you all took that in your stride – indeed, you spurred me on. Thank you. *And then*, Katy Corneli and Amber 'Bones' Crandell saved my bacon in Green River. I'm absolutely in your debt – love to the helpers of Helper. And thank you, dear Roz; familiar voice, distant star, Shanghai china. Hats off to all the Fishergate gang. Thanks too to Sam Bowser – ice diver and warm-hearted host.

Steve King was a excellent trouper and remains a staunch friend. Thanks for your help before, during and after our Rannoch odyssey. Love to you and to all the Kings of Aberdeen and London. Thanks also to David Greig, David Frew; Dominic Driver and all at the National Trust for Scotland.

Nick Herrmann – marvellous man, thank you. At the time it might have seemed like I put you through the wringer but I hope, having read the book and this list of acknowl-edgements, you'll see that worse things happened on land.

I am indebted to Liz Schaffer of *Lodestars Anthology* who first published a version of this chapter in 2018; Alaïs Perret at Bordeaux Tourisme and Magali Pautis – project and development manager at SMIDDEST (Joint Association for the Sustainable Development of the Gironde Estuary) – who was so phenomenally helpful and arranged for Jean-Marie Calbet, international lighthouse expert and all round excel-lent chap, to show me Cordouan. Thank you all so much for your help and generosity. I take my hat off to Martine

Macheras and the great Bruno Beurrier for their great knowledge, showmanship and humour. Thanks also to the crew of *La Bohème* and the Cordouan lighthouse keepers for their hospitality and care.

I fell on my feet in the most extraordinary way when Vera Michalski awarded me a place at FJM. Guillaume Dollmann took great care to make me feel at home, together with his tremendous team: Aurélie Baudrier, Natalia Granero, Mélanie Kensicher, Alexandra Pitonzo, Alexandre Miréno-wicz, Nathalie Plancherel, Shadi Saad, Ewa Surowska, Jessica Villat, and Ewa Zajac. Thanks to you, the charming reception ladies, maintenance, gallery and technical teams and everybody else at Fondation Jan Michalski. I had the great pleasure of residing alongside several other ply-lofted scribes – Nancy Campbell, Kristen Cosby, Perrine Le Querrec, Mikołaj Lozinski, Tanja Rahmy, Takashi Wakamatsu; cowbells, bouquets, and tiny trains to you all.

Thanks also to Jasmin and Titus Rowlandson, guardians of Walnut Tree Farm; Alex Lingford – affable motorist and wild swimmer; and Robert Macfarlane, fine friend to whom I owe so much.

In Japan I was lucky enough to travel in the company of Wondertrunk & Co. Deepest appreciation and respects to Megumi Ageishi, Renae Smith, Sakie Miya, Take Okamoto, Yoneda Ryojun, and Liz Schaffer of *Lodestars Anthology* – *Outpost*'s patron saint.

My Arctic dreams were made possible by Alex Edwards, Horatio Clare, and Erlend Øian. Horatio, fellow Walian, green man of letters, land and sea — thank you so much for your help and encouragement over the years. Alex, your kindness and generosity mean a huge amount. My best

ACKNOWLEDGEMENTS

wishes to you, Ralph and all at Natural High Safaris. Erlend, all credit for keeping our bonkers peloton in line, showing us wonders, and feeding us so well. The moment when you cheerily proffered smoked reindeer heart on the frozen sea in front of Fridtjovbreen will live long in the memory! Your enthusiasm, knowledge and knitwear were an utter joy.

Dominic Taylor, fellow dog-sledder; the man who woke me up for the Northern Lights. Thank you.

To Astrid Dillner and all at Svalbard Husky – human and hound – my thanks and admiration.

Nick Cox at the BAS Arctic Research Station in Ny-Ålesund Station, thank you for your patience and cordiality. Annette Scheepstra and Ronald Visser, Dr James Fenton, James Bulley, Dr Nick Crumpton, Katy MacMillan-Scott, Philip Pullman, and Rupert Thompson – I am grateful for all your contributions and advice.

Special thanks to Gonz Ferrero and Sebastian Herzén of Klättermusen, Sweden.

—

Thanks to my agent, Carrie Plitt at Felicity Bryan Associates. Excellent friend, guide and champion; lady whose name should arguably join mine on the front of this book. You're fantastic, thank you so much.

Simon Thorogood has walked the editing tightrope with great humour and equanimity. I am hugely grateful for his sympathetic suggestions, enthusiasm, counsel and care.

Thanks also to Leila Cruickshank, Vicki Rutherford, Annie Lee and Lorraine McCann for their work on the manuscript and Aa'Ishah Hawton for organising the quotations.

ACKNOWLEDGEMENTS

Jamie Byng and his Canongate team have made me feel incredibly welcome. Thank you all – particularly Anna Frame, who is fabulous.

Kristen Cosby and Jim Henterly ran their eyes over several early versions of this manuscript and *Outpost* is a much better book for their suggestions.

I am very lucky to have had the support of several publications whilst writing this book – many of whom carried early extracts or related material. My thanks to Jeff Barratt, Diva Harris and all at *Caught by the River*; Jo Tinsley and all at *Ernest Journal*; Jen Harrison Bunning, Anna Kirk and all at *Slightly Foxed*; Will Hudson at *It's Nice That*; Robert Bound and Ed Stocker at *Monocle*; and Clementine Macmillan-Scott and Sarah Odedina at *Scoop Magazine*.

I'd also like to thank Jeff Towns, Maggie James and Toby Nottage at Dylan Thomas' Boathouse, Laugharne; Louisa Yates, Peter Francis, Amy Sumner, and all at Gladstone's Library; Andrew and Laura Willan, Peregrine Massey and all at Wealden Lit Fest and Boldshaves; Julia Barnes and Kelly McDonald at Carriageworks, Sydney; and Rebecca Hage and Rebecca Hill at Sydney Harbour Trust.

Special thanks to Walter Donohue and Lauren Nicoll at Faber. Also all at Mr B's in Bath; Mairi Oliver, Andrew Scott, Artemis and all at the Lighthouse Bookshop, Edinburgh; The Bicycle Shop, Norwich; Hiut Denim Co., Cardigan; and KEX, Reykjavik.

ACKNOWLEDGEMENTS

My friends have been an endless source of kindness, support and encouragement during the writing of this book.

First, Kate Manning – brilliant, funny, humane. I know I was impossible. I'm sorry. Love and thanks to you.

Amy Alexander, Benedict Allen, Rachael Allen, Malú Ansaldo, Laven Arumugam, Will Ashon, Julia Barnes, Natalie Berry, Wendy Bevan-Mogg, Rosula Blanc, David Bramwell, Octavia Bright, Jamie Buchanan-Dunlop, Will Burns, Austen Capsey, Douglas H. Chadwick, Mathew Clayton, Will Connor, Clare Conville, Tim Dee, Louise Dennison, Mark Dishman, Prof. Gabor Domokos, Stanley Donwood, Jonty Driver, Abbie Garrington, Kirsty Gunn, Melissa Harrison, Bea Hemming, Nina Hervé, Werner Herzog, Philip Hoare, Will Jennings, David and Sandra Lees, Daisy Leitch, Melanie Lockwood, Trisha Loncraine, Sarah Lonsdale, Dr Richard Luckett, Lorna MacDougall, Amber Massie-Blomfield, Nelly Mukamurenzi, Maggie Nelson, Kate Norbury, C. C. O'Hanlon, Vaughan Oliver, Casey Perkis, Anthony and Christopher Pilley, Max Porter, Edward Posnett, David Potter, Alex Preston, Per Kyrre Reymert, David Richards, Dr John Paul Russo, Liz Schaffer and family, Kim Sherwood, Adam Smyth, Sally O. Smyth, Martha Sprackland, Polly Stenham, George Szirtes, Janine Ulfane, Emma Jane Unsworth, Patrick Walsh, Stephen Watts, Shane Winser, Magda Wojnowska – thank you all.

In memory of Denis Johnson (1949–2017) and Vaughan Oliver (1957–2019)

PERMISSION CREDITS

PERMISSION CREDITS

NOTES

EPIGRAPH

1 'The Peace of Wild Things', *The Peace of Wild Things: And Other Poems*, Wendell Berry, Penguin, London, 2018, p.25.

I HOTEL CALIFORNIA, NY-ÅLESUND

1 Extract from an email Werner Herzog sent to the author in June 2017.

2 'Home is so sad', *The Whitsun Weddings,* Philip Larkin, Faber, London, 1971, p.17.

3 Photograph caption opposite p.157, *Climbing Days*, Dorothy Pilley, Bell & Sons, London, 1935.

4 'Alone on a Mountaintop', *Lonesome Traveler,* Jack Kerouac, Penguin Classics, London, 2000, p.113.

5 *Wind, Sand and Stars*, Antoine de Saint-Exupéry, Penguin, London, 2000, p.91.

6 'The Latter Day Thoreau', *Five Dials* No. 2, Robert Macfarlane, Hamish Hamilton, London, 2008, p.10.

7 Pulitzer Prize-winning journalist and author David McCullough in conversation with National Endowment for the Humanities (NEH) Chairman Bruce Cole, *Humanities*, July/August 2002, Vol. 23/No. 4, p.23.

8 *Walden; or, Life in the Woods*, Henry David Thoreau, Penguin Illustrated Classics, London, 1938, p.42.

9 'Burnt Norton', *Four Quartets*, T.S. Eliot, Faber, London, 2001, p.4.

II SÆLUHÚS, ICELAND

1 'Lights Out', *Poems*, Edward Thomas, Selwyn & Blount, London, 1917.

2 *Questions of Travel: William Morris in Iceland*, Lavinia Greenlaw, Notting Hill Editions, London, 2011, p.xxiv.

3 Figures quoted relate to 'Iceland's tourism boom – and backlash', *The Financial Times*, Tim Moore, 7 March 2017, and 'Has Iceland's tourism bubble finally burst?', *The Daily Telegraph*, Hugh Morris, 8 March 2018.

4 *Questions of Travel: William Morris in Iceland*, Lavinia Greenlaw, Notting Hill Editions, London, 2011, p.xxiv.

5 *The Solace of Open Spaces*, Gretel Ehrlich, Penguin, London, 1986, p.8.

6 Ibid.

7 *A Field Guide to Getting Lost*, Rebecca Solnit, Canongate, Edinburgh, 2005, p.131.

8 'Spirits of the Land: A Tool for Social Education', *A Journey of International Children's Literature* (Vol. 37. No. 4), Ólina Thorvarðardóttir, Morgan State University, Baltimore, USA, 1999, p.33.

9 'In Iceland, "respect the elves – or else"', *The Guardian*, Oliver Wainwright, 5 March 2015.

10 *Call Them by Their True Names: American Crises (and Essays)*, Rebecca Solnit, Granta, London 2018, pp.11–12.

III SIMON STARLING – *SHEDBOATSHED*

1 *Duck Soup*, The Marx Brothers, Paramount Studios, 1933.

2 *Dart*, Alice Oswald, Faber, London, 2002, p.3.

3 www.tate.org.uk/whats-on/tate-britain/exhibition/turner-prize-2005

IV DESOLATION PEAK, WA, USA

1 *Lanark*, Alasdair Gray, Canongate, Edinburgh, 2016, p.6.

2 *Train Dreams*, Denis Johnson, Granta Books, London, 2011, p.113.

3 'Back to the start' – *Train Dreams*, by Denis Johnson, *The Spectator*, Jonathan McAloon, 22 October 2012.

4 *Continental Divide: A History of American Mountaineering*, Maurice Isserman, W. W. Norton & Company, New York, 2017.

5 *Poets on the Peaks: Gary Snyder, Philip Whalen & Jack Kerouac in the North Cascades*, John Suiter, Counterpoint, Washington DC, 2002, p.186.

6 'Alone on a Mountaintop', *Lonesome Traveler*, Jack Kerouac, Penguin, London, 2000, p.114.

7 Ibid.

8 *Some of the Dharma*, Jack Kerouac, Viking Press, New York, 1997, p.167. At this time Kerouac had only had one book published, *The Town and the City*, which had been put out by Harcourt Brace in 1950 to no great sales or acclaim.

9 *Poets on the Peaks: Gary Snyder, Philip Whalen & Jack Kerouac in the North Cascades,* John Suiter, Counterpoint, Washington DC, 2002.

10 'Howl', *Selected Poems 1947–1995*, Allen Ginsberg, Harper Perennial, London, 2001, p.49.

11 'Alone on a Mountaintop', *Lonesome Traveler*, Jack Kerouac, Penguin, London, 2000, p. 111.

12 *Fire Season*, Philip Connors, Harper Collins, London, 2011, p.4.

13 *Desolation Angels*, Jack Kerouac, Riverhead Books, New York, 1995, p.4.

14 Ibid., p.56.

15 'Alone on a Mountaintop', *Lonesome Traveler*, Jack Kerouac, Penguin, London, 2000, p.107.

16 'I Was Trying to Describe You to Someone', *Revenge of the Lawn: Stories 1962–1970*, Richard Brautigan, Canongate, Edinburgh, 2017, p.60.

17 'Alone on a Mountaintop', *Lonesome Traveler*, Jack Kerouac, Penguin, London, 2000, p.107.

18 'Alone on a Mountaintop', *Lonesome Traveler*, Jack Kerouac, Penguin, London, 2000, p.116.

19 'Alone on a Mountaintop', *Lonesome Traveler*, Jack Kerouac, Penguin, London, 2000, p.113.

V MARS, UTAH

1 *The Long Goodbye*, Raymond Chandler, Vintage, London, 2002, p.252.

2 ' "Not welcome here": Amazon faces growing resistance to its second home. As cities vie to host second campus, local activists say the *Hunger Games*-style competition is a bad deal for everyone – except Amazon', *The Guardian*, Julia Carrie Wong, 15 March 2018.

3 'Elon Musk: we must colonise Mars to preserve our species in a third world war – Founder of SpaceX, which is working on getting humans to the planet, speaks at SXSW amid rising nuclear tension', *The Guardian*, Olivia Solon, 11 March 2018.

4 'The Case for Mars: The Plan to Settle the Red Planet and Why We Must and The Case for Colonizing Mars', *Ad Astra/To the Stars* (National Space Society Magazine), Robert Zubrin, July/August 1996, p.240.

5 'Trump directs NASA to send astronauts to the moon and then Mars', *New Scientist*, Leah Crane, 11 December 2017.

6 'Scientists cautiously back Trump's moon plan', *Cosmos*, Richard A. Lovett, 19 December 2017.

7 As reported by ABC News.

8 'Four Changes', *Turtle Island*, Gary Snyder, New Direction Books, New York, 1974, p.35.

VI BOTHIES, SCOTLAND

1 *The House at Pooh Corner*, A.A. Milne, Penguin Books, London, 2011, p.81.

2 Reproduced from MBA Journal No. 33, Spring 1975.

3 Reproduced from MBA Journal No. 28, March 1973.

4 'Loch Avon', *In the Cairngorms*, Nan Shepherd, Galileo Publishers, Cambridge, 2015, p.2.

5 Apple Inc. Dictionary – Version 2.2.2 (203)

6 Merriam-Webster.com

7 'The Largesse of the Sea Maiden by Denis Johnson — Review', *The Guardian*, Geoff Dyer, 31 December 2017.

VII PHARE DE CORDOUAN, FRANCE

1 *Tim to the Lighthouse*, Edward Ardizzone, Oxford University Press, Oxford, 1979.

VIII SWITZERLAND

1 Speech at the Prussian Academy of Arts in Berlin, 22 January 1929.

2 *Walden; or, Life in the Woods*, Henry David Thoreau, Penguin Illustrated Classics, London, 1938, p.42.

3 *The Library of Ice – Readings from a Cold Climate*, Nancy Campbell, Scribner, London, 2018.

IX JAPAN

1 *Place, Time and Being in Japanese Architecture*, Kevin Nute, Routledge, London, 2004, p.18.

2 'Saying Farewell at the Monastery after Hearing the Old Master Lecture on "Return to the Source"', *No Nature: New and Selected Poems*, Gary Snyder, Counterpoint Press, Berkeley, California, 1992, p.342.

X SVALBARD, NORWAY

1 An extract from O'Keeffe's contribution to the exhibition catalogue of *An American Place*, New York City, 1944 – reprinted in *Georgia*

NOTES

O'Keeffe: Catalogue Raisonné (Vol. 2), Barbara Buhler Lunes, Yale University Press, New Haven and London, 1999, p.1099.

2   J.R.R. Tolkien to Rayner Unwin, 11 April 1953; *The Letters of J.R.R. Tolkien*, George Allen & Unwin, London, 1981, p.167.

3   Email from Katy MacMillan-Scott, 4 July 2017.

4   Although a Norwegian sovereign territory, Svalbard is open to citizens of forty-six nations. If your country has signed the Svalbard Treaty, pledging the demilitarisation and protection of the islands, you are free to come and make a life there. Non-treaty nationals may also live and work indefinitely, visa-free – however, the Governor of Svalbard's office warns that '[T]hose who consider living in Svalbard should be aware that it is difficult to find both work and housing, and the weather conditions are very challenging compared to most other places in the world. Living expenses are very high, and the Governor can reject persons without sufficient means to support themselves.' – www.sysselmannen.no/en/Visitors/Entry-and-residence/

The Svalbard Treaty gave signatory nations equal rights to engage in commercial activities on the islands which, from the early 1900s, generally meant mining. As of 2018, only Norway and Russia are making use of this right – the former operating a mine in Longyearbyen to extract coal for local use, the mine at Svea having closed in 2016; the latter in Barentsburg. – 'End comes to 100 years of Norwegian coal mining at Svalbard – Amid a boost in the geopolitical and strategic importance of the Arctic archipelago, the Norwegian government makes clear that the once so powerful industry must end', Atle Staalesen, *The Barents Observer*, 12 October 2017.

5   *Slaughterhouse 5*, Kurt Vonnegut, Vintage, London, 2000, p.116 (paraphrased).

6   *Destination Svalbard: Towards 2025* – en.visitsvalbard.com

7   whc.unesco.org/en/tentativelists/5161/

8   *Deep Green: The Living Mountain: Arne Naess 1912–2009* – www.
    greenpeace.org/colombia/es/Eco-Tips/deep-green/deep-green-feb-
    2009/

9   'Home is so sad', *The Whitsun Weddings*, Philip Larkin, Faber,
    London, 1971, p.17.

EPILOGUE

1   *About Looking*, John Berger, Penguin Books, London, 1980,
    p.14.

2   Gonz himself is CEO of Klättermusen, a company specialising
    in mountaineering equipment who have pioneered the use of
    environmentally sustainable fabrics and materials – durable
    textiles made of recycled plastic and wool, using old fishnets and
    carpets as sources of polyamide, and PET bottles as sources for
    polyester. Their waterproof zippers are manufactured without
    Fluorocarbons – a world first. The list goes on:

    'A small Swedish company toiling away in near complete silence
    for 40 years, using cutting edge science to create outdoor equip-
    ment of unparalleled durability with a minimal and sometimes
    even negative ecological footprint. The Skunkworks of the outdoor
    equipment world!'

    The first time I spoke to Gonz he told me his great hope was
    that climbers and explorers would pass their Klättermusen kit
    down several generations.

    www.klattermusen.com/en/

SELECT BIBLIOGRAPHY

A

California: With Selected Writings, Ansel Adams, Little, Brown, USA, 1997

The Endurance: Shackleton's Legendary Antarctic Expedition, Caroline Alexander, Bloomsbury, London, 1998

The Scottish Bothy Bible: The Complete Guide to Scotland's Bothies and How to Reach Them, Geoff Allan, Wild Things Publishing Ltd, Bath, 2017

The Faber Book of Exploration, Benedict Allen (ed.), Faber, London, 2002

The Earth Is Only a Little Dust Under Our Feet, Bego Antón, Overlapse, London, 2018

Tim to the Lighthouse, Edward Ardizzone, Oxford University Press, Oxford, 1979

Strange Labyrinth: Outlaws, Poets, Mystics, Murderers and a Coward in London's Great Forest, Will Ashon, Granta Books, London, 2017

The Man Who Walked Through Walls, Marcel Aymé, Pushkin Press, London, 2013

B

The Peregrine, The Hill of Summer & Diaries: The Complete Works of J.A. Baker, J.A. Baker, Collins, London, 2010

The Unlimited Dream Company, J.G. Ballard, Jonathan Cape, London, 1979

Levels of Life, Julian Barnes, Vintage Books, London, 2014

The Noise of Time, Julian Barnes, Vintage Books, London, 2017

About Looking, John Berger, Penguin Books, London, 1980

A Fortunate Man: The Story of a Country Doctor, John Berger, Canongate, Edinburgh, 2016

The Peace of Wild Things: And Other Poems, Wendell Berry, Penguin Books, London, 2018

Revenge of the Lawn: Stories 1692–1970, Richard Brautigan, Canongate, Edinburgh, 2017

Sombrero Fallout, Richard Brautigan, Canongate, Edinburgh, 2012

Around the World in Eighty Days, John Burningham, Jonathan Cape, London, 1972

Borka: The Adventures of a Goose with No Feathers, John Burningham, Jonathan Cape, London, 1963

C

The Library of Ice – Readings from a Cold Climate, Nancy Campbell, Scribner, London, 2018

The Long Goodbye, Raymond Chandler, Vintage Books, London, 2002

A Journey to the End of the Russian Empire, Anton Chekhov, Penguin Books, London, 2007

Icebreaker: A Voyage Far North, Horatio Clare, Chatto & Windus, London, 2017

Orison for a Curlew: In Search of a Bird on the Edge of Extinction, Horatio Clare, Little Toller Books, Dorset, 2015

Fire Season, Philip Connors, HarperCollins, London, 2011

Fence, Tim Cresswell, Penned in the Margins, London, 2015

The Modern Marvel Encyclopaedia, John R. Crossland (ed.), Collins Clear-Type Press, London & Glasgow, 1946

The Amazing Animal Atlas, Dr Nick Crumpton and Gaia Bordicchia, Flying Eye Books, London, 2017

SELECT BIBLIOGRAPHY

D

The Dahl Diary, 1992, Roald Dahl, Puffin Books, London, 1991

Kiss Kiss, Roald Dahl, Penguin Books, London, 2011

Over to You, Roald Dahl, Penguin Books, London, 2011

Notes from Walnut Tree Farm, Roger Deakin, Alison Hastie and Terence Blacker (eds); Penguin Books, London, 2008

Wildwood: A Journey Through Trees, Roger Deakin, Penguin Books, London, 2007

Slouching Towards Bethlehem, Joan Didion, Fourth Estate, London, 2017

The White Album, Joan Didion, Fourth Estate, London, 2017

The Abundance, Annie Dillard, Canongate, Edinburgh, 2017

Teaching a Stone to Talk, Annie Dillard, Canongate, Edinburgh, 2016

Essayism, Brian Dillon, Fitzcarraldo Editions, London, 2017

Deep Lane, Mark Doty, Cape Poetry, London, 2015

David Bowie: The Man Who Fell to Earth, Paul Duncan and David James, Taschen, Köln, 2017

E

The Solace of Open Spaces, Gretel Ehrlich, Penguin Books, London, 1986

Four Quartets, T.S. Eliot, Faber, London, 2001

Duck, Death and the Tulip, Wolf Erlbruch, Gecko Press, New Zealand, 2008

F

The Book of Strange New Things, Michel Faber, Canongate, Edinburgh, 2014

The Fatal Englishman: Three Short Lives, Sebastian Faulks, Penguin Books, London, 1996

The Snow Geese, William Fiennes, Picador Classic, London, 2015

SELECT BIBLIOGRAPHY

G

Jeremy Hutchinson's Case Histories, Thomas Grant, John Murray, London, 2015

Night Photograph, Lavinia Greenlaw, Faber, London, 1993

Questions of Travel – William Morris in Iceland, Lavinia Greenlaw, Notting Hill Editions, Devon, 2011

Swallowing Mercury, Wioletta Greg, Portobello Books, London, 2017

Selected Plays 1999–2009, David Greig, Faber, London, 2010

Shackleton's Journey, William Grill, Flying Eye Books, London, 2014

Caroline's Bikini, Kirsty Gunn, Faber, London, 2018

Infidelities, Kirsty Gunn, Faber, London, 2014

H

The Collected Essays of Elizabeth Hardwick, Elizabeth Hardwick, Darryl Pinckney (ed.), *New York Review of Books*, New York, 2017

Seeing Things, Seamus Heaney, Faber, London, 1991

Of Walking on Ice: Munich–Paris 11/23 to 12/14, 1974, Werner Herzog, Tanam Press, New York, 1980

Strange News from Another Star, Hermann Hesse, Penguin Books, London, 1976

RISINGTIDEFALLINGSTAR, Philip Hoare, Fourth Estate, London, 2017

The Meaning of Cricket, Jon Hotton, Yellow Jersey Press/Penguin, London, 2017

The Hawk in the Rain, Ted Hughes, Faber Modern Classics, London, 2015

I

Continental Divide: A History of American Mountaineering, Maurice Isserman, W.W. Norton & Company, New York, 2017

SELECT BIBLIOGRAPHY

The Roots of Japanese Architecture: A Photographic Quest, Teiji Itoh and
Isamu Noguchi, Harper & Row, New York, 1963

J

Cultural Amnesia: Notes in the Margin of My Time, Clive James,
Picador, London, 2012

B.S. Johnson Omnibus – Trawl, Albert Angelo, House Mother Normal,
B.S. Johnson, Picador, London, 2004

The Largesse of the Sea Maiden, Denis Johnson, Jonathan Cape, London,
2018

Train Dreams, Denis Johnson, Granta Books, London, 2011

K

Tove Jansson: Work and Love, Tuula Karjalainen, Particular Books,
London, 2014

Desolation Angels, Jack Kerouac, Riverhead Books, New York,
1995

Lonesome Traveler, Jack Kerouac, Penguin Books, London, 2000

Some of the Dharma, Jack Kerouac, Viking Press, New York, 1997

Beast, Paul Kingsnorth, Faber, London, 2016

Autumn, Karl Ove Knausgaard, Harvill Secker, Penguin Random
House, London, 2017

Winter, Karl Ove Knausgaard, Harvill Secker, Penguin Random
House, London, 2017

L

What We Really Talk About When We Talk About the Tube, John
Lanchester, Penguin Books, London, 2013

The Whitsun Weddings, Philip Larkin, Faber, London, 1971

The Dun Cow Rib: A Very Natural Childhood, John Lister-Kaye,
Canongate, Edinburgh, 2017

Georgia O'Keeffe: Catalogue Raisonné (Vol. 2), Barbara Buhler Lunes, Yale University Press, New Haven and London, 1999

M

The Crossing (The Border Trilogy, Vol. 2), Cormac McCarthy, Picador, London, 2010

Sky Nails: Poems 1979–1997, Jamie McKendrick, Faber, London, 2000

Kingdom of the Ice Bear: A Portrait of the Arctic, Hugh Mills and Mike Salisbury, BBC Books, London, 1985

Hons and Rebels, Jessica Mitford, Weidenfeld & Nicolson, London, 1999

Contact! – A Book of Glimpses, Jan Morris, Faber, London, 2009

In Scotland Again, H.V. Morton, Methuen & Co. Ltd, London, 1934

Curiosity: The Story of a Mars Rover, Markus Motum, Walker Books Ltd, 2017

The Importance of Being Iceland: Travel Essays in Art, Eileen Myles, Semiotexte, New York, 2009

N

The Ecology of Wisdom, Arne Naess, Penguin Classics, London, 2016

Farthest North: The Incredible Three-Year Voyage to the Frozen Latitudes of the North, Fridtjof Nansen, Skyhorse Publishing, New York, 2008

Bluets, Maggie Nelson, Wave Books, Seattle & New York, 2009

Place, Time and Being in Japanese Architecture, Kevin Nute, Routledge, London, 2004

O

Dart, Alice Oswald, Faber, London, 2002

Woods etc., Alice Oswald, Faber, London, 2005

SELECT BIBLIOGRAPHY

P

The Book of Disquiet, Fernando Pessoa, Penguin Books, London, 2002

Climbing Days, Dorothy Pilley, Bell & Sons, London, 1935

R

Ravilious, James Russell, Dulwich Picture Gallery/Philip Wilson Publishers, London & New York, 2015

S

The Mind's Eye, Oliver Sacks, Picador, London, 2010

Flight to Arras, Antoine de Saint-Exupéry, Penguin Modern Classics, London 1962

Wind, Sand and Stars, Antoine de Saint-Exupéry, Penguin Books, London, 2000

Notes on the Forest Flora of Japan, Charles Sprague Sargent, Houghton, Mifflin & Company, Boston & New York, 1894

Lincoln in the Bardo, George Saunders, Bloomsbury, London, 2017

My House of Sky – The Life and Work of J.A. Baker, Hetty Saunders, Little Toller Books, Dorset, 2017

Pocket Atlas of Remote Islands: Fifty Islands I Have Not Visited and Never Will, Judith Schalansky, Penguin Books, London, 2012

Apollo: The Extraordinary Visual History of the Iconic Space Programme, Zack Scott, Headline, London, 2017

Escape from the Antarctic, Ernest Shackleton, Penguin Modern Classics, London, 1999

In the Cairngorms, Nan Shepherd, Galileo Publishers, Cambridge, 2015

The Living Mountain, Nan Shepherd, Canongate, Edinburgh, 2011

The Quarry Wood, Nan Shepherd, Canongate, Edinburgh, 2018

The Hand, George Simenon, Penguin Modern Classics, London, 2016

A Berry Feast, Gary Snyder, Grove Press, New York, 1957

SELECT BIBLIOGRAPHY

Left Out in the Rain: New Poems 1947–1985, Gary Snyder, Counterpoint Press, Berkeley, California, 1992

No Nature: New and Selected Poems, Gary Snyder, Counterpoint Press, Berkeley, California, 1992

Turtle Island, Gary Snyder, New Direction Books, New York, 1974

A Field Guide to Getting Lost, Rebecca Solnit, Canongate, Edinburgh, 2005

Call Them by Their True Names: American Crises (and Essays), Rebecca Solnit, Granta, London, 2018

Men Explain Things to Me, Rebecca Solnit, Granta Books, London, 2014

The Mother of All Questions, Rebecca Solnit, Granta Books, London, 2017

Glass as Broken Glass, Martha Sprackland, Rack Press, London, 2017

Contemporary Artists Series – Simon Starling, Simon Starling, Dieter Roelstraete, Janet Harbord and Francesco Manacorda; Michele Robecchi and Craig Garrett (eds), Phaidon, London, 2012

The Moon Is Down, John Steinbeck, Penguin Modern Classics, London, 2014

The Life and Opinions of Tristram Shandy, Gentleman, Laurence Sterne, Wordsworth Classics, Hertfordshire, 1996

The Dead Mountaineer's Inn – One More Last Rite for the Detective Genre, Arkady and Boris Strugatsky, Melville House Publishing, London, 2015

Poets on the Peaks: Gary Snyder, Philip Whalen & Jack Kerouac in the North Cascades, John Suiter, Counterpoint, Washington DC, 2002

The Story of Mr Sommer, Patrick Süskind, Fox, Finch & Tepper, Bath, 2015

T

Memoirs of a Polar Bear, Yoko Tawada, Portobello Books, London, 2016

SELECT BIBLIOGRAPHY

Memories – From Moscow to the Black Sea, Teffi, Pushkin Press, London, 2016

Consolations of the Forest – Alone in a Cabin in the Middle Taiga, Sylvain Tesson, Penguin Books, London, 2013

Edward Thomas: Collected Poems, Edward Thomas, Faber, London, 2004

This Party's Got to Stop: A Memoir, Rupert Thomson, Granta Books, London, 2010

Walden; or, Life in the Woods, Henry David Thoreau, Penguin Illustrated Classics, London, 1938

And the Wind Sees All, Guðmundur Andri Thorsson, Peirene Press, London, 2018

The Letters of J.R.R. Tolkien, J.R.R. Tolkien; Humphrey Carpenter and Christopher Tolkien (eds), George Allen & Unwin, London, 1981

V

The Mussel Feast, Brigit Vanderbeke, Peirene Press, London, 2013

The Man I Became, Peter Verhelst, Peirene Press, London, 2016

Around the World in Eighty Days, Jules Verne, Penguin Classics, London, 2008

Slaughterhouse 5, Kurt Vonnegut, Vintage Books, London, 2000

Wampeters, Foma & Granfalloons (Opinions), Kurt Vonnegut, Delta, New York, 1974

W

Ancient Sunlight, Stephen Watts, Enitharmon Press, London, 2014

The Door in the Wall and Other Stories, H.G. Wells, Mitchell Kennerley, New York & London, 1911

Zoo, Christopher Wilson, Faber, London, 2017

The Invention of Nature: The Adventures of Alexander von Humboldt, the Lost Hero of Science, Andrea Wulf, John Murray, London, 2015

Z

The Wallcreeper, Nell Zink, Fourth Estate, London, 2015

The Case for Mars: The Plan to Settle the Red Planet and Why We Must, Dr Robert Zubrin, Simon & Schuster, New York, 2011

Messages From a Lost World: Europe on the Brink, Stefan Zweig, Pushkin Press, London, 2016

Shooting Stars: Ten Historical Miniatures, Stefan Zweig, Pushkin Press, London, 2013

EXPEDITION REPORTS

Joint Universities Spitsbergen Expedition: Final Report, 1973

Report of Brathay Spitsbergen Expedition, Brathay Trust, 1982

MAGAZINES

THE ALPINE REVIEW #3

AVAUNT – Issue 03, Spring 2013

FIVE DIALS #2, Hamish Hamilton, London, 2008

PAMPHLET

Soul of Japan: An Introduction to Shinto and Ise Jingu, Public Affair Headquarters for Shikinen-Swengu, Tokyo, 2013

THESIS

Draugasögur úr Hvítárnesskál / Ghost Stories of Hvítárnes Bowl, Halldór Óli Gunnarsson, University of Iceland, Reykjavik, 2012